# Canned Code for DOS and Windows

# Canned Code for DOS and Windows

Steve Rimmer

**Windcrest®/McGraw-Hill**

New York San Francisco Washington, D.C. Auckland Bogotá
Caracas Lisbon London Madrid Mexico City Milan
Montreal New Delhi San Juan Singapore
Sydney Tokyo Toronto

FIRST EDITION
SECOND PRINTING


Published by Windcrest, an imprint of McGraw-Hill, Inc.
The name "Windcrest" is a registered trademark of McGraw-Hill, Inc.



**Library of Congress Cataloging-in-Publication Data**

Rimmer, Steve.
Canned code for DOS and Windows / by Steve Rimmer
p. cm.
Includes index.
ISBN 0-8306-4511-X (h) ISBN 0-8306-4512-8 (p)
1. MS-DOS (Computer file) 2. PC-DOS (Computer file) 3. Microsoft Windows (Computer file) 4. Microcomputers—Programming. I. Title.
QA76.76.063R55 1993
005.26'2—dc20 93-34624
CIP

Acquisitions editor: Brad J. Schepp
Editorial team: Joanne Slike, Executive Editor
Lori Flaherty, Managing Editor
Laura J. Bader, Editor
Joann Woy, Indexer
Production team: Katherine G. Brown, Director
Patsy D. Harne, Desktop Operator
Lisa M. Mellott, Typesetting
Lori L. White, Proofreading
Design team: Jaclyn J. Boone, Designer
Brian Allison, Associate Designer
Cover design: Margaret Karczewski, Vienna, Va.
Marble paper background courtesy of Douglas M. Parks, Blue Ridge Summit, Pa.

WP1
4466

# Copyright Notice

If you have bought this book, you have bought the following rights to use the code herein for your applications.

- You are free to abstract code fragments from this book as you require and incorporate them into the programs you write. You can distribute these programs freely in their executable form, such that they can be run by other users but not readily decompiled, disassembled, or linked into other applications.
- You cannot distribute any of the source code from this book as source code, in either human or machine readable form.
- In distributing executable application files that contain functions or variations on functions from this book, you are not required to pay any additional royalties, nor do you require explicit written permission. No credit need be given to this book.
- You cannot distribute the shareware applications on the companion disc for this book without explicit written permission from Alchemy Mindworks Inc.

This one will be for Megan
as well, I think . . .

# Contents

# Introduction

*"If anyone in the room believes in telekinesis, raise my hand."*
—Graffiti

While not much to look at when it's complete, motel art seems to have become something of a late twentieth-century performance medium. If you've been to a mall of late you might have noticed a few of the proponents of the form—people who can complete a canvas in about 15 minutes, and who never get within 15 feet of a paintbrush. Motel art is done with palette knives and wads of Kleenex. As a rule, it's infinitely more interesting to watch it being wrought than it is to own—one generic landscape with moonlight on a lake and silhouetted trees looks pretty much like another.

That which differentiates motel art from conventional painting is to some extent the remarkable diversity of tricks that motel artists have evolved to paint very quickly and with predictable results. A good motel art painter can move quickly enough to make it impossible to see what his or her hands are doing. If allowed to paint continuously—and if enough paint and Kleenex were trucked in to support such an effort—a good motel artist could outfit an entire chain of nationwide motels in less than a day.

Most art is a fusion of inspiration and tricks. Writing computer software is one of the most complex art forms, and not surprisingly, it has a large bucket of tricks. In fact, unlike motel art, the unexpected things you can do with software is constantly expanding. There are only so many ways to hold a palette knife.

Knowing how the tricks of programming work and where to apply them is what distinguishes software mechanics from software artists. Unfortunately you can't take classes in advanced software trickery. The secrets of software experts are a complex oral tradition of the art form—bulletin boards, networks, things written down and then badly photocopied to be passed from hand to hand, and so on.

This book is a collection of a few of the countless tricks available to software authors. Some are fairly fundamental to making real-world software work—things like doing high-speed text mode screen access or handling simple graphics are important to most applications. Quite a few others are pointedly esoteric, and have their value in being well sought after and very nearly impossible to find. If you want to know how to read a DBF file or plot a fractal, you'll spend some time digging through C language primers trying to find anything.

Other wizardry, such as recursive graphics or playing annoying little tunes through your PC speaker, is interesting for its own sake. To be sure, however, they illustrate useful bits of programming you might find you can adapt for other, more productive uses.

## Of DOS and Windows

This is a book for programmers working on PC platforms, both in DOS and Microsoft Windows. Certainly not everything applies to both of these environments. For example, attempting any of the text mode tricks in chapter 1 in a Windows application will bring the wrath of the protected mode dragons down on your head. For the most part, however, functions that do things, such as reading a WordPerfect file or drawing a picture, will do them in any programming environment with a bit of fiddling.

The programs in this book can, to a large degree, be used in any environment you like. Specifically, much of the DOS code can be ported to Windows without substantial change.

One of the realities of publishing is that paper is expensive and so, in turn, are the books printed on it. In creating *Canned Code*, it seemed desirable to make it reasonably inexpensive as computer books go. This meant keeping the page count to something less than encyclopedic. Because DOS programs are typically a lot shorter than Windows programs, many of the example functions in this book that could have been illustrated in either a DOS or a Windows environment are in the former. Should you want to port things, however, you'll find several Windows applications to provide you with a framework for writing Windows code.

The code in this book assumes you know how to program in C, that you know how to set up and run your C compiler and, in a few instances, that you can use an assembler. While you'll get into some of the basic considerations of language inherent in *Canned Code*, this book won't teach you the C language. Some very good basic C language books are available, including using C under Windows.

One thing most software authors new to C find a bit troubling is that the C language was created before PCs were even a distant thundercloud on the horizon, and that books purporting to discuss C language programming often do so in a very system-independent way. This is the academically correct approach to learning C, but it won't set you up for writing Windows applications anytime soon. The basis of C under DOS and Windows is tangentially similar to the generic C that emerge from Bell Labs in the early 1970s in which a staggering amount of system-specific technique and code was added and still remains.

For example, the first program most introductory C language primers use to illustrate how the language is structured is `Hello`. Here it is, straight from the early 1970s:

```
main()
{
        printf("Hello");
}
```

This program can be compiled under DOS, although it illustrates an output technique of little use if you aspire to writing anything more complex than command line utilities. It can't be compiled under Windows, as Windows implementations of C lack a `printf` function. You can't do text output in an environment that doesn't really support text in the conventional sense. The Windows equivalent of `Hello` would require about 100 lines of code.

One often reads diatribes by users of other, non-PC operating systems that discourse on the generally miserable nature of DOS as a working environment. In a sense, much of this critique is justified—if you regard the function of an operating environment as being a collection of functions your applications can tap into to perform common tasks. In this case, DOS is about as powerful as a Honda driving into hurricane-force winds. Windows, by comparison, offers all sorts of canned magic for applications running under it.

The somewhat tenuous nature of DOS has meant that getting anything meaningful done under it requires an immense effort in cheating. Making DOS-based software work usually requires you to dispense with much of the portable, hardware-independent code that C primers offer in favor of code that does what it's told. The latter sort of code only works on a PC—porting PC applications to other environments, such as Macintosh or Unix systems, is usually unspeakably traumatic. However, once you have a good hammerlock on PC software cheating, you can make the insubstantial universe of DOS do some fairly amazing things.

Unfortunately the last thing a book about basic C programming is likely to do is tell you how to spoil the overall purity of C and break the rules. I have no such illusions, and you'll find at least one broken rule per page.

## DOS considerations

What makes writing DOS applications so challenging is that DOS insulates you very little from the cold reality of a PC's processor. A PC's processor is a nasty little toad, too, which isn't about to make the task of writing software for it any easier if it can help it.

The architecture of a PC's processor is based around the idea of segmented memory. *Segmented memory* allows a processor to address memory that would require 20-bit numbers using only 16-bit registers. It also allows code running under it to optimize itself and run faster if it's fairly small. The penalty is a memory architecture that seems like the theoretical equivalent of an Escher print.

Simple microprocessors, or almost all microprocessors except those that drive PCs, use what is called *linear,* or flat memory. The first byte of memory is called *byte zero,* and simple numbers can be used to address all the subsequent bytes. For example, if `p` pointed to the base of memory, `p[10000]` would point to the ten-thousandth byte of memory. It's a memory architecture even a Labrador retriever could understand.

The drawback to flat memory is that addressing lots of it requires numbers which must reside in uncomfortably large registers. A processor that can restrict itself to using 16-bit registers, for example, can do things more rapidly than one handling everything with 32-bit registers.

The original 8086 processor, which drove the first generation PCs, had 16-bit registers.

The original 8086 processor was about as fast as a sea turtle crawling up the beach with a boxcar strapped to its back, or if you like, about as fast as Windows booting up. Its designers were probably loath to consider making it any slower by giving it wide enough registers to do flat memory addressing. Later generations of its descendants did acquire 32-bit registers in a flat architecture and the capability of handling memory using a flat architecture. However, the primary PC operating environment had become entrenched in a segmented memory model, where it has remained.

In a segmented memory model, every byte in memory is addressed by two, 16-bit registers, called the *segment* and the *offset.* The segment register defines which "paragraph" of memory is being addressed. A paragraph is 64 kilobytes long, and each paragraph is removed from the previous one by 16 bytes. The segment value of an address, then, moves the absolute address in memory by 16-byte jumps. The offset value of an address defines where in the 64 kilobytes of the paragraph in question we'd like to point.

The powerful aspect of segment and offset addressing is that it allows small objects—those occupying less than 64 kilobytes—to be addressed using a single 16-bit register, even though they exist in enough memory to require a 20-bit number to fully address the lot. The drawback is in dealing with objects larger than 64 kilobytes, which can get extremely confusing.

Here's an example of the potential confusion. The `MK_FP` macro creates a pointer defined by a segment and an offset. Here's how you'd create a pointer to the sixteenth byte in segment 47104. This is, in fact, where the text mode screen memory of a PC usually resides. For reasons discussed later in the book, this pointer would actually address the eighth character on your screen when it's in text mode.

```
MK_FP (47104,16);
```

Here's another way to address the same byte:

```
MP_FP (47105,0);
```

The second case increments the segment value by one paragraph—16 bytes—and decrements the offset by 16. Using segmented memory pointers, multiple pointers can point to the same place in memory. If you checked to see if these two pointers were equal, C would say that they aren't, even though they both point to the same place.

The other catch in using segmented memory pointers under C is that you can only add simple integers to them, not long integers. For example, here's a pointer and an offset being added together:

```
p+=150;
```

What's really happening here is that 150 is being added to the offset component of p. If a sufficiently large value were to be added to p, such that its offset were to wrap past zero, p would wind up pointing lower in absolute memory than it did before the value was added to it. The mechanism for adding offsets to segmented memory pointers does not allow for carrying overflow to the segment. There's a way around this, and I'll get to this in a moment.

When you compile programs in the C language under DOS, you can choose the memory "model" you wish to use. This tells C how to treat the pointers that will exist within the executable version of your program. In the "small" model, all the code and data in your program are constrained to fit in one 64-kilobyte segment, and as such, everything can be addressed with 16-bit "near" pointers. This allows a small-model program to be very fast, but it limits the size of the program considerably.

In many applications, you can work with code that will fit in one segment, but with more data, or with fixed data objects that must be addressed with complete or "far" pointers. Programs of this sort should be compiled using the "medium" memory model.

Large applications that deal with both code and data that could exceed 64 kilobytes should be compiled under the "large" memory model. This makes all pointers 32-bit segment pointers.

Finally, if you'll be working with single data objects that could get larger than 64 kilobytes, and addressing them would cause the problem of adding numbers larger than an integer to a pointer, you can use the "huge" memory model. Huge pointers are converted to long integers before an offset is added and then back into conventional far pointers to actually address memory. This allows you to add long integers to huge pointers and access objects larger than 64 kilobytes.

Huge pointers are considerably slower to work with than are far pointers. All other things being equal, a program compiled in the huge memory model will be larger than one compiled in the far memory model.

You can also mix memory models under C, which is often the most practical way to work with some of these pointer types. For example, you can create a large-model program and declare a few select pointers that might have to address data objects larger than 64 kilobytes as being huge. If you compile a program in the large memory model, the following declaration will result in a far pointer:

```
char *p;
```

This results in a huge pointer:

```
char huge *p;
```

In using mixed model programming, you can often have the best of all worlds—small code size, fast code, and access to larger data objects.

## Compiler specifics for *Canned Code*

One of the things that's often cited as being a virtue of the C language is that it's ostensibly portable. This means that code written under one compiler or for one hardware platform can be easily ported to another. In a sense this is true, but in the real world it's exceedingly rare to find code that will move between compilers without requiring at least a bit of fine-tuning.

Proficient C language programmers who really understand what a C compiler does can refine the compiling process to suit the nature of the program being compiled. This is usually referred to as *optimization.* You can optimize for code size or execution speed, for better memory management, and so on.

Compilers that allow for this sort of optimization have all sorts of adjustable toggles and switches. It's very often the case that a program will only compile and run correctly if the compiler switches have been set up properly. You'll find this to be true for many of the example programs in this book.

To begin with, the DOS programs in this book are written in Borland C. You could certainly compile them under a different implementation of C—Microsoft C, for example—but you will probably run into a few things that require adjusting if you do. Most of Borland and Microsoft C are interchangeable, but there are functions that are unique to each. If you aren't all that fluent in the various dialects of C under DOS, there's a lot to be said for working with one of the Borland languages. Borland C and Borland Turbo C packages are largely interchangeable for this discussion.

First, I wrote all these programs using the Borland C integrated development environment. They should all compile correctly using the command line compiler as well.

Second, the code in this book is written in C, rather than in the currently trendy C++. The latter is an extension of C, and while it certainly has its uses, it represents considerable overkill for the sorts of small programs discussed here. If you like C++ you can certainly add the requisite C++ class declarations and such to the C language functions in this book for use in your own applications.

Third, the DOS-based code you'll encounter over the next few chapters was written in more or less pure Kernighan and Ritchie C, as opposed to ANSI C. This makes the code less complex and arguably easier to understand, but it assumes that you'll have your compiler set up correctly to deal with it. I'll discuss compiler setup in just a moment.

It's important to understand the distinction between the sort of C code that's used in this book and the more complex dialect of ANSI C. Neither is necessarily preferable to the other, as long as you understand what they're both up to.

Under C, everything is an integer unless you specifically tell C otherwise. In ages past, this was a fairly safe assumption because both integers and pointers could fit in 16-bit numbers, and, while occasionally interchanging them was reprehensible by C's standards, it was rarely fatal. Certainly in large-model programs in a DOS environment this is no longer true.

This is a legal C language function:

```
SellTheCat(cat)
{
        /* do something */
}
```

In the `SellTheCat` function, the argument `cat` is assumed to be an integer because it hasn't been declared as anything else. The function is assumed to return an integer because no mention has been made of it doing otherwise. The following are two obviously incorrect ways to call this function, but under simple C your compiler will not complain about either.

```
SellTheCat("Bad tempered tabby");

puts(SellTheCat());
```

In the first case, `SellTheCat` will be passed a pointer to a string when it's expecting an integer. In the second case, it won't be passed anything and its return value will be used as a pointer to a string. Neither misapplication of `SellTheCat` is likely to produce anything meaningful.

If you were to write a function called `SellTheCat`, and as such understand what it's supposed to do, it's unlikely that you'd deliberately call it incorrectly. To this end, C allows for prototypes.

Here's a more complete declaration for `SellTheCat`:

```
void SellTheCat(int n)
{
        /* do something */
}
```

This has declared that `SellTheCat` expects a single integer as an argument and that its return value is meaningless. You can tell any function about its nature by declaring a prototype for it at the top of your program's source code:

```
void SellTheCat(int n);
```

With these bits of code in place and the prototype checking switched on in your C compiler, attempting to use `SellTheCat` incorrectly would cause your compiler to issue suitable warnings or error messages.

There are two levels of prototype checking. The simplest is to have your compiler check any function calls for which prototypes exist. The somewhat more draconian one is to have your compiler refuse to compile any source code in which a prototype doesn't exist for every function within shouting distance. The latter, while certain to trap a few bugs for the habitually sloppy, is lethally frustrating after about 20 minutes.

The DOS-based code in this book does not declare function prototypes for all the functions it uses. You will find prototypes for functions that return values other than integers—where they're mandatory—and for those functions which if called incorrectly could spell the catastrophic demise of human civilization as we know it.

If you see warnings about "function does not return a value" or "function called with no prototypes" you should switch off the appropriate warning items in the configuration of your C compiler.

This is a complete list of the configuration items of your compiler that you should set up to correctly compile the DOS program examples in *Canned Code.*

- The memory model must be large.
- The default `char` type must be unsigned.
- All the ANSI C and C++ options must be off.
- Register and jump optimization must be off.
- Case-sensitive linking should be off.

You're free to change your compiler setup for your own applications based on the code in this book, of course, but if you start running into problems compiling the example programs begin with this configuration.

## Assembly language considerations

There are some things you just can't do in C, or that you can't do very well. Assembly language offers ways to get into the dark caverns and dungeons of DOS, as well as a path to optimize time-sensitive functions. While there is relatively little assembly language used in *Canned Code*, it does turn up occasionally.

The assembly language modules in this book that link to C programs assume that you'll be compiling your programs to work in the large memory model. They'll crash rather colorfully if they're used as they stand with other memory models. Whereas a C compiler will fiddle with its internal use of pointers to compensate for model changes, an assembler only knows how to do what you tell it to do.

Note that the assembly language modules in *Canned Code* assume that you'll have the register variables in your C compiler switched off.

In most cases you'll be able to use the assembly language modules in this book as they stand, even if you aren't wholly fluent in 8086 machine code. If you do decide to make changes to them, be sure you fully understand what they're up to. Assembly language offers you virtually none of the protection that C does, and it can crash your system in ways that C only dreams of doing.

The assembly language code in this book was assembled using the Borland TASM assembler. In using TASM, however, you should make sure you include the `/m3` command line switch to resolve any forward references in the source code.

# Windows considerations

Programming under Windows is decidedly more challenging than writing DOS applications, but it's not anywhere near as bound up in the complexities of different compiler standards. Because of the fairly rigid calling conventions of Windows' intrinsic functions, any language that wants to generate Windows applications pretty well has to behave itself.

Unless you're particularly daring, when you're dealing with Windows, it's a very good idea to ignore most of the foregoing discussion about prototypes being optional. The complexity of function calls and pointers under Windows makes using prototypes a very good idea—it's beyond all but the most organized software authors to keep track of all the nuances of calling Windows functions.

The Windows applications in this book were all compiled using Borland C++ 3.1 for Windows. You should set up your Windows compiler using the same defaults as were discussed in the foregoing section; however, the memory model should be medium, rather than large. Enable the Borland "smart callbacks" feature.

You'll find project files for the Borland integrated development environment on the companion disk for this book.

Note that most Windows applications are written in the medium memory model with far or huge pointers declared where they're required. Windows swaps code segments in and out of memory as an application runs, and as such you can have all the speed advantages of the medium model with no meaningful code or data size limitations.

## Using this book

It's unlikely that you'll find exactly the program you've always wanted to write in this book. *Canned Code* is a lot more likely to provide you with some of the harder-to-obtain pieces to build your application. As much as possible, the code in this book is fairly modular, and you should find it easy to pour into your own software.

If you're fairly new to C language programming, you might find that many of the examples in *Canned Code* will serve as more interesting exercises in the craft of creating software than the usual exercises in C primers. Dragon curves look a lot better than binary numbers, all other things being equal.

One of the most effective ways to learn how to write software is to begin with some existing code and modify it into what you require. You'll find a wealth of places to start from herein.

Having opened a can of worms, it's most often the case that the only way to recan them is to use a bigger can. The same is arguably true of canned code. You'll find it pretty easy to make much bigger things out of the contents of this book than exist between its pages at the moment. All it takes is some hard-drive space . . . and some imagination.

# 1
# Text wizardry

*"Once you pull the pin Mr. Hand Grenade is no longer your friend."*

—Graffiti

In many circles, the text modes of PC systems are regarded as some species of antediluvian reptile, something to be spoken of in polite whispers when civilized people are out of earshot. Microsoft ran an advertisement for Windows some while back that suggested that the DOS prompt, almost an icon of text mode, would hitherto be seen no more. One thing that the early Macintosh system developers were pleased to note was that Macintosh was modeless—text mode had never entered into the consciousness of the designers of the Mac.

In fact, text mode has its uses. It's fast and relatively easy to work with, and there are numerous applications for which text mode is quite adequate. Clearly, software that works solely with information—database managers, spreadsheets, and so on—can get along quite well in text mode, or in text mode with occasional recourse to graphics. The speed of text mode is often more than suitable compensation for the argument that it looks like something that should have been forgotten back in the early bronze age.

This chapter explores the tools required to make text mode applications look professional and do things that make dealing with text mode worthwhile.

It's possible to create very clever, user-friendly, interactive applications in text mode. It's also possible to create software that would have been cumbersome back when teletypes were state of the art. Unlike graphical user interface environments, such as Windows, a text mode screen is a blank canvas. You can paint anything you like on it, and it's up to you to keep it from being ugly.

## Do high-speed screen access

In support of their text modes, PC systems include BIOS calls to print characters to the screen. This relieves programmers of the task of knowing how to manage screen memory directly. At least, it would if the BIOS screen support was actually usable. Breathtakingly slow, the PC's BIOS seems perpetually stuck in first gear.

Contemporary PC text mode software can pop text, windows, menus, and other screen phenomena onto your tube in an immeasurably short time, even if your tube is connected to a relatively slow computer. It can do this through the miracle of direct screen access, a pretty refined name for cheating. Direct screen access abandons all manner of principles of good programming in favor of attractive software. The programmers responsible for the original PC BIOS would no doubt shake their prematurely bald heads in despair.

The correct and proper way to print a character to the PC screen from within a C language program is to do this:

```
putchar('A');
```

This would print the character A to the screen at the current cursor location. In fact, what will usually happen is that `putchar` will hand the character to DOS, which will hand it to the BIOS, which will think for a while and finally write the character to the screen. This involves at least two interrupt calls and an uncountable number of processor cycles. It's perhaps not surprising that it takes rather a while for the correct and proper method of printing text to actually get anything done.

The PC screen is a *memory mapped device*. This means that the memory that holds what's being displayed is actually just a block of memory on the processor bus. In text mode the screen memory begins at B000:0000H for Hercules and monochrome graphics adapters, and at B800:0000H for other display cards, such as EGA and VGA cards. If you write to memory beginning at one of these locations, as is appropriate, the contents of the screen will change. Knowing what to write to these locations allows you to change the screen contents in a predictable manner, arguably an asset.

A conventional PC text mode screen is set up as 25 columns of 80 characters each. Each character requires two bytes, or one word. As such, each row of text requires 160 bytes. A whole screen requires 4000 bytes of memory.

Each word of the screen memory holds the character being displayed in its low-order byte and the character's attribute in its high-order byte. We'll get back to this in a moment.

The easiest way to write to the screen is to cast a far pointer to the screen memory and copy data to where the pointer points. To begin with, let's find a way to derive this pointer.

```
char *screenPtr()
{
        union REGS r;

        r.x.ax=0x0f00;
        int86(0x10,&r,&r);

        if(r.h.al==0x07) return(MK_FP(0xb000,r.h.bh*0x1000));
        else return(MK_FP(0x800,r.h.bh*0x1000));
}
```

The screenPtr function will return a far pointer to the base of the screen text buffer, regardless of which segment value is being used. Note that on some display cards the text mode screen can have multiple pages, with each page being 4096 bytes long. This allows sufficiently crafty software to manage fast screen updates by writing to a hidden page and then making it the current visible page. This is a facility of questionable usefulness, as it's not available on all display adapters and it's not perceptibly faster than simply using a very fast screen display function, as I'll discuss in this chapter.

The interrupt call in screenPtr returns the current display mode number in the AL register and the current display page in the BH register. The mode will be seven if the card is a Hercules or monochrome display adapter, and something else—usually three—if the card is a CGA, EGA, or VGA display.

Prior to doing any high-speed screen updates, you should store the pointer returned by screenPtr in a global far pointer. Note that you must also have a prototype for screenPtr, as it returns something other than an integer. Here's the code involved:

```
char *screenPtr(void);  /* the prototype */

char *screen;           /* the pointer declaration */
screen=screen Ptr();    /* the assignment */
```

The pointer screen is of the type char, which means that it will address every byte in the screen buffer. To print simple text, you would actually only want to write to the even-numbered bytes, as the corresponding odd-numbered bytes store the character attributes. Here's a function to print a string this way:

```
DrawString(string,x,y)
        char *string;
        unsigned int x,y;
{
        char *p;

        p=screen+y*160+x*2;

        while(*string) {
```

```
                *p=*s++;
                p+=2;
        }
}
```

The DrawString function will print its string argument beginning at location (x,y) on the screen. It works out the initial location in the screen buffer based on there being 160 bytes per line and two bytes per character.

Note that this function does not allow for the sorts of string accommodations of dedicated string printing functions. Specifically, it will not correctly interpret control characters, such as carriage returns and tabs.

Here's a slightly different version of the previous function. This code will print a string with a defined character attribute. I'll discuss attributes in a moment.

```
DrawStringWithAttribute(string,x,y,attribute)
        char *string;
        unsigned int x,y,attribute;
{
        unsigned int *p;

        p=(unsigned int *)(screen+y*160+x*2);

        while(*string) *p++=*s++ | attribute << 8;
}
```

The DrawStringWithAttribute function is a bit more inscrutable, and uses even more cheating and underhandedness than its predecessor. When you write to the screen using a far pointer, as I've done thus far, what really happens in machine language is something like this:

```
    MOV ES,FP_SEG(screen)
    MOV DI,FP_OFF(screen)
    MOV AL,character
    STOSB
```

Writing a word rather than a byte this way involves using the STOSW instruction, not STOSB. Both require the same number of machine cycles, and there is no speed penalty—at least in theory—if you write text to the screen with an attribute byte attached. In fact, because the screen is really word oriented, it's actually a bit faster to handle text using DrawStringWithAttribute. In practice, you'll have a hard time coming up with a way to measure how long either of these calls requires.

Thus far, I have not really dealt with the nature of screen attributes. The attribute byte of each character defines its color and whether its highlighted or blinking. Specifically, the low-order four bits define the foreground color. The next three bits define the background color, and the high-order bit defines whether the character will be blinking or not. This can be used as a flag to determine whether a character is highlighted or not in some circumstances.

If you include the `conio.h` header file in a C program, you will have access to the following constants. They're shown as defines here—in most cases, they're actually declared as an `enum` in `conio.h`, although the effect is the same.

```
#define BLACK          0
#define BLUE           1
#define GREEN          2
#define CYAN           3
#define RED            4
#define MAGENTA        5
#define BROWN          6
#define LIGHTGRAY      7
#define DARKGRAY       8
#define LIGHTBLUE      9
#define LIGHTGREEN     10
#define LIGHTCYAN      11
#define LIGHTRED       12
#define LIGHTMAGENTA   13
#define YELLOW         14
#define WHITE          15
```

It takes a bit of cunning to use these defines correctly. To begin with, you can use any of these values as they stand to set the foreground color attribute of text. As such, this would print some text in magenta.

```
DrawStringWithAttribute("Some text",10,10,MAGENTA);
```

More specifically, it would print some text in magenta against a black background.

This is how you would print some text in blue against a light gray background. Note that light gray is what most people regard as normal intensity white.

```
DrawStringWithAttribute("Some text",10,10,BLUE | (LIGHTGRAY) <<4));
```

In this case, the value of BLUE will appear in the low-order four bits. The value of LIGHTGRAY is shifted left by four positions, and appears in the upper four bits. However, because LIGHTGRAY is less than eight, the high-order bit will be zero.

This is how you'd print some text in blue against light gray and make it blink.

```
DrawStringWithAttribute("Some text",10,10,BLUE | LIGHTGRAY << 4) | 0x80
```

When you OR 80H with an attribute value, you set the high-order bit, the flag for blinking text.

If you understand all this, you might well wonder what happens if you want to use a value between 8 and 15 as a background color, as these all have their high-order bits set. The answer is that you can't. If you use LIGHTMAGENTA, color 13, as a background color, it will be interpreted as MAGENTA, color 5, and the character will blink. You can use all 16 colors for a character's foreground, but only the first 8 as the background.

By default, the high-order bit of an attribute bit is interpreted as a flag to make the associated character blink. You can cause this to be regarded as a flag to indicate high intensity instead. This only works on EGA and VGA cards. Here's how to set up the screen for high intensity:

```
union REGS r;

r.x.ax=0x1003;
r.h.bl=0x00;
int86(0x10,&r,&r);
```

Having made this call, any characters that would normally blink because the high-order bits of their attribute values are high will be highlighted instead. This is arguably a much easier thing to look at than blinking text.

Here's how to return the screen to it's normal mode, such that the characters set to blink do so.

```
union REGS r;

r.x.ax=0x1003;
r.h.bl=0x01;
int86(0x10,&r,&r);
```

The previous discussion of character attributes applies to display adapters that support color; that is, CGA, EGA, and VGA cards. Hercules and monochrome display adapters support the same screen structure in text mode, but their attribute bytes are a little different. This is in keeping with the generally more limited range of display options available on a monochrome display.

On a monochrome display card, the following list of constants apply to character attributes:

```
#define UNDERLINE         1
#define NORMAL            7
#define REVERSE         112
#define BLINKING        128
#define HIGHINTENSITY     8
```

These constants are a bit tricky to use correctly. There are really only four valid attribute values, these being NORMAL, REVERSE, HIGHINTENSITY, and UNDERLINE. Note that REVERSE is actually NORMAL shifted left by four places. You can OR the BLINKING and HIGHINTENSITY constants with the four basic attributes. As such, you would print normal text like this:

```
DrawStringWithAttribute("Normal text",10,10,NORMAL);
```

You would print high-intensity text like this:

```
DrawStringWithAttribute("High intensity text",10,10,NORMAL |
HIGHINTENSITY);
```

The high-intensity flag is ignored if the REVERSE attribute is used.

Working with monochrome displays is a bit inconvenient, and for this reason, some applications that support text mode don't include drivers for monochrome cards. This will no doubt dismay the dwindling number of users with these cards, and you might find that complex screens created with the color facilities of a VGA card don't really translate to the few attributes of a monochrome card.

As a final note, in addition to printing text using the direct screen access techniques discussed here, you can also perform more rudimentary operations, such as clearing the screen. Here's how you'd do this:

```
unsigned int i,*ip;

ip=(unsigned int *)screen;
for(i=0;<2000;++i) *ip++=0x0720;
```

This bit of code writes 2000 identical words to the screen buffer. The low-order byte of the word in question is 20H, or 32, the ASCII value for a blank space. The high-order word is 07H, the screen attribute for light gray or normal text. This can be handled even more efficiently in assembly language:

```
         MOV   ES,FP_SEG(screen)
         MOV   DI,FP_OFF(screen)
         MOV   AX,0720H
         MOV   CX,2000
         CLD
REPNE    STOSW
```

Note that you must handle loading the ES and DI registers with the appropriate values, based on how you've stored the screen pointer.

## Determine the display card type

It's often handy to know what type of display card is in the machine your software is running on. There are, for example, some text mode display functions that work on EGA and VGA cards, but not on CGA cards.

As you saw in the previous section, you can determine whether the display is a monochrome or color card by having the BIOS return the current screen mode; monochrome cards can only support one text mode, this being mode seven. In fact, this is reliable if the card in question is a Hercules card in its graphics mode. Hercules graphics are not supported by PC BIOS and must be enabled by directly fiddling with the card's registers. As far as the BIOS is concerned, a Hercules card is in text mode when it's displaying graphics and, as such, the BIOS will still return mode seven. An old-style IBM monochrome display adapter doesn't have a graphics mode at all.

Refining your determination of the display card type beyond this might prove a bit more complex, and how you approach it will be determined to some extent by how you want the process to err if it encounters something unusual. There are a lot of unusual display cards—hardware that has been designed for laptops, terminals, PS/2 systems, and so on. Also keep in mind that most contemporary display cards have multiple modes. If you ask one, "Are you a VGA card or a Hercules card?" in the wrong way, it will reply "yes."

There are two approaches to determining whether your software is looking at a VGA card or not. The EGA and VGA cards have much more elaborate BIOS firmware than the original CGA and monochrome cards, requiring that the display card BIOS attach itself to the system BIOS. The display card BIOS usually resides in memory at C000:0000H. By convention, extension BIOSs begin with the bytes 55H and AAH. As such, the following should be a test for the existence of an extension BIOS for a display card, indicating the presence of either an EGA or VGA card:

```
char *p=MK_FP(0xc000,0x0000);

if(p[0]==0x55 && p[1]==0xaa /* it's an EGA or VGA card */
```

In practice, this isn't all that reliable. Some cards, such as the VGA displays of the IBM PS/2 machines, locate their extension BIOSs elsewhere, and this test will fail even if there really is a VGA card in place.

In fact, there's a much simpler way to perform this check. The EGA and VGA cards have their graphics buffers beginning at location A000:0000H. Older display cards begin their graphics buffers at the start of their text buffers. Looking for the existence of memory at A000:0000H will test for the presence of an EGA or VGA card.

There's a very reliable way to ascertain the existence of a VGA card. The BIOS will tell you, but only if you know how to ask.

```
union REGS r;
struct SREGS sr;
char b[64];

r.x.ax=0x1b00;
r.x.bx=0x0000;
```

```
r.x.di=FP_OFF(b);
sr.es=FP_SEG(b);
int86x(0x10,&r,&r,&sr);

if(r.h.al==0x1b) /* it's a VGA card */
```

This call is actually used to return information about the display functionality; that is, which modes are supported. However, because it only exists on a VGA card it's a pretty good indication as to whether one's present. It returns with 1BH in the AL register if it worked.

It seems fair to note that some of the more exotic display cards that IBM has released for its own systems—the 8514 and the XGA cards, for example—will look like a VGA card to this test as well. You'll have to get sneakier to be able to determine which type of VGA card is present. If you want to look at an example of such sneakiness, you might want to read my book *Super VGA Graphics*, published by Windcrest.

Determining whether a monochrome display is a Hercules card or an old-style IBM monochrome display adapter requires a degree of stealth that makes the previous bit of esoterica look like graffiti spray painted on the side of a Goodyear blimp. In their text modes, both cards look identical except a monochrome display adapter does not provide a way to know when the vertical retrace period of the display starts, while a Hercules card does. On a Hercules card, the high-order bit of port 03BAH will go high every time the vertical retrace interval begins. If you sample this port repeatedly for a sufficient interval—one-fifteenth of a second is more than long enough—and the high-order bit goes high at least once, the display is a Hercules card.

It makes you wonder how long someone had to think about that one. Here's the code to decide whether there's a Hercules card in your system. The `isHerc` function will return a true value if there is.

```
is Herc()        /* return true if there's Hercules card present */
{
        long ts;
        int r=0;

        ts=tick();
        do {
                if(inp(0x03ba) & 0x80) {
                        r=1;
                        break;
                }
        } while(ts==tick());
        return(r);
}

long tick()       /* fetch the BIOS tick count */
{
        union REGS r;

        r.x.ax = 0x0000;
```

```
        int86(0x1a,&r,&r);
        return(((long)r.x.cx<<16) | r.x.dx);
}
```

## Protect text strings from tampering

One of the unfortunate aspects of software is that it's often a lot softer than one would like it to be. While large-scale assaults on a complex application—disassembling one, for example—can be prohibitively difficult, it's often fairly easy to disable the copyright notices buried in code.

There are several ways to protect your applications from the machinations of hackers, cyberpunks, and the other denizens of the small hours of the morning. The simplest one is to use checksums.

A *checksum* of a block of data is a number that changes if the data changes. If you store a string and its checksum, your software can subsequently make sure the string hasn't changed by recalculating the checksum to see if it matches the original checksum. Here's a very simple function to calculate the checksum of a string:

```
unsigned int checksum(string)
        char *string;
{
        unsigned int a=0;

        while(*string) a+=*string++;
        return(a);
}
```

The `checksum` function will return a value that represents all the characters in a string added together. In fact, for long strings this will wrap around past zero, but it hardly matters. If the contents of a checksummed string change, the checksum will change.

At least, it should. This sort of checksum can be fooled fairly easily. For example, the two strings "Ac" and "cA" will have the same checksum, even though they contain different text. The ASCII values of the characters happen to add up to the same number.

Here's a checksum function that's quite a bit harder to fool:

```
unsigned int checksum(string)
        char *string;
{
        unsigned int j=0,i,n,a=0;

        n=strlen(string);

        for(i=0;i<n;++i) {
                switch(j) {
                        case 3:
                                a+=(((int)s[i] ^ 0x009b)<<j);
```

```
                        break;
                case 2:
                        a+=((~(int)s[i] & 0x005c)<< j);
                        break;
                case 1:
                        a+=((~(int)s[i] ^ 0x000e)<<j);
                        break;
                default:
                        a+=((int)s[i]*(int)s[i]);
                        break;
            }
            a &= 0x7fff;
            ++j;
            if(j > 3) j=0;
        }
        if(!a) ++a;
        return(a);
}
```

This version of the `checksum` function performs various bitwise operations on the characters of the string it checks. You can change the actual values involved to derive different checksums for different applications. Because different operations are performed on the characters of the string being checked depending on their position in the string, it's almost impossible to fool the checksum.

## Write a (martian) text filter

The DOS text filter facility is a relic dating back to the prehistory of PCs. It's a bit hard to fathom, and it's really only useful to people who like to play with unusual bits of computer lore. However, if you manipulate text files a lot, you'll probably find it handy, as it allows you to create various filters to manipulate text, objects that can be quickly combined into more complex processors with nothing more involved than a batch file.

By default, if you do this,

```
TYPE README.TXT
```

the text in the file README.TXT will be sent to your screen. However, you can also do this:

```
TYPE README.TXT | FILTER
```

This assumes the existence of a program called FILTER.COM or FILTER .EXE, which will accept text "piped" into it and will subsequently print it in some modified form. Here's a very simple filter:

```
#include "stdio.h"
#Include "ctype.h"
```

```
main()
{
        int c;

        while((c=getchar()) != EOF) putchar(toupper(c));
}
```

This filter is called TOUPPER.C; that is, it will result in a program called TOUPPER.EXE. If you pipe text through it, the text will be sent to your screen IN ALL UPPERCASE.

The TOUPPER filter looks impossibly simple. In fact, it uses some invisible hooks into DOS. It seems to do nothing more than accept keyboard input and print it to the screen after passing it through the `toupper` macro. If you run it like a conventional DOS application, that is precisely what it will do. However, if there is data being piped into it, the `getchar` function will read its characters from the piped source, rather than from your keyboard, and will return EOF when there are no more characters to be had.

Most DOS users have found that text printed to the screen can be redirected to a file using the > character. This is another aspect of the DOS filter mechanism. As such, you can use this filter to convert a text file to uppercase:

```
TYPE README.TXT | TOUPPER > README.TOO
```

The file README.TOO will contain the contents of README.TXT in uppercase.

Here's my favorite filter. It's called MARTIAN.C. It converts plain text to easily understandable martian, as found on any martian billboard or street sign.

```
/*
        Martian text filter

        Copyright (c) 1993 Alchemy Mindworks Inc.
*/

#include "stdio.h"

char lookup[]= {
        0x84,0xe1,0x9b,0xeb,0x89,0x9f,0x67,0x68,
        0x8b,0xf5,0x6b,0x9c,0x6d,0xef,0xed,0x9e,
        0x71,0xe2,0x24,0xe7,0xe6,0x76,0x77,0x78,
        0x9d,0x7a
        };

main()
{
        int c;

        while((c=getchar()) != EOF) putchar(tomartian(c));
}
```

```
tomartian(c)
        int c;
{
        if(c >= 'A' && c <='Z') return(lookup[c-'A']);
        else if(c >= 'a' && c <= 'z') return(lookup[c-'a']);
        else return(c);
}
```

The result of the martian filter is shown in 1-1.

```
H:\>type text
Once you open a can of worms the only practical
way to re-can them is to use a larger can.
                                - Martian proverb


H:\>type text | martian
ø∩¢ë ¥øµ ø₧ë∩ ä ¢ä∩ øf wøΓm$ τhë ø∩£¥ ₧Γä¢τï¢ä£
wä¥ τø Γë-¢ä∩ τhëm ï$ τø µ$ë ä £äΓgëΓ ¢ä∩.
                                - mäΓτïä∩ ₧ΓøvëΓß


H:\>
```

**1-1** Some text in English and its martian equivalent.

In fact, what MARTIAN does is to replace most of the conventional text characters with similar-looking symbols from the PC high-order character set. While peculiar, they do result in readable text—sort of.

Practical applications for MARTIAN might be fairly few—you can probably find uses for the DOS filter functions in general. Note that while they work on pure text files, you can't use filters with proprietary word processor files or other complex formatted documents.

## Create self-displaying text

The problem with READ.ME files is that half the people who should read them don't have a convenient way to do so and ignore them. A more useful form of READ.ME file might be one that displayed itself; that is, a program that showed text. While in theory a READ.ME file is a fairly simple thing to create, to really make such a function workable, you'd need a convenient process to integrate the text and the code to display it.

Here's a very simple assembly language program that will display text:

```
;
;       SELF DISPLAYING TEXT
;       COPYRIGHT (C) 1993 ALCHEMY MINDWORKS INC.
;
```

```
_TEXT           SEGMENT BYTE PUBLIC 'CODE'
                ASSUME  CS:_TEXT, DS:NOTHING, ES:NOTHING, SS:NOTHING
                ORG     100H

BEGIN:          JMP     START

LEN             DW      0000H

START:          MOV     AX,4000H
                MOV     BX,0001H
                MOV     CX,[LEN]
                MOV     DX,OFFSET ENDOFCODE
                INT     21H

                MOV     AX,4C00H
                INT     21H

ENDOFCODE       LABEL   BYTE

_TEXT           ENDS
                END     BEGIN
```

The SHOWTEXT.ASM file should be assembled into a COM file. It assumes that the text to be displayed will begin at the location ENDOFCODE, and that the number of characters to be displayed will be stored in LEN.

The SHOWTEXT.ASM program actually displays its text by writing it to file handle 1, which DOS leaves permanently connected to your screen. This is a lot faster than writing it one character at a time.

To integrate this bit of code with some text, you'll need SHOWTEXT.C. Here it is:

```
/*
        Self-displaying text generator
        Copyright (c) 1993 Alchemy Mindworks Inc.
*/

#include "stdio.h"
#include "alloc.h"

char comfile[]= {
        0xeb,0x03,0x90,0x00,0x00,0xb8,0x00,0x40,
        0xbb,0x01,0x00,0x2e,0x8b,0x0e,0x03,0x01,
        0xba,0x1a,0x01,0xcd,0x21,0xb8,0x00,0x4c,
        0xcd,0x21
        };

main(argc,argv)
        int argc;
        char *argv[];
{
        FILE *fp;
        char *p;
        unsigned long l;
        unsigned int *ip;

        puts ("Self-displaying text generator copyright "
```

```
                "(c) 1993 Alchemy Mindworks Inc.\n"
                "___________________________________________"
                "______________________________");

        if(argc <= 2) error("Arguments:          Text file to read\n"
                            "                    COM file to write\n";

        if((fp=fopen(argv[1],"rb")) == NULL)
            error("Error opening the source file");

        fseek(fp,0L,SEEK_END);

        l=ftell(fp);
        fseek(fp,0L,SEEK_SET);

        if(l > 32767L) error("The source file is a bit huge");

        if((p=malloc(unsigned int)l))==NULL) error("Can't allocate memo">;

        if(fread(p,1,(unsigned int)l,fp) != (unsigned int)l)
           error("Can't read the source file");

        fclose(fp);

        ip=(unsigned int *) (comfile+3);
        ip[0]=(unsigned int)l;

        if((fp=fopen(argv[2],"wb")) == NULL)
            error("Error creating the destination file");

        if(fwrite(comfile,1,sizeof(comfile),fp) != sizeof(comfile))
            error("Error writing the file header");

        if(fwrite(p,1,(unsigned int)l,fp) != (unsigned int)l)
            error("Error writing the text");

        fclose(fp);
        puts("All done");

        exit(0);
}

error(s)
        char *s;
{
        puts(s);
        exit(1);
}
```

The data in `comfile` at the top of SHOWTEXT.C is actually the assembled SHOWTEXT.ASM code. It's pretty easy to see what SHOWTEXT is up to. It will load a text file into memory, patch `comfile` with the length of the text it's read and then write `comfile` followed by the text to a destination file.

Assuming that TEXTFILE.TXT is a text file and that you'd like to create a program called README.COM, here's how you'd use SHOWTEXT:

```
SHOWTEXT TEXTFILE.TXT README.COM
```

Note that SHOWTEXT will only work with pure text files, rather than proprietary word processing documents. You can, however, include high-order IBM characters in its text files, and you can use ANSI escape sequences. The latter is a bit questionable, as it will make the programs SHOWTEXT creates a bit unreadable on machines without ANSI.SYS installed.

You might want to modify SHOWTEXT.ASM to handle paging if you anticipate displaying text files that are larger than one page. In this case, you'll need a way to convert the binary data of a COM file into a C language array. See the section of this book that deals with programmers' toys.

## Change the colors in the text mode palette

Earlier in this chapter I looked at writing text to the screen using the 16 available display colors. On the surface, it looks as if this list represents all the colors to be had in text mode, and in a sense, it does. Text mode doesn't have a dedicated palette per se. However, on a VGA card, the first 16 colors in the graphic mode palette also supply the colors for text mode. As such, you can add a few more colors to the earlier list—about a quarter of a million more.

Changing the colors in text mode is handled the same way as doing so in graphic mode for a VGA card, something that won't be dealt with in detail until the next chapter of this book. Colors can be defined as percentages of red, green, and blue light—this is called RGB color. On a PC, each color value can be stored in one byte, and as such it's convenient to represent colors as long integers, with one byte unused.

Here's a macro to create a long integer color value from percentages of red, green, and blue light:

```
#define RGB(r,g,b)      ((long)r | ((long)g << 8) | ((long)b <<16))
```

The values of `r`, `g`, and `b` should be in the range of 0 through 255.

Setting the VGA palette can be handled in either of two ways. The correct way—and, of course, the slowest—is to use BIOS calls to perform this function. A somewhat better approach is to manipulate the VGA card color registers directly. This is considerably faster than using a BIOS call to perform the same function—palette animation, where you change the colors on screen to make things appear to move, requires that you avoid using the BIOS to adjust the palette colors. The only catch is that it only works on VGA cards—other displays, such as IBM's mutant XGA cards, have different register layouts.

TEXTPAL.C, a demonstration program that exercises the text mode palette facilities of a VGA card, is illustrated in 1-2. Note that it will only run on VGA and super VGA cards. It begins by displaying the word BLUE in 16 gradations of the color blue. It will then animate this. Finally, it will display 15 colors not usually seen in text mode.

**1-2** The TEXTPAL.C source code.

```
/*
        text palette demo
        Copyright (c) 1993 Alchemy Mindworks Inc.
*/

#include "stdio.h"
#include "dos.h"
#include "colour.h"

#define RED(n)          ((int)(n & 0x0000ffL))
#define GREEN(n)        ((int)((n >> 8) & 0x0000ffL))
#define BLUE(n)         ((int)((n >> 16) & 0x0000ffL))
#define RGB(r,g,b)      ((long)r | ((long)g << 8) | ((long)b << 16))

long colourtable[]= {
        Black,
        ElectricBlue,
        OceanGreen,
        LightGreen,
        Chalk,
        AutumnOrange,
        Sand,
        Walnut,
        Crimson,
        DustyRose,
        NeonPurple,
        Black20,
        Cyan,
        Green,
        Yellow,
        White,
        };

main()
{
        union REGS r;
        char b[128];
        long table[16];
        int i,j,n;

        clrscr();

        initpalette();

        /* do a graduated screen of the blues */
        for(i=0;i<16;++i) table[i]=RGB(0,0,i<<4);
        setuppalette(table);

        /* unusual for loop, what... */
        for(b[0]=0;strlen(b)+4 <= 80;strcat(b,"BLUE"));

        /* show the blues */
        for(i=0;i<16;++i) putline(0,2+i,i,b);

        getch();
```

**1-2** Continued.

```
        /* animate the palette */
        for(n=0,j=1;!kbhit();n+=j){
                for(i=0;i<16;++i) table[i]=RGB(0,0,i*n);
                setuppalette(table);

                if(n >= 16) j=-1;
                else if(n <= 0) j=1;

                delay(50);
        }

        getch();

        clrscr();

        /* use a sophisticated designer palette */
        setuppalette(colourtable);

        putbanner(2,1,"Electric Blue");
        putbanner(3,2,"Ocean Green");
        putbanner(4,3,"Light Green");
        putbanner(5,4,"Chalk");
        putbanner(6,5,"Autumn Orange");
        putbanner(7,6,"Sand");
        putbanner(8,7,"Walnut");
        putbanner(9,8,"Crimson");
        putbanner(10,9,"Dusty Rose");
        putbanner(11,10,"Neon Purple");
        putbanner(12,11,"Black 20");
        putbanner(13,12,"Cyan");
        putbanner(14,13,"Green");
        putbanner(15,14,"Yellow");
        putbanner(16,15,"White");

        getch();

        clrscr();

        /* back to the same old colours */
        r.x.ax=0x0003;
        int86(0x10,&r,&r);

}

putbanner(y,attr,text)
        int y,attr;
        char *text;
{
        char *screen,b[64];
        int i;

        screen=MK_FP(0xb800,y*160);
        for(i=0;i<80;++i) {
                *screen++=219;
```

```
                *screen++=attr;
        }

        sprintf(b,"[ %s ]",text);

        putline((80-strlen(b))/2,y,attr,b);
}

putline(x,y,attr,text)
        int x,y,attr;
        char *text;
{
        char *screen;

        screen=MK_FP(0xb800,y*160+x*2);
        while(*text) {
                *screen++=*text++;
                *screen++=attr;
        }
}

initpalette()
{
        union REGS r;
        int i;
        for(i=0;i<16;++i) {
                r.x.ax=0x1000;
                r.h.bh=i;
                r.h.bl=i;
                int86(0x10,&r,&r);
        }
}

setuppalette(table)
        long *table;
{
        int i;

        outp(0x3c6,0xff);
        for(i=0;i<16;++i) {
                outp(0x3c8,i);
                outp(0x3c9,RED(table[i]) >> 2);
                outp(0x3c9,GREEN(table[i]) >> 2);
                outp(0x3c9,BLUE(table[i]) >> 2);
        }
}
```

Note that the `initpalette` function must be called prior to any palette changes.

The TEXTPAL program includes a file called COLOR.H. This defines the colors in the color palette used in the third section of the program. To be sure, the standard IBM color palette does not include shades such as "Dusty Rose" and "Desert Blue."

COLOR.H is illustrated in 1-3. It might require a bit of explanation.

**1-3** The COLOR.H header file.

```
/*        some interesting colours          */
#define CYMK(c,m,y,k)              ((((long)(100-(c+k))*255)/100) | \
                                   ((((long)(100-(m+k))*255)/100) << 8) | \
                                   ((((long)(100-(y+k))*255)/100) << 16))


#define Black                      CYMK(0,0,0,100)
#define Black80                    CYMK(0,0,0,80)
#define Black70                    CYMK(0,0,0,70)
#define Black60                    CYMK(0,0,0,60)
#define Black50                    CYMK(0,0,0,50)
#define Black40                    CYMK(0,0,0,40)
#define Black30                    CYMK(0,0,0,30)
#define Black20                    CYMK(0,0,0,20)
#define Black10                    CYMK(0,0,0,10)
#define White                      CYMK(0,0,0,0)
#define Blue                       CYMK(100,100,0,0)
#define Cyan                       CYMK(100,0,0,0)
#define Green                      CYMK(100,0,100,0)
#define Yellow                     CYMK(0,0,100,0)
#define Red                        CYMK(0,100,100,0)
#define Magenta                    CYMK(0,100,0,0)
#define Purple                     CYMK(20,80,0,20)
#define Orange                     CYMK(0,60,100,0)
#define Pink                       CYMK(0,40,20,0)
#define DarkBrown                  CYMK(0,20,20,60)
#define PowderBlue                 CYMK(20,20,0,0)
#define PastelBlue                 CYMK(40,40,0,0)
#define BabyBlue                   CYMK(60,40,0,0)
#define ElectricBlue               CYMK(60,60,0,0)
#define TwilightBlue               CYMK(40,40,0,20)
#define NavyBlue                   CYMK(60,40,0,40)
#define DeepNavy Blue              CYMK(40,40,0,60)
#define DesertBlue                 CYMK(40,20,0,40)
#define SkyBlue                    CYMK(100,20,0,0)
#define IceBlue                    CYMK(40,0,0,0)
#define LightBlueGreen             CYMK(20,0,0,20)
#define OceanGreen                 CYMK20,0,0,40)
#define MossGreen                  CYMK(20,0,0,60)
#define DarkGreen                  CYMK(20,0,0,80)
#define ForestGreen                CYMK(40,0,20,60)
#define GrassGreen                 CYMK(60,0,40,40)
#define KentuckyGreen              CYMK(40,0,20,40)
#define LightGreen                 CYMK(60,0,40,20)
#define SpringGreen                CYMK(60,0,60,20)
#define Turquoise                  CYMK(60,0,20,0)
#define SeaGreen                   CYMK(60,0,20,20)
#define FadedGreen                 CYMK(20,0,20,20)
#define GhostGreen                 CYMK(20,0,20,0)
#define MintGreen                  CYMK(40,0,40,0)
#define ArmyGreen                  CYMK(20,0,20,40)
#define AvocadoGreen               CYMK(20,0,40,40)
#define MartianGreen               CYMK(20,0,60,20)
#define DullGreen                  CYMK(20,0,40,20)
#define Chartreuse                 CYMK(40,0,100,0)
#define MoonGreen                  CYMK(20,0,60,0)
#define MurkyGreen                 CYMK(0,0,20,80)
```

```
#define OliveDrab            CYMK(0,0,20,60)
#define Khaki                CYMK(0,0,20,40)
#define Olive                CYMK(0,0,40,40)
#define BananaYellow         CYMK(0,0,60,20)
#define LightYellow          CYMK(0,0,60,0)
#define Chalk                CYMK(0,0,40,0)
#define PaleYellow           CYMK(0,0,20,0)
#define Brown                CYMK(0,20,40,40)
#define RedBrown             CYMK(0,40,60,20)
#define Gold                 CYMK(0,20,60,20)
#define AutumnOrange         CYMK(0,60,80,0)
#define LightOrange          CYMK(0,40,80,0)
#define Peach                CYMK(0,40,60,0)
#define DeepYellow           CYMK(0,20,100,0)
#define Sand                 CYMK(0,20,40,0)
#define Walnut               CYMK(0,20,40,60)
#define RubyRed              CYMK(0,60,60,40)
#define BrickRed             CYMK(0,60,80,20)
#define TropicalPink         CYMK(0,60,60,0)
#define SoftPink             CYMK(0,40,40,0)
#define FadedPink            CYMK(0,20,20,0)
#define Crimson              CYMK(0,40,20,40)
#define RegalRed             CYMK(0,60,40,20)
#define DeepRose             CYMK(0,60,20,20)
#define NeonRed              CYMK(0,100,60,0)
#define DeepPink             CYMK(0,60,40,0)
#define HotPink              CYMK(0,80,40,0)
#define DustyRose            CYMK(0,40,20,20)
#define Plum                 CYMK(0,40,0,60)
#define DeepViolet           CYMK(0,60,0,40)
#define LightViolet          CYMK(0,40,0,0)
#define Violet               CYMK(0,40,0,20)
#define DustyPlum            CYMK(0,20,0,40)
#define PalePurple           CYMK(0,20,0,20)
#define MajesticPurple       CYMK(20,60,0,20)
#define NeonPurple           CYMK(20,80,0,0)
#define LightPurple          CYMK(20,60,0,0)
#define TwilightViolet       CYMK(20,40,0,20)
#define EasterPurple         CYMK(20,40,0,0)
#define DeepPurple           CYMK(20,40,0,60)
#define Grape                CYMK(20,40,0,40)
#define BlueViolet           CYMK(40,60,0,0)
#define BluePurple           CYMK(40,100,0,0)
#define DeepRiver            CYMK(40,80,0,20)
#define DeepAzure            CYMK(60,80,0,0)
#define StormBlue            CYMK(40,60,0,40)
#define DeepBlue             CYMK(60,80,0,20)
```

The definitions for the colors in COLOR.H came from one of the palette files of an older copy of the Corel Draw Windows application, which are conveniently stored as simple ASCII text. Unfortunately, under Corel Draw, color is not defined as percentages of red, green, and blue light, but rather as cyan, magenta, yellow, and black ink. This is called CYMK color, where the K stands for black. It's beyond the scope of this book to deal with why color is structured this way under Corel Draw. It's also important to note that Corel Draw expresses its colors with values ranging from 0 to 100, rather than to 255.

It's fairly easy to translate CYMK color to RGB color for use in setting a VGA card's palette.

- Red = 100 – (Cyan + Black) * 2.55
- Green = 100 – (Magenta + Black) * 255
- Blue = 100 – (Yellow + Black) * 2.55

The macro CYMK in COLOR.H converts the CYMK colors in this header to the RGB colors stored as long integers in TEXTPAL.

With the COLOR.H header and the palette functions from TEXTPAL available to your text mode applications, you can have text in any color you like. In addition to these colors, of course, you can easily design your own. The Set Palette function of Desktop Paint 16, included with the companion disk for this book, is a good tool for quickly working out RGB color values.

## Draw boxes and three-dimensional boxes

The long-abused IBM graphics characters offer a limited range of expression to define screen graphics, and regrettably, most applications that use them look about the same as a result. You might want to look at the section later in this chapter that deals with defining your own characters if you'd like to improve on this situation. Be warned, however, designing characters isn't a simple undertaking.

In most cases you'll probably want to create text mode screen graphics using the existing PC high-order characters. One of the simplest functions of this sort is drawing boxes. The screen from the example program for this section is illustrated in 1-4.

The boxes in 1-4 were drawn with `DrawBox` and `Draw3DBox`, as illustrated in the demonstration program in 1-5. They're pretty simple functions, and the DRAWBOX.C listing is a pretty simple program.

Note that these box drawing functions draw single-line boxes. You can change the graphics characters they use to draw double-line boxes if you like, as follows:

| Single-line character | Double-line character | Function |
|---|---|---|
| 218 | 201 | Upper left corner |
| 191 | 187 | Upper right corner |
| 192 | 200 | Lower left corner |
| 217 | 188 | Lower right corner |
| 196 | 205 | Horizontal line |
| 179 | 186 | Vertical line |

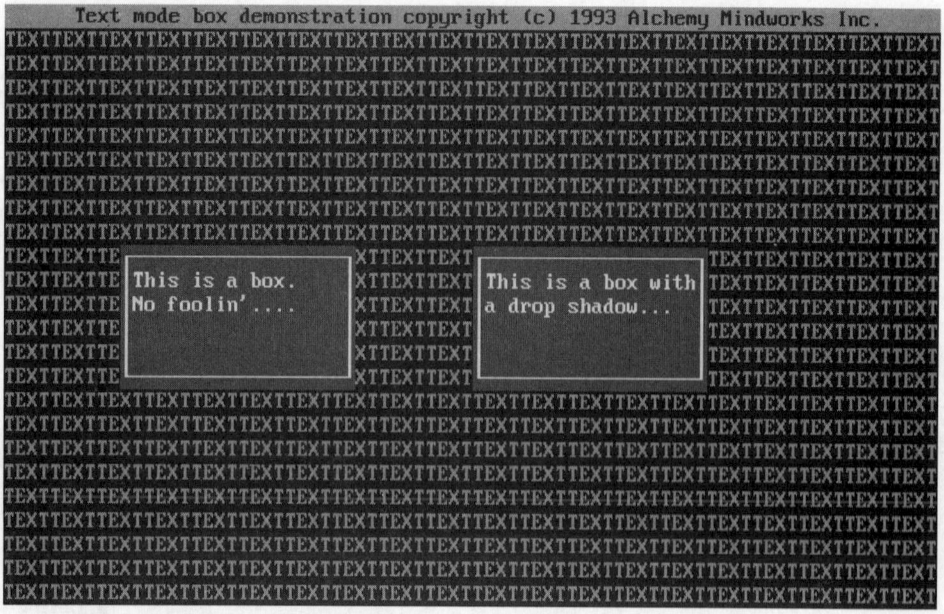


**1-4** The example box-drawing program.

**1-5** The DRAWBOX.C source code.

```
#include "stdio.h"
#include "dos.h"
#include "conio.h"

#define TEXTCOLOUR(foreground,background) (foreground | (background << 4))

char *screenPtr(void);

char *screen;

main()
{
        int i,j;
        screen=screenPtr();

        textattr(TEXTCOLOUR(BLACK,BLUE));
        clrscr();

        textattr(TEXTCOLOUR(BLUE,LIGHTGRAY));
        clreol();

        HideCursor();

        DrawString(0,0,"      Text mode box demonstration copyright (c) "
                "1993 Alchemy Mindworks Inc.",TEXTCOLOUR(BLUE,LIGHTGRAY));

        for(i=1;i<25;++i) {
                for(j=0;j<80;j+=4)
```

**1-5** Continued.

```
                DrawString(j,i,"TEXT",TEXTCOLOUR(LIGHTGRAY,BLUE));
        }

        DrawBox(10,10,30,16,TEXTCOLOUR(YELLOW,GREEN));
        DrawString(11,11,"This is a box.",TEXTCOLOUR(YELLOW,GREEN));
        DrawString(11,12,"No foolin'....",TEXTCOLOUR(YELLOW,GREEN));

        Draw3DBox(40,10,60,16,TEXTCOLOUR(YELLOW,GREEN));
        DrawString(41,11,"This is a box with",TEXTCOLOUR(YELLOW,GREEN));
        DrawString(41,12,"a drop shadow...",TEXTCOLOUR(YELLOW,GREEN));

        getch();

        textattr(WHITE);
        clrscr();
}

DrawString(x,y,text,attr)
        int x,y;
        char *text;
        int attr;
{
        unsigned int a,*ip;

        ip=(unsigned int *)(screen+(y*160+x*2));
        a=attr << 8;

        while(*text) *ip++=*text++ | a;
}

DrawBox(left,top,right,bottom,attr)
        int left,top,right,bottom,attr;
{
        unsigned int a,i,j,*ip;

        --bottom;
        --right;

        ip=(unsigned int *)(screen+top*160);
        a=attr << 8;

        ip[left]=218 | a;
        for(j=left+1;j<right;++j) ip[j]=196 | a;
        ip[right]=191 | a;

        for(i=top+1;i<bottom;++i) {
                ip+=80;
                ip[left]=179 | a;
                for(j=left+1;j<right;++j) ip[j]= 32 | a;
                ip[right]=179 | a;
        }

        ip+=80;

        ip[left]=192 | a;
        for(j=left+1;j<right;++j) ip[j]=196 | a;
```

```
        ip[right]=217 | a;
}

Draw3DBox(left,top,right,bottom,attr)
        int left,top,right,bottom,attr;
{
        unsigned int a,i,j,*ip;

        --bottom;
        --right;

        ip=(unsigned int *)(screen+top*160);
        a=attr << 8;

        ip[left]=218 | a;
        for(j=left+1;j<right;++j) ip[j]=196 | a;
        ip[right]=191 | a;
        ip[right+81]=(ip[right+81] & 0x00ff) | 0x0700;
        for(i=top+1;i<bottom;++i) {
                ip+=80;
                ip[left]=179 | a;
                        for(j=left+1;j<right;++j) ip[j]= 32 | a;
                ip[right]=179 | a;
                ip[right+81]=(ip[right+81] & 0x00ff) | 0x0700;
        }

        ip+=80;

        ip[left]=192 | a;
        ip[left+81]=(ip[left+81] & 0x00ff) | 0x0700;
        for(j=left+1;j<right;++j) {
                ip[j]=196 | a;
                ip[j+81]=(ip[j+81] & 0x00ff) | 0x0700;
        }

        ip[right]=217 | a;
        ip[right+81]=(ip[right+81] & 0x00ff) | 0x0700;

}

HideCursor()
{
        union REGS r;

        r.x.ax=0x0f00;
        int86(0x10,&r,&r);

        r.x.ax=0x0200;
        r.x.dx=0x1a00;
        int86(0x10,&r,&r);
}

char *screenPtr()
{
        union REGS r;

        r.x.ax=0x0f00;
        int86(0x10,&r,&r);
```

**1-5** Continued.

```
        if(r.h.al==0x07) return(MK_FP(0xb000,r.h.bh*0x1000));
        else return(MK_FP(0xb800,r.h.bh*0x1000));
}
```

## Use a mouse in text mode

A Microsoft-compatible mouse can manage a mouse cursor of sorts in text mode as well as under a GUI like Windows. While text mode mouse interfaces don't look quite as sophisticated as Windows might, they certainly represent a worthwhile extension for text-based applications. The text mode mouse functions offer a seamless way to integrate a mouse into your applications.

In order to use the text mode mouse functions, you must have a Microsoft-compatible mouse driver loaded in your system. The mouse driver will maintain a text cursor on the screen and allow you to interface to the mouse in a convenient way. All the mouse driver functions required to detect mouse clicks, locate the mouse cursor, and so on can be accessed by executing INT 33H instructions.

The mouse cursor is a rectangular block by default, but you can define it as any printable character you like. This includes things like the smiling face character, although by convention a diamond is usually used in this capacity. Following a smiling face around one's monitor for a while could get a bit distracting.

Clicking on the About button calls up a dialog box. Predictably, clicking on Quit returns you to DOS. The USEMOUSE program employs some of the screen access techniques discussed in this chapter. An example program that uses the text mode mouse interface is shown in 1-6. It displays two buttons, About and Quit.

**1-6** The USEMOUSE.C source code.

```
#include "stdio.h"
#include "dos.h"
#include "conio.h"
#include "alloc.h"

#define TEXTCOLOUR(foreground,background) (foreground | (background << 4))
#define WINDOWLEFT(p     ((int)p[2])
#define WINDOWTOP(p)     ((int)p[3])
#define WINDOWWIDE(p)    ((int)p[0])
#define WINDOWDEEP(p)    ((int)p[1])

typedef struct {
        int left,top,right,bottom;
        } RECT;

typedef struct {
        int x,y;
        } POINT;
```

```
char *screenPtr(void);
char *GetScreenText(int l,int t,int width,int depth);
char *OpenWindow(int left,int top,int right,int bottom,int attr);

char *screen;

int alive=1;

main()
{
        union REGS r;
        RECT quit,about;
        POINT point;

        screen=screenPtr();

        textattr(TEXTCOLOUR(BLACK,BLUE));
        clrscr();

        textattr(TEXTCOLOUR(BLUE,LIGHTGRAY));
        clreol();

        DrawString(0,0,"          Text mode mouse demonstration copyright (c) "
                "1993 Alchemy Mindworks Inc.",TEXTCOLOUR(BLUE,LIGHTGRAY));

        HideCursor();

        r.x.ax=0x0000;
        int86(0x33,&r,&r);

        if(!r.x.ax) {
                puts("No mouse driver found");
                exit(1);
        }

        r.x.ax=0x000a;
        r.x.bx=0x0000;
        r.x.cx=0xf000;
        r.x.dx=0x0f04;
        int86(0x33,&r,&r);

        MouseOn();

        MakeButton(60,20,"Quit",&quit,TEXTCOLOUR(BLUE,LIGHTGRAY));
        MakeButton(40,20,"About",&about,TEXTCOLOUR(BLUE,LIGHTGRAY));

        do {
                if(MouseDown(&point)) {
                        if(PointInRect(&point,&quit)) {
                                TrackMouse(&quit);
                                alive=0;
                        }
                        else if(PointInRect(&point,&about)) {
                                TrackMouse(&about);
                                DoAbout();
                        }
                        else putchar(7);
```

**1-6** Continued.

```
            }
        } while(alive);

        MouseOff();

        textattr(WHITE);
        clrscr();

        r.x.ax=0x0000;
        int86(0x33,&r,&r);
}

DoAbout()
{
        POINT point;
        RECT ok;
        char *p;
        int alive;

        if((p=OpenWindow(4,4,60,12,TEXTCOLOUR(BLUE,LIGHTGRAY))) != NULL) {
                DrawString(WINDOWLEFT(p)+2,WINDOWTOP(p)+1,
                      "Text mode mouse demonstration",
                      TEXTCOLOUR(BLUE,LIGHTGRAY));

                DrawString(WINDOWLEFT(p)+2,WINDOWTOP(p)+2,
                      "Copyright (c) 1903 Mother Martha's Software Inc.",
                      TEXTCOLOUR(BLUE,LIGHTGRAY));

                MakeButton(WINDOWLEFT(p)+WINDOWWIDE(p)-8,
                    WINDOWTOP(p)+4,"Ok",&ok,TEXTCOLOUR(BLUE,LIGHTGRAY));
                do {
                        if(MouseDown(&point)) {
                                if(PointInRect(&point,&ok)) {
                                        TrackMouse(&ok);
                                        alive=0;
                                } else putchar(7);
                        }
                } while(alive);

                CloseWindow(p);
        } else putchar(7);
}

char *OpenWindow(left,top,right,bottom,attr)
        int left,top,right,bottom,attr;
{
        char *p;

        if((p=GetScreenText(left,top,right-left,bottom-top)) == NULL)
            return(NULL);

        DrawBox(left,top,right,bottom,attr);

        return(p);
}
```

```
CloseWindow(p)
        char *p;
{
        PutScreenText(p);
        free(p);
}

TrackMouse(rect)
        RECT *rect;
{
        POINT point;
        char *p;
        int i,j,x,y;

        MouseOff();

        p=(screen+(rect->top*160+rect->left*2))+1;

        x=(rect->right-rect->left)<<1;
        y=rect->bottom-rect->top;
        for(i=0;i<y;++i) {
                for(j=0;j<x;j+=2) p[j] = (p[j] >> 4) | (p[j] << 4);
                p+=160;
        }

        MouseOn();

        while(MouseDown(&point));

        MouseOff();

        p=(screen+(rect->top*160+rect->left*2))+1;

        x=(rect->right-rect->left)<<1;
        y=rect->bottom-rect->top;
        for(i=0;i<y;++i) {
                for(j=0;j<x;j+=2) p[j] = (p[j] >> 4) | (p[j] << 4);
                p+=160;
        }

        MouseOn();
}

MakeButton(left,top,text,rect,attr)
        int left,top;
        char *text;
        RECT *rect;
        int attr;
{
        int n;

        n=strlen(text);

        SetRect(rect,left,top,left+4+n,top+3);
        DrawBox(left,top,left+4+n,top+3,attr);
        DrawString(left+2,top+1,text,attr);
}
```

**1-6** Continued.

```
DrawString(x,y,text,attr)
        int x,y;
        char *text;
        int attr;
{
        unsigned int a,*ip;

        MouseOff();
        ip=(unsigned int *)(screen+(y*160+x*2));
        a=attr << 8;

        while(*text) *ip++=*text++ | a;

        MouseOn();
}

DrawBox(left,top,right,bottom,attr)
        int left,top,right,bottom,attr;
{
        unsigned int a,i,j,*ip;

        MouseOff();

        --bottom;
        --right;

        ip=(unsigned int *)(screen+top*160);
        a=attr << 8;

        ip[left]=218 | a;
        for(j=left+1;j<right;++j) ip[j]=196 | a;
        ip[right]=191 | a;

        for(i=top+1;i<bottom;++i) {
                ip+=80;
                ip[left]=179 | a;
                for(j=left+1;j<right;++j) ip[j]= 32 | a;
                ip[right]=179 | a;
        }

        ip+=80;

        ip[left]=192 | a;
        for(j=left+1;j<right;++j) ip[j]=196 | a;
        ip[right]=217 | a;
        MouseOn();
}

MouseOn()
{
        union REGS r;

        r.x.ax=0x0001;
        int86(0x33,&r,&r);
}
```

```
MouseOff()
{
        union REGS r;

        r.x.ax=0x0002;
        int86(0x33,&r,&r);
}
MouseDown(p)
        POINT *p;
{
        union REGS r;

        r.x.ax=0x0003;
        int86(0x33,&r,&r);

        p->x=r.x.cx>>3;
        p->y=r.x.dx>>3;
        return(r.x.bx & 0x03);
}

HideCursor()
{
        union REGS r;

        r.x.ax=0x0f00;
        int86(0x10,&r,&r);

        r.x.ax=0x0200;
        r.x.dx=0x1a00;
        int86(0x10,&r,&r);
}

PointInRect(p,r)
        POINT *p;
        RECT *r;
{
        if(p->x >= r->left && p->x < r->right &&
           p->y >= r->>top  && p->y < r->bottom) return(1);
        else return(0);
}

char *screenPtr()
{
        union REGS r;

        r.x.ax=0x0f00;
        int86(0x10,&r,&r);

        if(r.h.al==0x07) return(MK_FP(0xb000,r.h.bh*0x1000));
        else return(MK_FP(0xb800,r.h.bh*0x1000));
}

SetRect(r,left,top,right,bottom)        /* set a rectangle */
        RECT *r;
        int left,top,right,bottom;
{
        r->left=left;
```

**1-6** Continued.

```
        r->top=top;
        r->right=right;
        r->bottom=bottom;
}

char *GetScreenText(l,t,width,depth)
        int l,t,width,depth;
{
        char *p,*sp,*dp;
        int i;

        if((p=malloc(4+(width*depth*2))) == NULL) return(NULL);

        MouseOff();
        p[0]=width;
        p[1]=depth;
        p[2]=l;
        p[3]=t;

        sp=screen+(160*t)+(l<<1);
        dp=p+4;
        width=width<<1;
        for(i=0;i<depth;++i) {
                memcpy(dp,sp,width);
                sp+=160;
                dp+=width;
        }
        MouseOn();
        return(p);
}

PutScreenText(p)
        char *p;
{
        char *dp;
        int i,width,depth,l,t;

        MouseOff();
        width=*p++;
        depth=*p++;
        l=*p++;
        t=*p++;

        dp=screen+(160*t)+(l<<1);

        width=width<<1;
        for(i=0;i<depth;++i) {
                memcpy(dp,p,width);
                p+=width;
                dp+=160;
        }
        MouseOn();
}
```

There are several bits of code you'll need to communicate with a mouse. All of them use INT 33H calls, as expedited through the `int86` function in C. This is a somewhat abbreviated list of mouse functions—see the Microsoft Mouse Programmer's Reference Guide for a complete description of the mouse driver interface.

To begin with, you must initialize the mouse. This is the call to do so:

```
union REGS r;

r.x.ax=0x0000;
int86(0x33,&r,&r);
```

If `r.x.ax` contains zero after this call there's no mouse driver present in the system.

Here's how to turn on the mouse cursor; that is, to make it visible on screen:

```
union REGS r;

r.x.ax=0x0001;
int86(0x33,&r,&r);
```

This is the call to turn the mouse cursor off:

```
union REGS r;

r.x.ax=0x0002;
int86(0x33,&r,&r);
```

It's important to turn the mouse cursor off when you write text to the screen and to turn it on again when you're done. The mouse cursor is just a character animated on screen by the mouse driver. If you print text over it, the cursor will vanish and then leave a divot in your screen when it moves.

The default square block mouse cursor is a bit ugly. Here's the call to turn it into a white diamond:

```
union REGS r;

r.x.ax=0x000a;
r.x.bx=0x0000;
r.x.cx=0xf000;
r.x.dx=0x0f04;
int86(0x33,&r,&r);
```

The argument stored in the DX register defines the character code for your mouse cursor in its low-order word and the character attribute in its high-order word.

Finally, here's some code to ascertain the state of the mouse; that is, to see if one of its buttons has been clicked and where it's located.

```
union REGS r;

r.x.ax=0x0003;
int86(0x33,&r,&r);
```

Having executed this call, `r.x.cx >> 3` will be the horizontal position of the mouse, `r.x.dx >> 3` will be the vertical position of the mouse, and `r.x.bx` will hold flags that represent the button positions. It allows for a mouse with up to 16 buttons. If `r.x.bx & 0x0001` is true the left button has been clicked. If `r.x.bx & 0x0002` is true the next button over—typically the right one on a two-button mouse—has been clicked.

The tricky part in using a mouse is not in knowing how to make these calls, which is pretty elementary, but rather in devising workable functions to manage the items that will be clicked in.

The USEMOUSE program in 1-6 illustrates a text mode version of a very simple GUI. If you'd like to learn more about constructing a user interface of this type, you might want to consult one of my books on the subject, *Graphical User Interface Programming* or *Super VGA Graphics*, both published by Windcrest.

Having set up the mouse and the screen, the USEMOUSE program falls into a loop in which it calls `MouseDown` repeatedly. The `MouseDown` function returns a true value when a mouse button has been clicked and stores the location of the mouse cursor in a POINT object. A POINT defines *x* and *y* coordinates on your screen.

Objects to click in are defined by RECT objects, as set up by `MakeButton`. When you call `MakeButton`, a rectangular button is drawn on the screen and its position is stored in the RECT object passed to the `MakeButton` function.

When a mouse click is detected, the `PointInRect` function can be used to see whether it has occurred within one of the RECTs that defines an on-screen button. If it has, the `TrackButton` will invert the button to indicate that the click has been noticed, and suitable action can be taken to respond to the click.

There are only two buttons in USEMOUSE. The About button will call up an About dialog, which has a button of its own. The About dialog involves capturing the screen area behind where the box will go, as handled by `GetScreenText`, drawing a box with some text, and then falling into another loop to wait for a mouse click. When the dialog is closed the original screen area beneath the box must be replaced by a call to `PutScreenText`.

You can expand on the mouse functions considerably, creating a complete user interface if you like.

## Change the appearance of characters in VGA text modes

The PC character set is a bit pedestrian; at least, it has grown to be that way through years of use. There are good arguments for changing all or part of this font, which a VGA card allows you to do.

The ability to redefine a VGA card's characters under software control allows you to generate specific characters for your applications—for example, symbols that don't exist in the default IBM character set—or to use more interesting looking fonts in general. In redefining the character set you won't be affecting the internal character set in your system per se. Returning to the default character set is even easier than defining a new one.

The process of defining a new character set, or more correctly, of downloading a character set to the VGA BIOS, is handled by an INT 21H call. Unfortunately, it's a somewhat peculiar call in that it involves modifying the BP register. Programs written in C make extensive use of the BP register, as it's the pointer that deals with the stack. The BP register is where local variables are stored and arguments are passed between functions. Most C implementations take great offense at anything that attempts to meddle with it.

For this reason, I'll begin with a short assembly language module, CHNGFNT1.ASM, as seen in 1-7. This will provide you with a function called `DownloadFont`, which handles the process in such a way so as not to upset C. The DOS call in `DownloadFont` is structured like this:

- AX = 1110H
- BX = Point size of the font * 256
- CX = The number of characters to download
- DX = The number of the first character to be replaced
- ES:BP = A pointer to the new font bitmap table

**1-7** The CHNGFNT1.ASM source code.

```
;
;                MACHINE LANGUAGE MODULE FOR CHNAGEFONT
;

_AOFF           EQU      6       ;STACK OFFSET TO FIRST ARG


_TEXT           SEGMENT BYTE PUBLIC 'CODE'
                ASSUME  CS:_TEXT,DS:_DATA

; REPROGRAM THE FONT CONTROLLER
;               ARG1 = POINTER TO NEW FONT        [0]
;               ARG2 = FIRST CHARACTER            [4]
;               ARG3 = NUMBER OF CHARACTERS       [6]
;               ARG4 = POINTS                     [8]
```

1-7 Continued.

```
;               ARG5 = BLOCK                        [10]
                PUBLIC   _DownloadFont
_DownloadFont   PROC     FAR
                PUSH     BP
                MOV      BP,SP
                PUSH     DS
                PUSH     ES

                MOV      AX,1110H
                MOV      BH,BYTE PTR [BP + _AOFF + 8]
                MOV      BL,BYTE PTR [BP + _AOFF + 10]
                AND      BL,07H
                MOV      CX,[BP + _AOFF + 6]
                MOV      DX,[BP + _AOFF + 4]
                MOV      ES,[BP + _AOFF + 2]
                MOV      BP,[BP + _AOFF + 0]
                INT      10H

                POP      ES
                POP      DS

                POP      BP
                RET
_DownloadFont   ENDP

_TEXT    ENDS

DGROUP          GROUP    _DATA,_BSS
_DATA           SEGMENT WORD PUBLIC 'DATA'

_DATA           ENDS

_BSS            SEGMENT WORD PUBLIC 'BSS'

_BSS            ENDS

                END
```

The point size is typically 14 or 16. A character font table consists of 14 or 16 bytes for each character, with each character being 8 bits wide.

Multiple character table blocks are available in the VGA BIOS, which allow you to download several fonts at once and switch among them. This is somewhat beyond the scope of this discussion, and I'll allow that one block, block 0, which is adequate for simple font manipulation. Note, however, that in the previous table the BX register really contains the point size in its high-order byte and the block number in its low-order byte.

The CHNGFONT.H header file defines three complete alternate fonts. It's not reproduced here, being a fairly huge list of meaningless hex numbers, but you can find it on the companion disk for this book. Prior to including it you should have one of the symbols FONT1, FONT2, or FONT3 defined in your source code.

Of the three fonts, the first is a slightly spindly version of the standard PC font, the second is a very extreme font drawn in characters that drip blood, and the third is a thin sans serif font.

The font change demonstration program, CHNGFONT.C, is illustrated in 1-8. A project or MAKE file is required to link this to CHNGFNT1.ASM from 1-7.

**1-8** The CHNGFONT.C source code.

```
#include "stdio.h"
#include "dos.h"
#include "conio.h"
#define FONT3
#include "chngfont.h"

#define TEXTCOLOUR(foreground,background) (foreground | (background << 4))
#define BOXTEXT          TEXTCOLOUR(LIGHTGREEN,BROWN)
#define BACKTEXT         TEXTCOLOUR(BLACK,GREEN)
#define POEMTEXT         TEXTCOLOUR(YELLOW,BLACK)
#define LINETEXT         TEXTCOLOUR(YELLOW,GREEN)

void DownloadFont(char *font,int first,int chars,int charsize,int block);
char *screenPtr(void);

char *screen;
main()
{
        char b[81];
        union REGS r;
        int i,j,n;

        screen=screenPtr();

        DownloadFont(font,FONTFIRST,FONTCHARS,FONTSIZE,0);
        HideCursor();

        ClearScreen(BACKTEXT);
        DrawBox(3,3,21,21,BOXTEXT);
        for(i=0;i<256;++i)
            DrawChar(4+(i % 16),4+(i/16),i,BOXTEXT);

        i=3;
        /* this bit is copyright (c) Alfred Lord Tennyson, 1843 */
        DrawString(30,i++,"                                        ",POEMTEXT);
        DrawString(30,i++," On either side of the river lie        ",POEMTEXT);
        DrawString(30,i++," Long fields of barley and of rye       ",POEMTEXT);
        DrawString(30,i++," To clothe the wold and meet the sky    ",POEMTEXT);
        DrawString(30,i++," And through the field the road run by  ",POEMTEXT);
        DrawString(30,i++," To many-towered Camelot                ",POEMTEXT);
        DrawString(30,i++,"                                        ",POEMTEXT);
        DrawString(30,i++," And up and down the people go          ",POEMTEXT);
        DrawString(30,i++," Gazing where the lilies blow           ",POEMTEXT);
        DrawString(30,i++," Round an island there below            ",POEMTEXT);
        DrawString(30,i++," The island of Shalott                  ",POEMTEXT);
        DrawString(30,i++,"                                        ",POEMTEXT);
```

**1-8** Continued.

```
        DrawString(30,i++," Willows whiten, aspens quiver          ",POEMTEXT);
        DrawString(30,i++," Little breezes dusk and shiver         ",POEMTEXT);
        DrawString(30,i++," Through the wave that runs forever     ",POEMTEXT);
        DrawString(30,i++," By the island in the river             ",POEMTEXT);
        DrawString(30,i++," Flowing down to Camelot                ",POEMTEXT);
        DrawString(30,i++,"                                        ",POEMTEXT);

        for(n=j=1;!kbhit();n+=j) {
                memset(b,32,80);
                for(i=0;i<n;++i) {
                        b[40+i]=219;
                        b[40-i]=219;
                        b[40+n+i]=178;
                        b[40-n-i]=178;
                        b[40+(n*2)+i]=177;
                        b[40-(n*2)-i]=177;
                        b[40+(n*3)+i]=176;
                        b[40-(n*3)-i]=176;
                }
                b[80]=0;
                DrawString(0,24,b,LINETEXT);
                DrawString(0,0,b,LINETEXT);
                if(n > 7 || n < 1) j*=-1;
                delay(100);
        }

        getch();

        r.x.ax=0x1104;
        r.x.bx=0x0000;
        int86(0x10,&r,&r);
}

ClearScreen(attr)
        int attr;
{
        unsigned int i,a,*ip;

        ip=(unsigned int *)screen;
        a=attr << 8;

        for(i=0;i<4000;++i) *ip++=32 | a;
}

DrawChar(x,y,chr,attr)
        int x,y,chr,attr;
{
        unsigned int a,*ip;

        ip=(unsigned int *)(screen+(y*160+x*2));
        a=attr << 8;

        *ip=chr | a;
}

DrawString(x,y,text,attr)
```

```
        int x,y;
        char *text;
        int attr;
{
        unsigned int a,*ip;

        ip=(unsigned int *)(screen+(y*160+x*2));
        a=attr << 8;

        while(*text) *ip++=*text++ | a;
}

DrawBox(left,top,right,bottom,attr)
        int left,top,right,bottom,attr;
{
        unsigned int a,i,j,*ip;

        --bottom;
        --right;

        ip=(unsigned int *)(screen+top*160);
        a=attr << 8;

        ip[left]=218 | a;
        for(j=left+1;j<right;++j) ip[j]=196 | a;
        ip[right]=191 | a;

        for(i=top+1;i<bottom;++i) {
                ip+=80;
                ip[left]=179 | a;
                for(j=left+1;j<right;++j) ip[j]= 32 | a;
                ip[right]=179 | a;
        }

        ip+=80;

        ip[left]=192 | a;
        for(j=left+1;j<right;++j) ip[j]=196 | a;
        ip[right]=217 | a;
}

char *screenPtr()
{
        union REGS r;

        r.x.ax=0x0f00;
        int86(0x10,&r,&r);

        if(r.h.al==0x07) return(MK_FP(0xb000,r.h.bh*0x1000));
        else return(MK_FP(0xb800,r.h.bh*0x1000));
}

HideCursor()
{
        union REGS r;

        r.x.ax=0x0f00;
        int86(0x10,&r,&r);
```

**1-8** Continued.

```
        r.x.ax=0x0200;
        r.x.dx=0x1a00;
        int86(0x10,&r,&r);
}
```

The CHNGFONT program doesn't do very much, but it does it in a different font. Specifically, it displays the current character set, three verses of a Tennyson poem, and animated bars at the top and bottom of your screen. It then waits for a key press and quits to DOS. Notice the final call to `int86`; this reloads the standard VGA screen font.

Two functions that haven't been discussed in this chapter are `HideCursor` and `ClearScreen`. The `HideCursor` function makes the text mode hardware cursor vanish by parking it on the twenty-sixth line; that is, one line below the bottom of the screen. You can't do this with the Turbo C `gotoxy` function, as it traps for illegal arguments, of which this would be one. The `ClearScreen` function clears the screen to the attribute of your choice by filling it with blanks.

## Use 50-line text on a VGA card

While most PC users are familiar with the conventional 80-×-25-character text mode, there are other text modes available. We'll ignore the antediluvian 40-×-25-character mode in this discussion. The 50-line mode, however, can be genuinely useful if you have a lot of text to view at once. This mode is only available on a VGA or super VGA card. In fact, it's not really a mode at all. It's a by-product.

As discussed in the previous section of this chapter, you can redefine the fonts on a VGA card. You can also select among three internal fonts, which all VGA cards provide. These are 8-, 14-, and 16-points deep, respectively. The latter is the usual VGA text mode font.

If you select the 8-point font, each character will occupy only half as much vertical space as it would in the normal screen font, and as such, twice as many lines will fit on the screen. They won't look as attractive, of course—the 8-point font is a bit chunky.

The only catch to using 50-line text is that most of the conventional ways to manage the screen—through BIOS calls, for example—won't work in this mode. At least they can't be counted on to work reliably. This isn't much of a catch as catches go; the high-speed screen functions used throughout this chapter can deal with 50-line text.

Enabling the 50-line text mode on a VGA card entails a bit of BIOS tickling—as with many VGA card tricks, it's only tangentially documented.

```
Set50()
{
        union REGS r;
        int cpage;
```

```
        r.x.ax=0x0f00;
        int86(0x10,&r,&r);
        cpage=r.h.bh;

        r.x.ax=0x0500;
        int86(0x10,&r,&r);

        r.x.ax=0x1112;
        r.h.bl=0;
        int86(0x10,&r,&r);

        r.x.ax=0x0500+cpage;
        int86(0x10,&r,&r);
}
```

The first `int86` call fetches the current display page. The second one sets the display page to zero, which is necessary for the font change. The third one actually selects the 8-point font. The final one reselects the current display page again. In most cases the current display page will be zero.

Reverting to the normal VGA screen font uses much the same code. Note that the third `int86` call is slightly different.

```
Set25()
{
        union REGS r;
        int cpage;

        r.x.ax=0x0f00;
        int86(0x10,&r,&r);
        cpage=r.h.bh;

        r.x.ax=0x0500;
        int86(0x10,&r,&r);

        r.x.ax=0x1114;
        r.h.bl=0;
        int86(0x10,&r,&r);

        r.x.ax=0x0500+cpage;
        int86(0x10,&r,&r);
}
```

The example program in 1-9 is VIEW50, a 50-line text file viewer. It will accept a path to a text file as its command line argument and display the file's contents in 50-line mode. It assumes that it will be fed pure text files rather than proprietary word processor files or other complex documents.

**1-9** The VIEW50.C source code.

```
/*
        50-line text file viewer
        Copyright (c) 1993 Alchemy Mindworks Inc.
*/

#include "stdio.h"
```

**1-9** Continued.

```
#include "alloc.h"
#include "conio.h"
#include "dos.h"

#define TEXTCOLOUR(foreground,background) (foreground | (background << 4))

#define BACKGROUND      TEXTCOLOUR(WHITE,BLUE)
#define BANNER          TEXTCOLOUR(BLACK,RED)

#define SCREENWIDE      80
#define SCREENDEEP      50
#define TEXTBLOCK       0xfff0

#define HOME            0x4700
#define CURSOR_UP       0x4800
#define END             0x4f00
#define CURSOR_DOWN     0x5000
#define PG_UP           0x4900
#define PG_DOWN         0x5100

char *screenPtr();
char *LoadFile(char *path,int *linecount);

char *screen;

main(argc,argv)
        int argc;
        char *argv[];
{
        char *text,b[16];
        int c,line=0,linecount;

        screen=screenPtr();

        if(argc <= 1) error("Argument:                Path to a text file");

        puts("Wait...");

        if((text=LoadFile(argv[1],&linecount)) == NULL)
            error("Error loading text file");

        HideCursor();

        Set50();
        ClearScreen(BACKGROUND);

        DrawString(0,0," 50-line text file viewer copyright (c) 1993 "
                   "Alchemy Mindworks Inc.                ",BANNER);

        do {
                DrawPage(text,line);
                sprintf(b,"%-4.4u/%-4.4u",line+1,linecount+1);
                DrawString(70,0,b,BANNER);
                c=GetKey();

                switch(c) {
```

```
                        case 27:
                                break;
                        case CURSOR_UP:
                                if(line > 0) —line;
                                break;
                        case CURSOR_DOWN:
                                if(line < (linecount-SCREENDEEP)) ++line;
                                break;
                        case PG_UP:
                                if((line-(SCREENDEEP-4)) < 0) line=0;
                                else line-=(SCREENDEEP-4);
                                break;
                        case PG_DOWN:
                                if((line+(SCREENDEEP-4)) >= (linecount-SCREENDEEP))
                                    line=linecount-SCREENDEEP;
                                else line+=(SCREENDEEP-4);
                                break;
                        case HOME:
                                line=0;
                                break;
                        case END:
                                line=linecount-SCREENDEEP;
                                break;
                }

        } while(c != 27);

        free(text);

        Set25();
        textattr(7);
        clrscr();
}

DrawPage(text,start)
        char *text;
        unsigned int start;
{
        unsigned i;

        for(i=0;i<start;++i) {
                if(*text==0) break;
                text+=strlen(text)+1;
        }

        for(i=1;i<SCREENDEEP;++i) {
                if(*text==0) break;
                ClearLine(i,BACKGROUND);
                DrawString(0,i,text,BACKGROUND);
                text+=strlen(text)+1;
        }
}

ClearLine(y,attr)
        int y,attr;
{
```

**1-9** Continued.

```
        unsigned int a,i,*ip;

        ip=(unsigned int *)(screen+(y*160));
        a=(attr << 8) | 32;

        for(i=0;i<SCREENWIDE;++i) *ip++=a;
}

char *LoadFile(path,linecount)
        char *path;
        int *linecount;
{
        FILE *fp;
        char *text,*p;
        long blocksize=0L;
        unsigned int linesize;
        int c;

        if((fp=fopen(path,"ra"))==NULL) return(NULL);

        *linecount=0;

        if((text=malloc((unsigned int)TEXTBLOCK))==NULL) {
                fclose(fp);
                return(NULL);
        }

        p=text;

        do {
                linesize=0;
                while((c=fgetc(fp)) != '\n' && c != EOF) {
                        if(c==9) {
                                while((linesize+1) % 8) {
                                        if(linesize < SCREENWIDE)
                                            p[linesize]=32;
                                        ++linesize;
                                }
                        }
                        else if(c >= 32 &&
                                c != EOF &&
                                linesize < SCREENWIDE)
                             p[linesize++]=c;

                        /* if you want to view WordStar 3.3 files,
                           make the previous line
                           p[linesize++]=c & 0x7f;
                        */
                }

                if(linesize==0) p[linesize++]=32;

                p[linesize++]=0;
                p+=linesize;
                blocksize+=(long)linesize;
                (*linecount)++;
```

```
        } while(c != EOF &&
                blocksize < (long)(TEXTBLOCK-SCREENWIDE-1));
        *p++=0;

        fclose(fp);
        return(text);
}

Set50()
{
        union REGS r;
        int cpage;
        r.x.ax=0x0f00;
        int86(0x10,&r,&r);
        cpage=r.h.bh;

        r.x.ax=0x0500;
        int86(0x10,&r,&r);

        r.x.ax=0x1112;
        r.h.bl=0;
        int86(0x10,&r,&r);

        r.x.ax=0x0500+cpage;
        int86(0x10,&r,&r);
}

Set25()
{
        union REGS r;
        int cpage;

        r.x.ax=0x0f00;
        int86(0x10,&r,&r);
        cpage=r.h.bh;

        r.x.ax=0x0500;
        int86(0x10,&r,&r);

        r.x.ax=0x1114;
        r.h.bl=0;
        int86(0x10,&r,&r);

        r.x.ax=0x0500+cpage;
        int86(0x10,&r,&r);
}

DrawString(x,y,text,attr)
        int x,y;
        char *text;
        int attr;
{
        unsigned int a,*ip;

        ip=(unsigned int *)(screen+(y*160+x*2));
        a=attr << 8;

        while(*text) *ip++=*text++ | a;
```

**1-9** Continued.

```
}

HideCursor()
{
        union REGS r;

        r.x.ax=0x0f00;
        int86(0x10,&r,&r);

        r.x.ax=0x0200;
        r.x.dx=(SCREENDEEP+1)<<8;
        int86(0x10,&r,&r);
}
char *screenPtr()
{
        union REGS r;

        r.x.ax=0x0f00;
        int86(0x10,&r,&r);

        if(r.h.al==0x07) return(MK_FP(0xb000,r.h.bh*0x1000));
        else return(MK_FP(0xb800,r.h.bh*0x1000));
}

ClearScreen(attr)
        int attr;
{
        unsigned int i,a,*ip;

        ip=(unsigned int *)screen;
        a=attr << 8;

        for(i=0;i<SCREENWIDE*SCREENDEEP;++i) *ip++=32 | a;
}

error(s)
        char *s;
{
        puts(s);
        exit(1);
}

GetKey()
{
        int c;

        c = getch();
        if(!(c & 0x00ff)) c = getch() << 8;
        return(c);
}
```

The VIEW50 program is a fairly simple example of text file handling. It won't display more than 64 kilobytes worth of text and, as such, can get away with some fairly sloppy data handling. The `LoadFile` function reads the source file and stores it in a buffer as sequential null-terminated language strings. The end of the buffer is indicated by a zero-length string; that is, by two zero bytes in succession. Because a blank line would look like the end of the buffer under these conditions, blank lines are padded out to lines containing one space character.

To locate line `n` in a buffer of this sort, you would do the following. In this example, the buffer is addressed by a pointer called `text`.

```
int i;

for(i=0;i<n;++i) {
        if(*text==0) break;
        text+=strlen(text)+1;
}
```

When this loop is complete, `text` will point either to line `n` or to a zero-length string at the end of the buffer, if `n` specified a line number beyond what the buffer contained.

This is a sort of idiot's linked list—it represents a very space-efficient way to store text but a relatively slow way to access it. If `text` points to a line partway through the buffer and you'd like to find a previous line, you must return to the beginning and count again. In addition, spanning from line to line involves a lot of calculation.

In dealing with larger lists you'd probably use a real linked list; that is, each data element preceded by a pointer to the next element such that a function that wanted to find a particular element could "walk" the list fairly quickly. This would arguably be overkill in this example. I'll have a look at a real double-linked list with a side of fries later in this chapter when I deal with WordPerfect files. It will be severe overkill there too, of course.

Once `LoadFile` has returned a pointer to a buffer that contains the text, VIEW50 calls `DrawPage` repeatedly to display the text in the buffer. This function uses the previous bit of code to find the top line to be displayed and then repeatedly calls `DrawString` to display the text. The `ClearLine` call is necessary to erase whatever was previously on the line in question, as it might have been longer than the line to be drawn.

The `do` loop in the `main` function of VIEW50 adjusts the value in `line`, the current top line to be displayed, based on the keyboard input returned by `GetKey`. It will fall out and return to DOS when Esc, character 27, is hit.

If you decide to use VIEW50 for something more than an example of implementing 50-line text, you might want to make it a bit more bulletproof than it is here. For one thing, it could use some code to make sure that it's running on a VGA card, as its requests to initialize this mode on other display adapters won't be greeted with favor.

## Work with WordPerfect files

I don't use WordPerfect if I can help it, and I usually can. I could never remember all those alternate shifted function key combinations. This book was written using a really dusty copy of WordStar 3.3. They don't make word processors with few enough features for writing books, but pre-Columbian WordStar comes close.

As with most word processing packages, a WordPerfect file doesn't contain anything like simple ASCII. The file structure is outlined in WordPerfect's technical documentation, but implementing a function to read WordPerfect files is a bit of an undertaking.

The WP-VIEW program discussed in this section includes a function to read a WordPerfect file into a buffer as simple ASCII and to make sense of the elementary text formatting codes of WordPerfect. It also illustrates how linked lists work and how to deal with data objects larger than 64 kilobytes.

As is apparent if you've read through the preceding section of this chapter, text files are awkward things to deal with. They consist of discrete data objects—the individual text lines—but the objects are of varying sizes. Finding a specific line quickly requires some cunning.

If the lines were all the same length, you could index them as the line length multiplied by the line number you were after. You could arrange this by padding all the lines out to a fixed length, but this is exceedingly wasteful of memory.

Another approach would be to put all the lines in memory and create a table of pointers at the start of each one. This, too, has its difficulties. It involves making multiple passes through the text buffer and juggling several potentially large memory blocks, as it's impossible to initially know the number of lines in a text file.

The way around this seemingly inflexible set of restrictions is to use a linked list. One of the more exotic approaches to managing data, a linked list has numerous advantages when you're dealing with blocks of data of no fixed size. It allows you to locate any line in a buffer quickly and imposes only a minimum of overhead on the whole effort. It doesn't require a separate table. It also lets you find lines relative to other lines—for example, moving back by one line does not involve counting your way through the entire previous section of the file, as was undertaken earlier in the simple text file viewer.

In a linked list, each line in the text buffer is preceded by a data structure like this one:

```
typedef struct LINK {
        struct LINK *prev;
        struct LINK *next;
        unsigned int length;
        } LINK;
```

The length element indicates the number of characters in the line in question. The prev element points to the LINK object for the preceding line, or to NULL if this is the first object in the list. The next element points to the next LINK object in the list, or to NULL if this is the last object in the list.

Allowing that p is a pointer to a buffer of linked lines—each line being preceded by a LINK object—and lnk is a pointer of the type LINK, here's how you'd find the nth line in the buffer.

```
int i;

lnk=(LINK *)p;
for(i=0;i<<n;++i) lnk=lnk->>next;
```

This bit of code will work its way through each link in the list by finding the link it points to. In fact, this is a bit simplified. It should check to make sure that lnk->next doesn't point to NULL, indicating that there are fewer than *n* lines in the list.

You can work backwards in a linked list just as easily. If lnk points to the LINK object of a particular line, here's how you'd find the line *n* lines earlier.

```
int i;

for(i=0;i<<n;++i) lnk=lnk->>prev;
```

Again, this code should check to make sure that lnk->prev doesn't equal NULL with each pass through the loop.

This approach to managing lines of text for a file viewer works well because there are only 25 lines of interest at any time—the ones on the screen. Most movement in the file is relative to the currently visible part of it; you'll want to view the next line or the next page, for example.

In fact, you can find the extremes of a linked list quickly by simply walking the list until the appropriate LINK pointer turns out to be NULL.

It's worth noting that the prev and next elements in a LINK are 32-bit pointers. A linked list can occupy more than a single memory segment, and very often will if you want to look at large WordPerfect documents. Because the large memory model does not allow long integers to be added to pointers, the actual offsets from one link to the next are handled by a function that does, this being farPtr. It can be found in the WP-VIEW program.

Understanding WordPerfect document files is a bit more involved than understanding linked lists. A WP file always starts with the four-byte string "\377WPC," where the first element is shown as an octal constant that works out to 255. The four bytes after this string are a long integer representing the offset into the file for the start of its text. You should seek to this point before you read anything else.

WordPerfect text is stored in something like ASCII once you seek past the header and whatever else is lurking at the start of the file. Paragraphs run without any returns except at a hard end, which is indicated by a line feed (character 10). Traditional carriage returns (character 13) occur as soft returns for formatting, such as around a graphic frame. For the purpose of viewing WordPerfect text, these should be treated as spaces.

This explanation ignores formatting blocks, which I'll get to in a moment. Inasmuch as the text in a WordPerfect document is stored unformatted, a text viewer must format it to fit on a text mode screen. The text that emerges from a document file must be broken up into 80-character lines so that each line ends with the end of a word.

Formatting text in text mode is relatively easy. Beginning with the start of the text, you would read characters into a buffer until you encountered a space character (character 32). You would then continue to read characters until something other than a space was encountered. This buffer now contains one word. If its length plus the length of the current line is less than the width of the screen, the word can be added to the current line. If not, the current line should be ended, a new line created, and the word added to it. This process is repeated until the whole file is read. A line can also be ended if a line feed is encountered at the end of a word, indicating that the end of a paragraph has been reached.

The process of reading a WP file can be complicated somewhat by the existence of formatting codes and blocks imbedded in the text. These handle things like justification, font changes and effects, tabbing, and so on. They're identified by characters with ASCII values greater than 127.

Characters in the range of 128 through 191 are single-byte commands. If one of these is encountered, it can be ignored. These commands perform all sorts of functions, such as columnar math, table of contents entries, and the setting of WordPerfect's internal flags.

Characters in the range of 192 through 207 are fixed-size blocks that handle things like changing text effects. Each of the seven currently defined codes in this range has a specific length. You can skip the code and get on to the next bit of readable text by seeking forward by the size of the block in question.

The WP-VIEW program keeps track of the state of these effects flags. Text that WordPerfect would print with an effect is displayed in a different color than that which would be printed normally.

There are 16 effects, with codes running from 0 through 15. This makes keeping track of the ones that have been set on pretty easy. If `effects` is an integer, `effects | (1 << code)` says that a specific effect has been switched on by a 195 block, and `effects & ~(1 << code)` says that it has been switched off.

Characters from 208 on up indicate the beginning of variable-length blocks. Fortunately each of these blocks knows what its variable length is.

Having found a character in this range, you can waste the ensuing one-byte subcode and then read an integer, which represents the length of the block in bytes. Seek forward by this many more characters and you'll be looking at text again—or perhaps at the start of yet another block if you're reading a particularly complex WordPerfect document.

While a dissertation on the meanings of all the WordPerfect blocks and codes would run for chapters, knowing this much about them makes it possible to ignore them.

The `loadfile` function in WP-VIEW unpacks a WP file into a buffer as a linked list. The text is stored as conventional ASCII, except that any text that would print with an effect has its high-order bits set.

The source code for WP-VIEW is illustrated in 1-10. It expects to see a path to a WordPerfect document file as its command line argument.

The WP-VIEW application is a decidedly rudimentary application of WordPerfect document files. You can certainly do a lot more with them if you like. For an oppressively thorough discussion of the WordPerfect document file structure, order the WordPerfect Developer's Toolkit from WordPerfect Corporation, 1555 North Technology Way, Orem, Utah 84057.

**1-10** The WP-VIEW source code.

```
    /*
        WordPerfect document file viewer
        Copyright (c) 1991 Alchemy Mindworks Inc.
*/

#include "stdio.h"
#include "alloc.h"
#include "conio.h"
#include "dos.h"

#define HOME            71 * 256
#define CURSOR_UP       72 * 256
#define PG_UP           73 * 256
#define END             79 * 256
#define CURSOR_DOWN     80 * 256
#define PG_DOWN         81 * 256

/* screen colours... change these if you like */
#define SCREENBACK      BLUE
#define NORMAL          (YELLOW + (SCREENBACK << 4))
#define INVERSE         (SCREENBACK + (LIGHTGRAY << 4))
#define BRIGHT          (LIGHTCYAN + (SCREENBACK << 4))

/* screen dimensions */
#define SCREENWIDE      80
#define SCREENDEEP      25
#define SCREENTOP       1

/* how big one word can get */
#define WORDSIZE        32
```

**1-10** Continued.

```
/* one linked list link */
typedef struct LINK {
        struct LINK *prev;
        struct LINK *next;
        unsigned int length;
        } LINK;

/* some prototypes */
char *loadfile(char *s);
char *farPtr(char *p,unsigned long l);
unsigned int *screenptr();

main(argc,argv)
        int argc;
        char *argv[];
{
        char *p;

        clrscr();
        textattr(INVERSE);
        clreol();
        cprintf("  WordPerfect file viewer version 1.0 copyright "
                "(c) 1993 Alchemy Mindworks Inc.");
        textattr(NORMAL);

        if(argc <= 1) error("Argument              "
                    "path to a WordPerfect document");

        if((p=loadfile(argv[1])) != NULL) showfile(p);

        farfree(p);

        textattr(0x07);
        clrscr();
}

showfile(p)
        char *p;
{
        LINK *lnk,*nextlnk;
        unsigned int c,i,j,*screenbase,*screen[SCREENDEEP];

        hidecursor();
        nextlnk=lnk=(LINK *)p;

        screenbase=screenptr();
        for(i=0;i<SCREENDEEP;++i)
                screen[i]=screenbase+SCREENWIDE*i;

        do {
                nextlnk=lnk;
                for(i=1;i<SCREENDEEP;++i) {
                        if(nextlnk==NULL) blankline(screen[i]);
                        else {
                                showline(screen[i],nextlnk);
                                nextlnk=nextlnk->next;
```

```
                }
            }

            switch(c=GetKey()) {
                case HOME:
                    while(lnk->prev != NULL)
                        lnk=lnk->prev;
                    break;
                case END:
                    while(lnk->next != NULL) lnk=lnk->next;
                    for(i=0;i<(SCREENDEEP-SCREENTOP);++i) {
                        if(lnk->prev != NULL)
                            lnk=lnk->prev;
                    }
                    break;
                case CURSOR_DOWN:
                    nextlnk=lnk;
                    for(i=0;i<(SCREENDEEP-SCREENTOP);++i) {
                        if(nextlnk->next != NULL)
                            nextlnk=nextlnk->next;
                    }
                    if(nextlnk->next != NULL) lnk=lnk->next;
                    break;
                case CURSOR_UP:
                    if(lnk->prev != NULL) lnk=lnk->prev;
                    break;
                case PG_UP:
                    for(i=0;i<(SCREENDEEP-SCREENTOP);++i) {
                        if(lnk->prev != NULL)
                            lnk=lnk->prev;
                        else break;
                    }
                    break;
                case PG_DOWN:
                    for(i=0;i<(SCREENDEEP-SCREENTOP);++i) {
                        nextlnk=lnk;
                        for(j=0;j<(SCREENDEEP-SCREENTOP);++j) {
                            if(nextlnk->next != NULL)
                                nextlnk=nextlnk->next;
                        }
                        if(nextlnk->next==NULL) break;
                        if(lnk->next != NULL)
                            lnk=lnk->next;
                        else break;
                    }
                    break;
            }
        } while(c != 27);
}

showline(line,lnk)
        unsigned int *line;
        LINK *lnk;
{
        char *p;
        int i,c;

        p=(char *)lnk+sizeof(LINK);
```

**1-10** Continued.

```
        for(i=0;i<SCREENWIDE;++i) {
                if(i < lnk->length) {
                        c=*p++;
                        if(c & 0x0080) *line++ = ((c & 0x7f) | (BRIGHT << 8));
                        else *line++ = (c | (NORMAL << 8));
                }
                else *line++ = (32 | (NORMAL << 8));
        }
}

blankline(line)
        unsigned int *line;
{
        int i;
        for(i=0;i<SCREENWIDE;++i) *line++ = (32 | (NORMAL << 8));
}

char *loadfile(s)
        char *s;
{
        LINK *lnk,*nextlnk;
        FILE *fp;
        char *p,*line,b[WORDSIZE];
        unsigned long freemem,offset;
        unsigned int wordindex=0,effects=0;
        int i,n,c=0;

        freemem=coreleft()-2048L;

        if((p=farmalloc(freemem)) == NULL) {
                error("Can't allocate memory");
                return(NULL);
        }

        if((fp=fopen(s,"rb")) == NULL) {
                error("Can't open source file");
                farfree(p);
                return(NULL);
        }

        if(fread(b,1,4,fp) != 4 || memcmp(b,"\377WPC",4)) {
                error("Bad WordPerfect file header");
                fclose(fp);
                farfree(p);
                return(NULL);
        }

        if(fread((char *)&offset,1,sizeof(unsigned long),fp)
            != sizeof(unsigned long)) {
                error("Bad file offset");
                fclose(fp);
                farfree(p);
                return(NULL);
        }

        fseek(fp,offset,SEEK_SET);
```

```
lnk=(LINK *)p;

line=farPtr(p,(unsigned long)sizeof(LINK));

memset((char *)lnk,0,sizeof(LINK));

do {
        do {
                if(c > 0x007f && c != EOF) {
                        switch(c) {
                                /* special character */
                                case 0x00c0:
                                        for(i=0;i<3;++i) fgetc(fp);
                                        break;
                                /* alignment */
                                case 0x00c1:
                                        for(i=0;i<8;++i) fgetc(fp);
                                        break;
                                /* indent */
                                case 0x00c2:
                                        for(i=0;i<8;++i) fgetc(fp);
                                        break;
                                /* effect on */
                                case 0x00c3:
                                        effects |= (1<<fgetc(fp));
                                        fgetc(fp);
                                        break;
                                /* effect off */
                                case 0x00c4:
                                        effects &= ~(1<<fgetc(fp));
                                        fgetc(fp);
                                        break;
                                /* block protect */
                                case 0x00c5:
                                        for(i=0;i<4;++i) fgetc(fp);
                                        break;
                                /* end of indent */
                                case 0x00c6:
                                        for(i=0;i<5;++i) fgetc(fp);
                                        break;
                                /* different display when hypenated */
                                case 0x00c7:
                                        for(i=0;i<6;++i) fgetc(fp);
                                        break;
                                /* must be a subfunction code */
                                default:
                                        if(c >= 0x00d0) {
                                                fgetc(fp);
                                                n=fgetc(fp)+(fgetc(fp)<<8);
                                                for(i=0;i<n;++i)fgetc(fp);
                                        }
                                        break;
                        }
                }
                else {
                        if(c != EOF && c > 32) {
                                if(effects) c |= 0x0080;
                                b[wordindex++]=c;
```

**1-10** Continued.

```
                                }
                        }
                        c=fgetc(fp);
                        if(c==0x000d) c=32;
                } while(wordindex < WORDSIZE && c > 32 && c != EOF);

                while(wordindex < WORDSIZE && c == 32) {
                        if(effects) c |= 0x0080;
                        b[wordindex++]=c;
                        c=fgetc(fp);
                }
                /* try to add the current word to this line */
                if((lnk->length+wordindex) < SCREENWIDE) {
                        memcpy(line+lnk->length,b,wordindex);
                        lnk->length+=wordindex;
                        freemem-=((long)sizeof(LINK)+(long)wordindex);
                }

                /* if it won't fit... or if it ended with a hard
                   return... finish this line and link to the
                   next line */
                if(c == 0x0a || (lnk->length+wordindex) >= SCREENWIDE) {
                        if(c != EOF) {
                                lnk->next=(LINK *)farPtr((char *)lnk,(unsigned long)(lnk->length+sizeof(LINK)))
                                nextlnk=lnk->next;
                                memset((char *)nextlnk,0,sizeof(LINK));
                                nextlnk->prev=lnk;
                                lnk=nextlnk;
                                line=(char *)lnk+sizeof(LINK);
                        }
                }
                wordindex=0;

        } while(c != EOF && freemem > (long)WORDSIZE);
        fclose(fp);
        return(p);
}

/* say goodbye... it's independance day */
error(s)
        char *s;
{
        printf("\r\nERROR: %s\r\n",s);
        exit(1);
}

/* retrun a far pointer plus a long integer */
char *farPtr(p,l)
        char *p;
        unsigned long l;
{
        unsigned int seg,off;

        seg = FP_SEG(p);
        off = FP_OFF(p);
        seg += (off / 16);
```

```
        off &= 0x000f;
        off += (unsigned int)(l & 0x000fL);
        seg += (l / 16L);
        p = MK_FP(seg,off);
        return(p);
}

unsigned int *screenptr()
{
        union REGS r;
        r.x.ax=0x0f00;
        int86(0x10,&r,&r);

        if(r.h.al==0x07) return(MK_FP(0xb000,r.h.bh*0x1000));
        else return(MK_FP(0xb800,r.h.bh*0x1000));
}

GetKey()
{
        int c;

        c = getch();
        if(!(c & 0x00ff)) c = getch() << 8;
        return(c);
}

hidecursor()
{
        union REGS r;

        r.x.ax=0x0f00;
        int86(0x10,&r,&r);

        r.x.ax=0x0200;
        r.x.dx=0x1a00;
        int86(0x10,&r,&r);
}
```

## Get text input with editing

The standard C language `get` function will allow your applications to fetch strings from the keyboard, but only in the crudest, most primitive way possible. Aside from being awkward to work with, it's anything but bulletproof. A better string `get` function is essential for any application that requires input more complex than "press any key."

The `getst` function will implement really elegant keyboard line editing of the sort found at the DOS prompt, if you have the DOSKEY program installed. Specifically, the following editing functions are recognized by `getst`:

| | |
|---|---|
| Left arrow | moves the cursor left |
| Right arrow | moves the cursor right |
| Home | moves the cursor to the first character in the string |
| End | moves the cursor to the last character in the string |

| | |
|---|---|
| Esc | deletes all the characters in the string |
| Enter | terminates entry |
| Backspace | deletes the character to the left of the cursor |
| Del | deletes the character to the right of the cursor |
| Ins | toggles between insert and overwrite mode |

In using `getst`, you can define an initial string for the editing field. You can also define a filter procedure, which will modify the characters that are typed or which will exclude certain characters from the entry field. For example, you could create a filter that only allowed digits to be typed to create a numeric entry field.

Finally, I should note that I wrote `getst` a long time ago, and it has been in service in numerous applications. It's a really well-debugged bit of code. The complete function is shown in 1-11.

**1-11** The GETST.C source code.

```
#define INS             (82 * 256)
#define DEL             (83 * 256)
#define HOME            (71 * 256)
#define CURSOR_LEFT     (75 * 256)
#define CURSOR_RIGHT    (77 * 256)
#define END             (79 * 256)

getst(size,deflt,buffer,proc)    /* get a string */
        int size;
        char *deflt,*buffer;
        int (*proc)();
{
        char *p;
        int i,l,c,cursor=0,insert=0,rval=1;

        *buffer = 0;
        if((p=malloc(size+1)) != NULL) {
                small_cursor();
                for(c=0;c<size;++c) putch(' ');
                for(c=0;c<size;++c) putch(0x08);

                do {
                        l = strlen(buffer);
                        if(*(deflt) == 0) c = GetKey();
                        else c = *deflt++;
                        switch(c) {
                                case DEL:
                                        if(cursor < l) {
                                                memcpy(p,buffer,cursor);
                                                memcpy(p+cursor,buffer+cursor+1,(l-cursor)+1);
                                                strcpy(buffer,p);
                                                i=printf("%s%c",buffer+cursor,' ');
                                                while(i) {
                                                        putch(0x08);
                                                        --i;
                                                }
                                        }
```

```
    break;
case INS:
        if(insert) {
                insert = 0;
                small_cursor();
        }
        else {
                insert = 1;
                big_cursor();
        }
        break;
case HOME:
        while(cursor) {
                putch(0x08);
                --cursor;
        }
        break;
case END:
        while(cursor < l) {
                putch(*(buffer+cursor));
                ++cursor;
        }
        break;
case CURSOR_RIGHT:
        if(cursor < l) {
                putch(*(buffer+cursor));
                ++cursor;
        }
        break;
case CURSOR_LEFT:
        if(cursor) {
                putch(0x08);
                --cursor;
        }
        break;
case 0x08:
        if(cursor == l) {
                if(l) {
                        --l;
                        --cursor;
                        *(buffer+l) = 0;
                        putch(0x08);
                        putch(' ');
                        putch(0x08);
                }
        }
        else if(cursor < l && cursor > 0) {
                --cursor;
                memcpy(p,buffer,cursor);
                memcpy(p+cursor,buffer+cursor+1,(l-cursor)+1);
                strcpy(buffer,p);
                i=printf("%c%s%c",0x08,buffer+cursor,' ')-1;
                while(i) {
                         putch(0x08);
                         --i;
                }
        }
        break;
```

**1-11** Continued.

```
                    case 0x1b:
                            while(cursor < l) {
                                    putch(*(buffer+cursor));
                                    ++cursor;
                            }
                            while(l--) {
                                    putch(0x08);
                                    putch(' ');
                                    putch(0x08);
                            }
                            cursor = 0;
                            *buffer = 0;
                            break;
                    default:
                            if(proc != NULL) c=(proc)(c,&rval);
                            if(c >= 0x20 && c <= 0x7f) {
                            if(cursor == l && l < size) {
                                     *(buffer + l++) = c;
                                     *(buffer + l) = 0;
                                     putch(c);
                                     ++cursor;
                            }
                            else if(cursor < l) {
                                    if(!insert) {
                                            *(buffer + cursor++) = c;
                                            putch(c);
                                    }
                                    else if(l < size) {
                                            memcpy(p,buffer,cursor);
                                            *(p+cursor) = c;
                                            memcpy(p+cursor+1,
                                                buffer+cursor,(l-cursor)+1);
                                            strcpy(buffer,p);
                                            i=printf("%s",buffer+cursor)-1;
                                            while(i--) putch(0x08);
                                            ++cursor;
                                    }
                            }
                    }
                    break;
            }
        } while(c != 0x0d && rval != 0);
        free(p);
        small_cursor();
        return(c);
    }
    else return(-1);
}

big_cursor()    /* make the cursor big */
{
    union REGS r;

    r.h.ah = 15;
    int86(0x10,&r,&r);
```

```
        r.h.ah = 1;
        r.h.cl = 7;
        r.h.ch = 3;
        int86(0x10,&r,&r);
}

small_cursor()     /* make the cursor small */
{
        union REGS r;

        r.h.ah = 15;
        int86(0x10,&r,&r);

        r.h.ah = 1;
        r.h.cl = 6;
        r.h.ch = 5;
        int86(0x10,&r,&r);
}
```

The getst function also calls GetKey. This function will return the next key press, as its name implies, but it keeps track of the PC extended keyboard characters as well. As such, if you hit the Home key, GetKey will return the HOME constant.

In fact, these extended keys are actually the keyboard scan codes. Specifically, if a normal alphabetic key is hit, GetKey will store its ASCII value in the low-order byte of the integer it returns and zero in the high-order byte. If an extended key is struck, the scan mode of the extended key will be stored in the high-order byte and zero should be stored in the low-order byte.

Here are two versions of GetKey:

```
GetKey()
{
        int c;

        c = getch();
        if(!(c & 0x00ff) c = getch() << 8;
        return(c);
}

GetKey()
{
        int c;

        c=bioskey(0);
        if(c & 0x00ff) c &= 0x00ff;
        return(c);
}
```

The first GetKey uses a peculiarity of the standard C language getch function as it's implemented on a PC. If a call to getch returns zero, you should call getch a second time and treat the value it returns as the scan code of an extended keyboard character. If the first call doesn't return zero it can be treated as a normal ASCII value.

This is arguably the correct way to implement GetKey, but it has a catch, if rather an obscure one. If you have the dreaded ANSI.SYS driver installed in your system and use it to assign strings to the function keys of your keyboard, the first character of each string will be returned by GetKey when you hit one of your function keys, rather than the scan code for the key.

The second GetKey gets around this problem by getting around DOS entirely. It makes a direct call to the BIOS. In theory this could cause problems with some distant revision of DOS, although it's highly unlikely.

Note that in addition to GetKey, the getst function also makes calls to big-cursor and small-cursor. As you might expect, these functions change the size of the DOS text mode cursor. The small cursor is used to indicate the normal overwrite text entry mode—if you type text over existing characters, the existing characters will be replaced. Hitting the Ins key will toggle getst into its insert mode, and the cursor will get bigger to indicate this. In insert mode, typing text with the cursor midway through the existing string will push the text to the right of the cursor ahead of it.

The getst function itself is fairly easy to understand, although it might seem to be more complex than it needs to be. Part of the reason for this is that it does all its line editing and juggling with no cursor positioning functions. It moves the cursor backwards by issuing nondestructive backspace characters and forward by printing the text of the string being edited. As such, it's very easy to implement in environments other than the DOS text mode.

There are four arguments to getst, as follows:

```
getst(size,deflt,buffer,proc)
        int size;
        char *deflt,*buffer;
        int (*proc) ();
```

The size argument should be set to the maximum size of the string you'd like to get. If someone attempts to type more characters than size specifies, the getst function will ignore them.

The deflt argument is the default string to be placed in the editing field before users have a chance to type their own input. For example, if you wanted to prompt for a file name using getst you might set this argument to "UNTITLED.TXT." Users of your application could hit Enter to accept this name, or they could edit the field to set up a new name.

The buffer argument is where getst will store the string it gets when it terminates.

Finally, proc is a filter. You can pass NULL for this argument if you don't want to use a character filter, in which case getst will allow any character you want to enter in its text field. A filter is of the following form:

```
int filter(c)
        int c;
{
        /* do something with c */
        return(c);
}
```

A filter will pass each keyboard character that's entered. It can return a modified character, which will turn up in the entry field, or zero if the character is to be ignored. Here are a few examples of filters:

```
int filter(c)
        int c;
{
        return(toupper(c));
}
```

This filter will make all the alphabetic characters typed into the `getst` entry field uppercase. In theory you could just pass `toupper` as the `proc` argument to `getst`, but in most compilers `toupper` is actually implemented as a macro rather than as a function.

This next filter will only allow numeric input:

```
int filter(c)
        int c;
{
        if(isdigit(c)) return(c);
        else return (0);
}
```

Here's a complete invocation of `getst`:

```
int filter();
char buffer[129];
getst(128,"UNTITLED.TXT",buffer,filter);
```

This assumes the existence of a suitable filter function. Because this call to `getst` looks like it will be used to fetch a DOS file name, you might want to create a filter that refuses to accept illegal characters for file names, such as spaces.

Note that the buffer passed to `getst` as its `buffer` argument should be one byte bigger than the value in the `size` argument to allow for the final zero byte if the string is filled. The `getst` will return the length of the string it finally stores in its `buffer` argument, or –1 if it couldn't allocate its internal scratch buffer.

# 2
# Canned graphics

*"Discoveries are made by not following instructions."*
—Graffiti

Text is businesslike and productive. Graphics are fun. As a rule, software that's fun usually comes out on top. Microsoft Windows, for example, is popular at least in part because it's graphic and fun. You can make it look distinctive and visually interesting, and perhaps more to the point, you can make it look unlike what's running on everyone else's computer. People used to do this by gluing rubber spiders to their monitors.

Graphics is a rather larger area than text—I've written a number of dedicated books about it, as listed later in this chapter. While you'll find a pretty worthwhile can of graphic paraphernalia herein, it seems fair to note that it's anything but exhaustive. The default 640-×-480 pixel, 16-color Windows display offers something more than $6^{87}$ different permutations of pixels. You can do quite a lot with something like this.

A portion of this chapter is dedicated to graphics as they appear under Windows. This should not be seen to suggest that DOS doesn't support graphics, only that it supports them fairly poorly. Displaying graphics in a Windows application is typically very easy, as that's what Windows does even when it isn't actually doing anything at all. By comparison, DOS offers no meaningful graphics facilities, and it offers them in a chaotic and poorly defined environment that requires all sorts of libraries and drivers and mystic secrets to get even fairly trivial graphics together.

This is not altogether bad, of course. Well-crafted graphics under DOS look eye-catching, as much of the DOS-based software that most people run is either wholly mired in text mode or uses very crude, ugly graphics. Users of Lotus 1-2-3, with its spindly monochrome chart graphics, are usually singularly impressed by even fairly coarse full-color photorealistic bitmaps, for example. I'll get into these first—torrid things, those photorealistic bitmaps.

## Displaying PCX files

One of the sources of confusion in using graphics on a PC—and more specifically, graphics files—is that there's nothing like a standard graphics file format. Whereas Macintosh systems have MacPaint files and Amigas have IFF files, PCs offer a choice of more than a dozen possible formats in which to store a picture. PC display adapters employ a welter of display modes, most of which are incompatible. Having a picture appear on your screen can be a challenge of epic dimensions, rivaling the ancient deeds of legend.

In fact, you can simplify the problem a bit if you know where to cheat. While there are lots of image file formats about, you need only be able to work with one to get graphics to display. Likewise, you can choose standard display modes that are common to almost all contemporary display devices.

The program in this example will display a PCX file on any VGA card. The PCX format is one of the more popular PC image file formats, and almost all display adapters in use at the moment are VGA cards. The exceptions are earlier CGA, EGA, and Hercules cards, whose numbers grow fewer with the passage of time, and a few IBM creations, such as the XGA and 8514 cards.

In order to display a PCX file you must know how to unpack the file into a format that's compatible with a VGA card's graphics mode display, how to set the color palette of your VGA card to match that of the PCX file being unpacked, and finally, how to get image data from the PCX file onto your screen. None of these things is particularly difficult if you know where all the trap doors and secret passages are.

A PCX file consists of a header that defines information such as the dimensions of the file followed by image data that is "run length" encoded, or compressed, to make it smaller. The header is a fairly simple object that looks like this:

```
typedef struct {
        char manufacturer;
        char version;
        char encoding;
        char bits_per_pixel;
        int xmin,ymin;
        int xmax,ymax;
        int hres;
        int vres;
        char palette[48];
        char reserved;
        char color_planes;
        int bytes_per_line;
        int palette_type;
        char filler[58];
        } PCXHEAD;
```

I won't deal with all the fields in a PCXHEAD object here. Many of them can be ignored unless you get into more complex graphics applications. The ones that matter are:

- `manufacturer`: This will always be 10. It serves as a signature to verify that you're actually reading a PCX file.
- `bits_per_pixel`: This is the number of bits of color depth represented by the file in question—sort of.
- `xmin` and `xmax`: The width of the picture in pixels will be `xmax – xmin`.
- `ymin` and `ymax`: The depth of the picture in pixels will be `ymax – ymin`.
- `palette`: If the picture has 16 or fewer colors, the color information will be stored in this field.
- `bytes_per_line`: This will be the actual number of bytes of information required to store one line of image data.

The PCX files discussed in this section all support between 2 and 256 colors. In fact, the PCX standard allows for up to 16 million colors, but I won't deal with the really high-end aspects of the format here. A 256-color palette requires 768 bytes of data to support it, which would take some doing to squeeze into a 128-byte header. As such, 256-color PCX files have their palettes at the end of the file, after the image data. The palette data is always preceded by a byte that holds the value 12.

The image data itself is stored using a very simple form of compression that reduces the amount of space required by areas of a picture that are all the same color. You can see how a PCX line is unpacked by having a look at the `readpcxline` function in the program I'll look at in a moment.

Color palette information is stored as three bytes per color, just as it was in the example text mode palettes from the last chapter. In graphics applications it's usually the case that color values won't be packed into long integers, but will be dealt with as separate bytes arranged in the order red, green, blue. Windows programmers should note that under Windows the order is usually reversed.

The `setpalette` function in the code to follow will set the current VGA palette based on an array of three-byte color values passed to it.

Finally, there are two VGA graphics modes of interest to this application. They are mode 12H, which allows for 640-×-480 pixels in 16 colors, and mode 13H, which allows for 320-×-200 pixels in 256 colors. The former mode is useful for displaying simple black-and-white graphics and for doing drawn mechanical graphics, such as business charts or Windows screens. The latter mode can display photorealistic images, albeit at a fairly coarse resolution.

The SHOWPCX program, illustrated in 2-1, is a simple command line PCX file viewer. Given the path to a PCX file and a VGA card to display it on, it will show the picture on your screen and wait for a key press, at which time it will return to DOS.

**2-1** The SHOWPCX.C source code.

```
/*
        Simple PCX reader
        Copyright (c) 1993 Alchemy Mindworks Inc.

        Make sure the default char type is UNSIGNED and
        the memory model is LARGE when you compile this.
*/

#include "stdio.h"
#include "dos.h"
#include "alloc.h"
#include "stdlib.h"

#define pixels2bytes(n)         ((n+7)/8)
#define plane(n)            { outp(0x3c4,2); outp(0x3c5,(n)); }

typedef struct {
        char manufacturer;
        char version;
        char encoding;
        char bits_per_pixel;
        int xmin,ymin;
        int xmax,ymax;
        int hres;
        int vres;
        char palette[48];
        char reserved;
        char colour_planes;
        int bytes_per_line;
        int palette_type;
        char filler[58];
        } PCXHEAD;

main(argc,argv)
        int argc;
        char *argv[];
{
        FILE *fp;
        PCXHEAD pcx;
        union REGS r;
        char *screen=MK_FP(0xa000,0x0000);
        char *p,*pr,palette[768];
        unsigned int width,depth,bytes,bits,planebytes;
        unsigned int screenwidth,screendepth,screenbytes,screenmode;
        unsigned int i,j;

        if(argc <= 1)
            error("Argument:             path to a PCX file");

        if((fp=fopen(argv[1],"rb"))==NULL)
            error("Can't open the PCX file.");

        if(fread((char *)&pcx,1,sizeof(PCXHEAD),fp) != sizeof(PCXHEAD))
            error("Can't read the PCX header.");

        if(pcx.manufacturer != 10)
```

```
     error("This isn't a PCX file.");

if(pcx.bits_per_pixel==1) bits=pcx.colour_planes;
else bits=pcx.bits_per_pixel;

width=pcx.xmax-pcx.xmin;
depth=pcx.ymax-pcx.ymin;

bytes=pcx.bytes_per_line;

if(bits==1) {
        screenwidth=640;
        screendepth=480;
        screenbytes=80;
        screenmode=0x0012;
        memcpy(palette,"\000\000\000\377\377\377",6);
}
else if(bits <= 4) {
        screenwidth=640;
        screendepth=480;
        screenbytes=80;
        planebytes=pixels2bytes(width);
        screenmode=0x0012;
        memcpy(palette,pcx.palette,48);
        bytes*=bits;
}
else {
        screenwidth=320;
        screendepth=200;
        screenbytes=320;
        screenmode=0x0013;
        fseek(fp,-769L,SEEK_END);
        if(fgetc(fp) != 12)
            error("Can't find the palette");

        if(fread(palette,1,768,fp) != 768)
            error("Can't read the palette");

        fseek(fp,(long)sizeof(PCXHEAD),SEEK_SET);
}

if((p=malloc(bytes))==NULL)
    error("Can't allocate memory.");

r.x.ax=screenmode;
int86(0x10,&r,&r);

setpalette(palette,bits);

for(i=0;i<depth && i<screendepth;++i) {
        if(readpcxline(p,fp,bytes) != bytes) {
                r.x.ax=0x0003;
                int86(0x10,&r,&r);
                error("The PCX file is damaged.");
        }
        if(bits==1) memcpy(screen,p,min(screenbytes,bytes));
        else if(bits==8) memcpy(screen,p,min(screenwidth,bytes));
        else {
```

**2-1** Continued.

```
                        pr=p;
                        for(j=0;j<bits;++j) {
                                plane(1<<j);
                                memcpy(screen,pr,min(screenbytes,planebytes));
                                pr+=planebytes;
                        }
                        plane(0x0f);
                }
                screen+=screenbytes;
        }
        getch();

        r.x.ax=0x0003;
        int86(0x10,&r,&r);
}

readpcxline(p,fp,bytes)
        char *p;
        FILE *fp;
        unsigned int bytes;
{
        int n=0,c,i;

        memset(p,0,bytes);
        do {
                c=fgetc(fp) & 0xff;
                if((c & 0xc0) == 0xc0) {
                        i=c & 0x3f;
                        c=fgetc(fp);
                        while(i--) p[n++]=c;
                }
                else p[n++]=c;
        } while(n < bytes);
        return(n);
}

setpalette(p,bits)
        char *p;
        int bits;
{
        union REGS r;
        int i,n;

        n=1<<bits;
        if(bits <= 4) {
                for(i=0;i<n;++i) {
                        r.x.ax=0x1000;
                        r.h.bh=i;
                        r.h.bl=i;
                        int86(0x10,&r,&r);
                }
        }

        outp(0x3c6,0xff);
        for(i=0;i<n;++i) {
                outp(0x3c8,i);
```

```
                outp(0x3c9,(*p++) >> 2);
                outp(0x3c9,(*p++) >> 2);
                outp(0x3c9,(*p++) >> 2);
        }
}

error(s)
        char *s;
{
        puts(s);
        exit(1);
}
```

SHOWPCX assumes you won't attempt to feed it a PCX file of a type it can't fathom. This includes PCX files with 16 million colors, as well as some 16-color PCX files that have been created incorrectly. Quite a few applications that export PCX files do so in a form that well-behaved PCX readers like SHOWPCX will not handle correctly.

The SHOWPCX program also assumes that you really do have a VGA card in your system. Nothing good will happen if you attempt to run it on a computer with an EGA card in it, for example. If you choose to make some serious use of SHOWPCX, you might want to add traps for these exceptions.

Finally, note that the SHOWPCX program will always display an image in the upper left corner of your screen. If the picture is smaller than your screen, it will pad out the extra space with black, or more properly, with color zero in your picture's palette. If it's too large, it will only display that portion that fits on your screen.

The Graphic Workshop shareware package, included on the companion disk for this book, can be used to convert pictures from other formats into PCX for use with this program. If you encounter a PCX file that SHOWPCX won't read—one of the many slightly funky variations on the PCX format—use Graphic Workshop to convert from PCX to PCX. Graphic Workshop reads almost any PCX file, and it always writes correct ones.

## Generating a maze in Windows

A maze is illustrated in 2-2. Perhaps more specifically, it illustrates a Windows application that has generated a maze. Mazes have a long history, dating back to classical mythology and English formal gardens. The creation of mazes is an art form, or at least it was until software that could create them turned up. It's a lot easier to create mazes out of pixels than by using hedge clippers.

In fact, a maze is a very simple mathematical model. The definition of a maze for this discussion is a path having one entrance, one exit, and lots of twists and dead ends in-between.

The maze generation algorithm is fairly easy to understand—and perhaps even more so if you watch the program at work. It begins by drawing

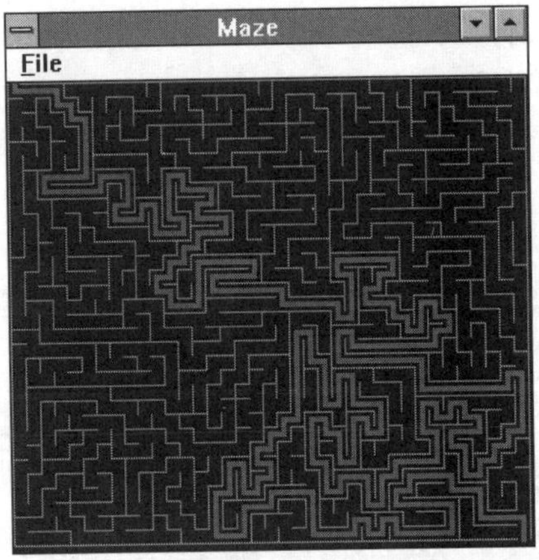


**2-2** A Windows maze.

a grid in the application window. It then recursively walks through the grid, knocking out sections of the walls. Beginning with a random direction, it works its way along, changing direction as it goes, until it runs out of places to turn. At each turn it keeps a record of where it has come from as an entry on its private stack. It will run out of places when it either hits a wall or when it hits a path that's already been taken. At such time as there's nowhere else to go, it collapses its stack by one and tries another direction.

Solving the maze is handled in much the same way. Inasmuch as the maze has been created randomly, there's no logical way to solve it based on an algorithm. Rather, it can only be worked out by trial and error. Beginning at the start of the maze, an imaginary character ventures into the maze, once again keeping track of its progress on a local stack. When it meets a dead end, it collapses its stack by one level, back tracks, and tries another direction. It continues to do this until it finally reaches the lower right corner of the maze, at which time it can consider the puzzle solved.

The C language source code, MAZE.CPP, for the MAZE application is illustrated in 2-3.

**2-3** The MAZE.CPP source code.

```
/*
        Maze generator for Windows
        version 1.0 Copyright (c) 1992
        Alchemy Mindworks Inc.

        From MAZE.C by James L. Dean.
*/

#include <windows.h>
#include <dir.h>
#include <alloc.h>
#include <stdio.h>
#include <stdlib.h>
```

```
/* defines */
#define MINMAZESIZE    16
#define CELLSIZE        8
#define PATHPEN         3

/* constants for the File menu */
#define         FILE_ABOUT         103
#define         FILE_EXIT         104

#ifndef max
#define max(a,b)                (((a)>(b))?(a):(b))
#endif
#ifndef min
#define min(a,b)                (((a)<(b))?(a):(b))
#endif

/* some data structures */
typedef struct STACK1REC {
        unsigned char index_1;
        struct STACK1REC *next_ptr;
        } *STACK1RECPTR;

typedef struct STACK2REC {
        unsigned char index_1;
        unsigned char index_2;
        struct STACK2REC *next_ptr;
        } *STACK2RECPTR;

typedef struct {
        int delta_x[96];
        int delta_y[96];
        int fatal_error;
        int magnitude_delta_x;
        int magnitude_delta_y;
        int num_columns;
        int num_rows;
        int r_n[8];
        int twice_magnitude_delta_x;
        int twice_magnitude_delta_y;
        int x_max;
        int y_max;
        DWORD passage;
        DWORD path;
        DWORD wall;
        HPEN solve_pen;
        HPEN passage_pen;
        HPEN path_pen;
        HPEN wall_pen;
        HBRUSH passage_brush;
        HBRUSH path_brush;
        } MAZE;

/* draw a line */
#define Line(hdc,l,t,r,b) { MoveTo(hdc,l,t); LineTo(hdc,r,b); }

/* this is a crude way to slow down the maze solving
   function so you can see what it's up to. Uncomment
   second version of Wait to drop into first.
```

**2-3** Continued.

```
*/
#define Wait()                  { for(int n=0;n<10000;++n); }
/*
#define Wait()                  { for(long n=0;n<100000L;++n); }
*/

/* prototypes */
long FAR PASCAL WndProc(HWND,unsigned int,unsigned int,long);
DWORD FAR PASCAL AboutDlgProc(HWND hwnd,WORD message,WORD wParam,LONG lParam);
void DoMaze(HDC hdc,RECT *rect);
void InitializeMaze(MAZE *maze,HDC hdc,RECT *rect);
void GenerateMaze(MAZE *maze,HDC hdc,RECT *rect);
void SolveMaze(MAZE *maze,HDC hdc);

char szAppName[]="Maze";
HANDLE hInst;

/* this is where the maze lives */
MAZE maze;

#pragma warn -par
int PASCAL WinMain(HANDLE hInstance,HANDLE hPrevInstance,
                   LPSTR lpszCmdParam,int nCmdShow)
{
        RECT rect;
        HWND hwnd;
        MSG msg;
        HDC hdc;
        WNDCLASS wndclass;

        if(!hPrevInstance) {
                wndclass.style          = CS_HREDRAW | CS_VREDRAW;
                wndclass.lpfnWndProc    = WndProc;
                wndclass.cbClsExtra     = 0;
                wndclass.cbWndExtra     = 0;
                wndclass.hInstance      = hInstance;
                wndclass.hIcon          = LoadIcon(hInstance,szAppName);

                wndclass.hCursor        = LoadCursor(NULL,IDC_ARROW);
                wndclass.hbrBackground  = GetStockObject(WHITE_BRUSH);
                wndclass.lpszMenuName   = szAppName;
                wndclass.lpszClassName  = szAppName;

                RegisterClass(&wndclass);
        }

        hInst=hInstance;

        /* create a window */
        hwnd = CreateWindow(szAppName,
                        "Maze",
                        WS_OVERLAPPED | WS_CAPTION | WS_SYSMENU|
                        WS_MINIMIZEBOX | WS_MAXIMIZEBOX,
                        100,100,300,300,
                        NULL,
```

```
                        NULL,
                        hInstance,
                        NULL);

        ShowWindow(hwnd,nCmdShow);
        UpdateWindow(hwnd);

        /* every chance we get, either process a message or create a maze. */
        for(;;) {
                if(PeekMessage(&msg,NULL,0,0,PM_REMOVE)) {
                        if(msg.message==WM_QUIT) break;
                        TranslateMessage(&msg);
                        DispatchMessage(&msg);
                }
                else {
                        hdc=GetDC(hwnd);
                        GetClientRect(hwnd,&rect);
                        DoMaze(hdc,&rect);
                        ReleaseDC(hwnd,hdc);
                }
        }

        return(msg.wParam);
}

long FAR PASCAL WndProc(HWND hwnd,unsigned int message,unsigned int wParam,long lParam)
{
        FARPROC lpfnDlgProc;
        PAINTSTRUCT ps;

        switch(message) {
                case WM_COMMAND:
                        switch(wParam) {
                                case FILE_ABOUT:
                                        if((lpfnDlgProc=MakeProcInstance((FARPROC)
                                        AboutDlgProc,hInst)) != NULL) {
                                                DialogBox(hInst,"AboutBox",hwnd,
                                                lpfnDlgProc);
                                                FreeProcInstance(lpfnDlgProc);
                                        }
                                        return(0);
                                case FILE_EXIT:
                                        if(MessageBox(hwnd,"Had enough mazes?",
                                        "Exit...",MB_OKCANCEL | MB_ICONINFORMATION) ==
                                        IDOK)
                                                PostQuitMessage(0);
                                        break;
                        }
                        break;
                case WM_SIZE:
                case WM_ACTIVATE:
                        maze.fatal_error=TRUE;
                        return(0);
                case WM_CREATE:
                        maze.wall=RGB(0,255,0);
                        maze.passage=RGB(0,0,0);
                        maze.path=RGB(0,128,0);
```

**2-3** Continued.

```
                        maze.wall_pen=CreatePen(PS_SOLID,1,maze.wall);
                        maze.passage_pen=CreatePen(PS_SOLID,1,maze.passage);
                        maze.path_pen=CreatePen(PS_SOLID,PATHPEN,maze.path);
                        maze.solve_pen=CreatePen(PS_SOLID,PATHPEN,maze.passage);
                        maze.passage_brush=CreateSolidBrush(maze.passage);
                        maze.path_brush=CreateSolidBrush(maze.path);
                        return(0);
                case WM_PAINT:
                        BeginPaint(hwnd,&ps);
                        maze.fatal_error=TRUE;
                        EndPaint(hwnd,&ps);
                        return(0);
                case WM_DESTROY:
                        DeleteObject(maze.wall_pen);
                        DeleteObject(maze.passage_pen);
                        DeleteObject(maze.path_pen);
                        DeleteObject(maze.solve_pen);
                        DeleteObject(maze.passage_brush);
                        DeleteObject(maze.path_brush);
                        PostQuitMessage(0);
                        break;
        }

        return(DefWindowProc(hwnd,message,wParam,lParam));
}

/* handle messages to the About dialog */
DWORD FAR PASCAL AboutDlgProc(HWND hwnd,WORD message,WORD wParam,LONG lParam)
{
        POINT point;

        switch(message) {
                case WM_INITDIALOG:
                        return(TRUE);
                case WM_CTLCOLOR:
                        if(HIWORD(lParam)==CTLCOLOR_STATIC ||
                          HIWORD(lParam)==CTLCOLOR_DLG) {
                                SetBkColor(wParam,RGB(192,192,192));
                                SetTextColor(wParam,RGB(0,0,0));

                                ClientToScreen(hwnd,&point);
                                UnrealizeObject(GetStockObject(LTGRAY_BRUSH));
                                SetBrushOrg(wParam,point.x,point.y);

                                return((DWORD)GetStockObject(LTGRAY_BRUSH));

                        }
                        if(HIWORD(lParam)==CTLCOLOR_BTN) {
                                SetBkColor(wParam,RGB(192,192,192));
                                SetTextColor(wParam,RGB(0,0,0));

                                ClientToScreen(hwnd,&point);
                                UnrealizeObject(GetStockObject(BLACK_BRUSH));
                                SetBrushOrg(wParam,point.x,point.y);

                                return((DWORD)GetStockObject(BLACK_BRUSH));
```

```
                    }
                    break;
                case WM_COMMAND:
                    switch(wParam) {
                        case IDOK:
                            EndDialog(hwnd,wParam);
                            return(TRUE);
                    }
                    break;
        }

        return(FALSE);
}

void DoMaze(HDC hdc,RECT *rect)
{
        maze.fatal_error=FALSE;

        InitializeMaze(&maze,hdc,rect);
        if(!maze.fatal_error) GenerateMaze(&maze,hdc,rect);
        if(!maze.fatal_error) SolveMaze(&maze,hdc);
}

void InitializeMaze(MAZE *maze,HDC hdc,RECT *rect)
{
        int delta_index_1a;
        int delta_index_1b;
        int delta_index_1c;
        int delta_index_1d;
        int delta_index_2;
        int max_num_columns;
        int max_num_rows;
        int max_x;
        int max_y;
        int r_n_index_1;
        int r_n_index_2;
        char seed[256];
        int tem_int;

        max_x=rect->right-rect->left;
        max_y=rect->bottom-rect->top;
        max_num_columns=max_x/CELLSIZE;
        max_num_rows=max_y/CELLSIZE;

        randomize();
        maze->num_rows=max_num_rows;
        maze->num_columns=max_num_columns;

        sprintf(seed,"%u",random(32767));

        for(r_n_index_1=0;
            r_n_index_1 < 8 && seed[r_n_index_1] != 0;
            r_n_index_1++) {
                tem_int=seed[r_n_index_1];
                while(tem_int >= 29) tem_int-=29;
                maze->r_n[r_n_index_1]=tem_int;
        }
```

**2-3** Continued.

```
r_n_index_2=7;
while (r_n_index_1 > 0) {
        r_n_index_1--;
        maze->r_n[r_n_index_2]=maze->r_n[r_n_index_1];
        r_n_index_2--;
}

while (r_n_index_2 >= 0) {
        maze->r_n[r_n_index_2]=19;
        r_n_index_2--;
}

maze->magnitude_delta_x=max_x/maze->num_columns/2;
maze->twice_magnitude_delta_x=maze->magnitude_delta_x+
    maze->magnitude_delta_x;
maze->magnitude_delta_y=max_y/maze->num_rows/2;
maze->twice_magnitude_delta_y=maze->magnitude_delta_y+
    maze->magnitude_delta_y;
maze->x_max=maze->twice_magnitude_delta_x*maze->num_columns;
maze->y_max=maze->twice_magnitude_delta_y*maze->num_rows;
maze->delta_x[0]=maze->magnitude_delta_x;
maze->delta_y[24]=maze->magnitude_delta_y;
maze->delta_x[48]=-maze->magnitude_delta_x;
maze->delta_y[72]=-maze->magnitude_delta_y;
maze->delta_y[0]=0;
maze->delta_x[24]=0;
maze->delta_y[48]=0;
maze->delta_x[72]=0;
delta_index_2=-1;
for(delta_index_1a=0;delta_index_1a < 4;delta_index_1a++) {
        for(delta_index_1b=0;delta_index_1b < 4;delta_index_1b++) {
                if(delta_index_1a != delta_index_1b) {
                        for(delta_index_1c=0;delta_index_1c <
                        4;delta_index_1c++) {
                                if((delta_index_1a != delta_index_1c) &&
                                (delta_index_1b != delta_index_1c)) {
                                        for(delta_index_1d=0; delta_index_1d <
                                        4;delta_index_1d++) {
                                                if(delta_index_1a !=delta_index
                                                _1d && delta_index_1b !=
                                                 delta_index_1d && delta
                                                _index_1c != delta_index_1d) {
                                                        delta_index_2=delta
                                                       _index_2+1;
                                                        maze->delta_x[(24*delta
                                                        _index_1a+delta_index
                                                        _2)]=maze->delta_x[0];
                                                        maze->delta_y[(24*delta
                                                        _index_1a+delta_index
                                                        _2)]=maze->delta_y[0];
                                                        maze->delta_x[(24*delta
                                                        _index_1b+delta_index
                                                        _2)]=maze->delta_x[24];
                                                        maze->delta_y[(24*delta
```

```
                                                                _index_1b+delta_index
                                                                  _2)]=maze->delta_y[24];
                                                                maze->delta_x[(24*delta
                                                                  _index_1c+delta_index
                                                                  _2)]=maze->delta_x[48];
                                                                maze->delta_y[(24*delta
                                                                  _index_1c+delta_index
                                                                  _2)]=maze->delta_y[48];
                                                                maze->delta_x[(24*delta
                                                                  _index_1d+delta_index
                                                                  _2)]=maze->delta_x[72];
                                                                maze->delta_y[(24*delta
                                                                  _index_1d+delta_index
                                                                  _2)]=maze->delta_y[72];
                                                        }
                                                }
                                        }
                                }
                        }
                }
        }
}

void GenerateMaze(MAZE *maze,HDC hdc,RECT *rect)
{
        int finished;
        int delta_index_1;
        int delta_index_2;
        int digit;
        int digit_num;
        int recurse;
        int r_n_index_1;
        int r_n_index_2;
        STACK2RECPTR stack_head=NULL;
        STACK2RECPTR stack_ptr=NULL;
        int sum;
        int tem_int;
        int x;
        int x_next;
        int x_out;
        int y;
        int y_next;
        int y_out;

        SelectObject(hdc,maze->passage_pen);
        SelectObject(hdc,maze->passage_brush);
        Rectangle(hdc,rect->left,rect->top,rect->right,rect->bottom);

        SelectObject(hdc,maze->path_pen);
        SelectObject(hdc,maze->path_brush);
        Rectangle(hdc,0,0,maze->x_max,maze->y_max);

        if(maze->path != maze->wall) {
                SelectObject(hdc,maze->wall_pen);
                x_out=0;
                while(x_out <= maze->x_max) {
                        Line(hdc,x_out,0,x_out,maze->y_max);
```

**2-3** Continued.

```
                x_out+=(maze->twice_magnitude_delta_x);
        }
        y_out=0;
        while (y_out <= maze->y_max) {
                Line(hdc,0,y_out,maze->x_max,y_out);
                y_out+=(maze->twice_magnitude_delta_y);
        }
}
sum=0;
for(digit_num=1;digit_num <= 3;digit_num++) {
        digit=maze->r_n[0];
        r_n_index_1=0;
        for(r_n_index_2=1;r_n_index_2 < 8;r_n_index_2++) {
                tem_int=maze->r_n[r_n_index_2];
                maze->r_n[r_n_index_1]=tem_int;
                r_n_index_1++;
                digit+=tem_int;
                if(digit >= 29) digit-=29;
        }
        maze->r_n[7]=digit;
        sum=29*sum+digit;
}
x=(2*(sum%(maze->num_columns))+1)*maze->magnitude_delta_x;
sum=0;
for(digit_num=1; digit_num <= 3; digit_num++) {
        digit=maze->r_n[0];
        r_n_index_1=0;
        for(r_n_index_2=1; r_n_index_2 < 8; r_n_index_2++) {
                tem_int=maze->r_n[r_n_index_2];
                maze->r_n[r_n_index_1]=tem_int;
                r_n_index_1++;
                digit+=tem_int;
                if(digit >= 29) digit-=29;
        }
        maze->r_n[7]=digit;
        sum=29*sum+digit;
}
y=(2*(sum%(maze->num_rows))+1)*maze->magnitude_delta_y;

SelectObject(hdc,maze->passage_brush);
SelectObject(hdc,maze->passage_pen);

finished=FALSE;
recurse=TRUE;
stack_head=NULL;
while(!finished && !maze->fatal_error) {
        Yield();
        if(recurse) {
                Rectangle(hdc,x-maze->magnitude_delta_x+1,y-maze-
                >magnitude_delta_y+1,
                           x+maze->magnitude_delta_x,y+maze-
                           >magnitude_delta_y);

                delta_index_1=0;
                do {
                        delta_index_2=maze->r_n[0];
```

```
                r_n_index_1=0;
                for(r_n_index_2=1;r_n_index_2<8;r_n_index_2++) {
                        tem_int=maze->r_n[r_n_index_2];
                        maze->r_n[r_n_index_1]=tem_int;
                        r_n_index_1++;
                        delta_index_2+=tem_int;
                        if(delta_index_2 >= 29) delta_index_2-=29;
                }
                maze->r_n[7]=delta_index_2;
        } while (delta_index_2 >= 24);
        recurse=FALSE;
}
while((delta_index_1 < 4) && !recurse && !maze->fatal_error) {
        x_next=x+2*maze->delta_x[24*delta_index_1+delta_index_2];
        if((x_next <= 0) || (x_next >= maze->x_max)) delta_index_1++;
        else {
                y_next=y+2*maze->delta_y[24*delta_index_1+delta
                _index_2];
                if((y_next <= 0) || (y_next >= maze->y_max))
                    delta_index_1++;
                else if(GetPixel(hdc,x_next,y_next)==maze->path) {
                        if(x == x_next) {
                                y_out=(y+y_next)/2;
                                Line(hdc,x-maze->magnitude_delta
                                _x+1,y_out,
                                         x+maze->magnitude_delta
                                         _x,y_out);
                        }
                        else {
                                x_out=(x+x_next)/2;
                                Line(hdc,x_out,y-maze->magnitude_delta
                                _y+1,
                                         x_out,y+maze->magnitude
                                         _delta_y);
                        }

                        x=x_next;
                        y=y_next;
                        if((stack_ptr=(struct STACK2REC *)malloc(
                        (unsigned) sizeof(struct STACK2REC))) == NULL)
                            maze->fatal_error=TRUE;
                        else {
                                stack_ptr->next_ptr=stack_head;
                                stack_head=stack_ptr;
                                stack_head->index_1=(unsigned char)
                                delta_index_1;
                                stack_head->index_2=(unsigned char)
                                delta_index_2;
                                recurse=TRUE;
                        }
                }
                else delta_index_1++;
        }
}
if((!recurse) && (!maze->fatal_error)) {
        delta_index_1=(int) stack_head->index_1;
        delta_index_2=(int) stack_head->index_2;
```

**2-3** Continued.

```
                        stack_ptr=stack_head;
                        stack_head=stack_head->next_ptr;
                        free((char *)stack_ptr);
                        stack_ptr=NULL;
                        if(stack_head == NULL) finished=TRUE;
                        else {
                                x-= (2*maze->delta_x[24*delta_index_1+delta_index_2]);
                                y-= (2*maze->delta_y[24*delta_index_1+delta_index_2]);
                        }
                }
        }
        if(!maze->fatal_error) {
                Line(hdc,1,0,(maze->twice_magnitude_delta_x)-1,0);
                Line(hdc,maze->x_max-(maze->twice_magnitude_delta_x)+1,maze->y_max,maze
                ->x_max,maze->y_max);
        }
        if(stack_ptr != NULL) free(stack_ptr);
}

void SolveMaze(MAZE *maze,HDC hdc)
{
        int finished;
        unsigned char delta_index_1;
        int recurse;
        STACK1RECPTR stack_head=NULL;
        STACK1RECPTR stack_ptr=NULL;
        int x;
        int x_next;
        int y;
        int y_next;
        int stack_size=0;

        x=maze->magnitude_delta_x;
        y=maze->magnitude_delta_y;
        y_next=y+(maze->magnitude_delta_y);

        SelectObject(hdc,maze->path_pen);
        Line(hdc,x,0,x,y);

        finished=FALSE;
        recurse=TRUE;
        stack_head=NULL;

        while(!finished && !maze->fatal_error) {
                Wait();
                Yield();
                if(recurse) {
                        delta_index_1=0;
                        recurse=FALSE;
                }
                while((delta_index_1 < 4) && !finished && !recurse && !maze->fatal
                _error) {
                        x_next=x+maze->delta_x[24*delta_index_1];
                        y_next=y+maze->delta_y[24*delta_index_1];
```

```
                    if(GetPixel(hdc,x_next,y_next)==maze->passage) {
                            x_next+=maze->delta_x[24*delta_index_1];
                            y_next+=maze->delta_y[24*delta_index_1];
                            if(y_next <= maze->y_max) {

                                    SelectObject(hdc,maze->path_pen);
                                    Line(hdc,x,y,x_next,y_next);

                                    x=x_next;
                                    y=y_next;
                                    if((stack_ptr=(struct STACK1REC *)malloc
                                    (sizeof(struct STACK1REC)))==NULL)
                                        maze->fatal_error=TRUE;
                                    else {
                                            stack_ptr->next_ptr=stack_head;
                                            stack_head=stack_ptr;
                                            stack_head->index_1=delta_index_1;
                                            recurse=TRUE;
                                            ++stack_size;
                                    }
                            } else finished=TRUE;
                    } else delta_index_1++;
            }
            if(delta_index_1 >= 4 && !maze->fatal_error) {
                    x_next=x;
                    y_next=y;
                    delta_index_1=stack_head->index_1;
                    stack_ptr=stack_head;
                    stack_head=stack_head->next_ptr;
                    free((char *)stack_ptr);
                    stack_ptr=NULL;
                    --stack_size;
                    x-=(2*maze->delta_x[24*delta_index_1]);
                    y-=(2*maze->delta_y[24*delta_index_1]);

                    SelectObject(hdc,maze->solve_pen);
                    Line(hdc,x,y,x_next,y_next);

                    delta_index_1++;
            }
    }
    if(!maze->fatal_error) {
            SelectObject(hdc,maze->path_pen);
            Line(hdc,x,y,x,maze->y_max);
    }

    /* free any unused stack elements */
    while(stack_size--) {
            stack_ptr=stack_head;
            stack_head=stack_head->next_ptr;
            free((char *)stack_ptr);
    }
}

/* that's it... */
```

In addition, you'll need MAZE.RC, MAZE.PRJ, and MAZE.DEF, as illustrated in 2-4(a), 2-4(b), and 2-4(c).

**2-4(a)** The MAZE.RC file.

```
Maze MENU
BEGIN
        POPUP "&File"
        BEGIN
                MENUITEM "&About...", 103
                MENUITEM "E&xit", 104
        END

END



Maze ICON
BEGIN
'00 00 01 00 01 00 20 20 10 00 00 00 00 00 E8 02'
'00 00 16 00 00 00 28 00 00 00 20 00 00 00 40 00'
'00 00 01 00 04 00 00 00 00 00 80 02 00 00 00 00'
'00 00 00 00 00 00 00 00 00 00 00 00 00 00 00 00'
'00 00 00 00 80 00 00 80 00 00 00 80 80 00 80 00'
'00 00 80 00 80 00 80 80 00 00 80 80 80 00 C0 C0'
'C0 00 00 00 FF 00 00 FF 00 00 00 FF FF 00 FF 00'
'00 00 FF 00 FF 00 FF FF 00 00 FF FF FF 00 9C CC'
'CC CC CC CC C9 CC CC CC CC C9 CC CC CC CC 9C 99'
'99 99 99 99 C9 C9 99 99 99 C9 C9 99 99 99 9C 99'
'C9 99 99 99 C9 C9 99 99 C9 C9 C9 99 99 99 9C 99'
'CC CC CC CC C9 C9 9C CC C9 C9 CC CC C9 99 9C 99'
'99 99 99 99 C9 C9 9C 99 99 C9 99 99 C9 99 9C CC'
'CC CC CC C9 C9 C9 9C CC CC C9 CC CC C9 99 99 99'
'99 99 99 C9 C9 C9 99 99 99 C9 C9 99 99 99 9C CC'
'CC CC C9 C9 C9 C9 9C CC C9 C9 CC CC C9 99 9C 99'
'99 99 C9 C9 C9 C9 9C 99 C9 C9 99 99 C9 99 9C 99'
'99 99 C9 C9 C9 C9 9C 99 C9 C9 CC CC C9 99 9C 99'
'99 99 C9 C9 C9 C9 9C 99 CC C9 C9 99 99 99 9C 99'
'99 99 C9 C9 C9 C9 9C 99 99 99 CC CC C9 99 9C 99'
'99 99 C9 C9 C9 C9 9C CC CC C9 99 99 C9 99 9C 99'
'CC CC C9 C9 C9 C9 99 99 99 C9 CC CC C9 99 9C 99'
'C9 99 99 C9 C9 C9 99 99 CC C9 C9 99 99 99 9C 99'
'CC CC CC C9 C9 CC CC 99 C9 99 CC CC C9 99 9C 99'
'99 99 99 99 C9 99 9C 99 C9 99 99 99 C9 99 9C 99'
'99 99 99 99 CC CC 9C 99 C9 99 CC CC C9 99 9C CC'
'CC CC C9 99 99 9C 9C 99 CC 99 C9 99 99 99 99 99'
'99 99 CC 99 99 9C 9C 99 9C 99 C9 9C CC CC 9C CC'
'C9 99 9C CC CC 9C 9C C9 9C C9 C9 9C 99 9C 9C 99'
'CC C9 99 99 9C 9C 99 C9 99 C9 C9 9C 99 9C 9C 99'
'99 CC CC C9 9C 9C C9 CC 99 C9 C9 9C 99 9C 9C CC'
'99 99 99 C9 9C 99 C9 9C 99 C9 C9 9C CC 9C 99 9C'
'9C CC C9 C9 9C 99 CC 9C 99 C9 C9 99 9C 9C 99 9C'
'9C 99 C9 C9 9C C9 9C 9C 99 C9 C9 99 9C 9C 99 9C'
'CC 99 C9 C9 99 C9 9C 9C 99 C9 C9 99 9C 9C 99 99'
'99 99 C9 CC 99 C9 9C 9C 99 C9 C9 99 9C 9C CC CC'
'CC CC C9 9C 99 C9 9C 9C 99 C9 CC CC CC 9C 99 99'
'99 99 99 9C 99 C9 9C 9C 99 C9 99 99 99 9C 99 99'
```

```
'99 99 99 9C CC C9 9C CC 99 CC CC CC CC CC 99 99'
'99 99 99 99 99 99 99 99 99 99 99 99 99 99 00 00'
'00 00 00 00 00 00 00 00 00 00 00 00 00 00 00 00'
'00 00 00 00 00 00 00 00 00 00 00 00 00 00 00 00'
'00 00 00 00 00 00 00 00 00 00 00 00 00 00 00 00'
'00 00 00 00 00 00 00 00 00 00 00 00 00 00 00 00'
'00 00 00 00 00 00 00 00 00 00 00 00 00 00 00 00'
'00 00 00 00 00 00 00 00 00 00 00 00 00 00 00 00'
'00 00 00 00 00 00 00 00 00 00 00 00 00 00 00 00'
'00 00 00 00 00 00 00 00 00 00 00 00 00 00'

END

AboutBox DIALOG 86, 56, 200, 116
STYLE WS_POPUP | WS_CAPTION
CAPTION "About..."
BEGIN
        DEFPUSHBUTTON "Ok", IDOK, 88, 96, 24, 12, WS_CHILD | WS_VISIBLE | WS_TABSTOP
        CTEXT "Copyright \251 1993 Alchemy Mindworks Inc.", 102, 8, 40, 184, 8, WS
        _CHILD | WS_VISIBLE | WS_GROUP
        CTEXT "Maze 1.0", 101, 8, 8, 184, 8, WS_CHILD | WS_VISIBLE | WS_GROUP
        ICON "Maze", 101, 92, 20, 16, 16, WS_CHILD | WS_VISIBLE
        CONTROL "The source code for this application... and numerous others... can be
found in the book Canned Code, by Steve Rimmer, published by Windcrest/McGraw Hill
(ISBN 0-8306-4512-8)", 103, "STATIC", SS_CENTER | WS_CHILD | WS_VISIBLE | WS_BORDER |
WS_GROUP, 8, 52, 184, 36
END
```

**2-4(b)** The MAZE.PRJ file.

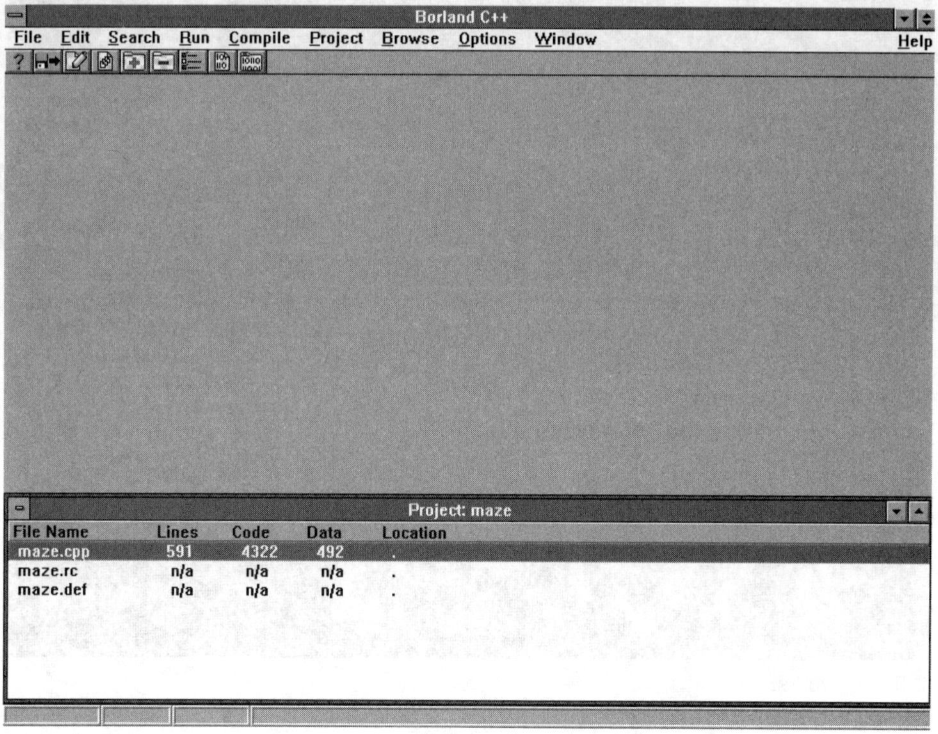

**2-4(c)** The MAZE.DEF file.

```
NAME            MAZE
DESCRIPTION     'Maze'
EXETYPE         WINDOWS
CODE            PRELOAD MOVEABLE
DATA            PRELOAD MOVEABLE MULTIPLE
HEAPSIZE        16384
STACKSIZE       8092
```

There's nothing in the MAZE application that's particularly tricky, except for the actual function to generate and subsequently solve mazes. It serves to illustrate that most volatile of all programming techniques, recursion. I'll look at a few more applications of recursion later in this book. It's a wonderful approach to problem solving when you can find a problem to solve with it.

## Draw some fireworks

The result of a program called FIREWORK is illustrated in 2-5. The complete FIREWORK program generates a constantly shifting display of digital pyrotechnics, accompanied by suitable explosions now and again.

**2-5** Fireworks.

The FIREWORK program is based in part on an old program called Pyro that I found on a bulletin board, written by K. G. Shields.

The complete source code for FIREWORK.C is illustrated in 2-6. As with all the DOS-based programs in this section, it's very important that this one be compiled using the large memory model. Once compiled, it will produce FIREWORK.EXE, which can be run from the DOS prompt to generate images like the one in 2-5. While arguably not of any practical use, it's fun to watch. As it's structured now, FIREWORK runs through its performance of effects and returns to DOS—you can easily modify it to run continuously if you like.

**2-6** The FIREWORK.C source code.

```
/*
        Fireworks, copyright 1993 Alchemy Mindworks Inc.
        Based in part on Pyro, copyright (c) 1987 K.G. Shields
*/

#include <stdlib.h>
#include <dos.h>
#include <math.h>

#define NI              6               /*Number of items*/
#define NP              60              /*Number of points per item*/
#define TP              400             /*Total number of points*/

#define SPURT           1
#define FLARE           2
#define BURST           3
#define ROCKET          4
#define ROMANCANDLE     5

#define SCREENWIDE      640
#define SCREENDEEP      480

#define writeplane(n)           { outp(0x3c4,2); outp(0x3c5,(n)); }
#define setbitmask(n)       { outp(0x3ce,8); outp(0x3cf,(n)); }
#define setwritemode(n)         { outp(0x3ce,5); outp(0x3cf,(n)); }
#define setdatarot(n)           { outp(0x3ce,3); outp(0x3cf,(n)); }

#define clearscreen()           memset(screen,0,(SCREENWIDE>>3)
                                *SCREENDEEP)


int xl[NI],xh[NI],yl[NI],yh[NI],vell[NI],velh[NI],angl[NI];
int angh[NI],alivel[NI],aliveh[NI],coll[NI],colh[NI],sizel[NI];
int sizeh[NI],fadev[NI],item_alive[NI],devicetype[NI],wait[NI];
int master[NI],g[TP],x[TP],y[TP],xvel[TP],yvel[TP],alive[TP];
int col[TP],size[TP],fade[TP],itemno[TP],next[TP],state[TP];
int im,jm,km,xmin,xmax,ymin,ymax,xend,yend,newpt,endpt,ci;
int num_active,num_dormant,freep,mastercol,sh=5,spurt=1;
int flare=2,burst=3,rocket=4,roman=5,sep=180,scan=179;
int gv=2,slowdown=80,statev=0,burstlife=10,noise=0;
int inkey;

float sina[361],cosa[361];
```

**2-6** Continued.

```
char *screen=MK_FP(0xa000,0x0000);

main()
{
        union REGS inr,outr;

        inr.x.ax=0x0012;
        int86(0x10,&inr,&outr);

        inr.x.ax=0x1000;
        inr.x.bx=0;
        int86(0x10,&inr,&outr);

        inr.x.ax=0x2c00;
        int86(0x21,&inr,&outr);

        srand(outr.x.dx);

        setrange(&xmin,&xmax,5<<sh,(SCREENWIDE-6)<<sh);
        setrange(&ymin,&ymax,5<<sh,(SCREENDEEP-6)<<sh);

        for(im=0;im<NI;item_alive[im]=0,im++) {
                for(jm=0;jm<TP;alive[jm]=0,next[jm]=jm+1,jm++); /*List of
                free points*/

                freep=0;
                next[sep-1]=-1;
                for (im=0;im<=90;im++) {
                        sina[180+im]=sin(im/57.29578);
                        sina[180+-im]=-sina[180+im];
                        sina[180+180-im]=sina[180+im];
                        sina[180+im-180]=-sina[180+im];
                        cosa[180+im]=cos(im/57.29578);
                        cosa[180+-im]=cosa[180+im];
                        cosa[180+180-im]=-cosa[180+im];
                        cosa[180+im-180]=-cosa[180+im];
                }

                multiple(flare,3,1,200,20,150);
                multiple(spurt,1,1,450,20,500);
                multiple(burst,5,1,100,10,75);
                multiple(rocket,5,3,100,10,0);
                multiple(burst,5,1,100,10,35);
                multiple(spurt,2,1,450,20,500);
                multiple(flare,4,1,200,20,150);
                multiple(burst,5,1,100,10,25);
                multiple(roman,5,3,100,10,60);
                statev=-1;

                /*Set up for finale*/
                burstlife=20;
                startup(burst,150,200,100,1,3,3,5,-1);
                process(30,-1);
                startup(burst,500,100,100,1,3,3,5,-1);
                process(50,-1);
                startup(burst,250, 50,100,1,3,3,5,-1);
```

```
            process(180,-1);
            statev=0;
            burstlife=10;
            clearscreen();
        }
        terminate();
}

setrange(d1,d2,s1,s2) /*Store limits information*/
        int *d1,*d2,s1,s2;
{
        if (s1<=s2) {
                *d1=s1;
                *d2=s2;
        }
        else {
                *d1=s2;
                *d2=s1;
        }
}

limits(it,lxl,lxh,lyl,lyh,lvell,lvelh,langl,langh,lalivel,laliveh,
    lcoll,lcolh,lsizel,lsizeh,lfade) /*Set limits for point generation for
    item it*/
        int it,lxl,lxh,lyl,lyh,lvell,lvelh,langl,langh;
        int lalivel,laliveh,lcoll,lcolh,lsizel,lsizeh,lfade;
{
        setrange(&xl[it],&xh[it],lxl<<sh,lxh<<sh);
        setrange(&yl[it],&yh[it],lyl<<sh,lyh<<sh);
        setrange(&vell[it],&velh[it],lvell<<sh,lvelh<<sh);
        setrange(&angl[it],&angh[it],langl,langh);
        setrange(&alivel[it],&aliveh[it],lalivel,laliveh);
        setrange(&coll[it],&colh[it],lcoll,lcolh);
        setrange(&sizel[it],&sizeh[it],lsizel,lsizeh);
        fadev[it]=lfade;
}

int rnd(int low,int high) /*Returns a value between low and high (inclusive)*/
{
        return low+(((long)rand()*(high-low+1))>>15);
}

#pragma warn -aus
void show(int x,int y,int col,int size) /*Show (or remove) point x,y if it is visible*/
{
        int i,x1,x2,dummy,address,lbit,rbit;

        if(y >= ymin) {
                if(y <= ymax) {
                        if(x >= xmin) {
                                if(x <= xmax) {
                                        setdatarot(0x18);
                                        for(i=-(size-1); i<=size-1; i++) {
                                                x1=(x>>sh)-(size-1-abs(i));
                                                x2=(x>>sh)+(size-1-abs(i));
                                                while (x1 <= x2) {
                                                        lbit=x1 & 7;
```

**2-6** Continued.

```
                                                            rbit=(x2>=(x1 | 7))
                                                            ? 7 : lbit+x2-x1;
                                                            setbitmask(
                                                            (unsigned char )
                                                            (0xff<<(7-rbit+
                                                            lbit))>>lbit);
                                                            address=((y>>
                                                            sh)+i)*80+(x1>>3);
                                                            dummy=screen
                                                            [address];
                                                            writeplane(col);
                                                            screen[address]
                                                            =0xff;
                                                            x1=x1+rbit-lbit+1;
                                                    }
                                            }
                                            setdatarot(0);
                                            setbitmask(0xff);
                                            writeplane(0x0f);
                                    }
                            }
                    }
            }
}
#pragma warn +aus

void release(pt) /*Release point pt*/
        int pt;
{
        alive[pt]=abs(alive[pt]);
        scan=max(scan,pt);
}

void create(it,pt) /*Create a point for item it*/
        int it,*pt;
{
        int vel,angle;
        if (freep>=0) {
                *pt=freep;
                freep=next[*pt];
        }
        else {
                for (*pt=sep;(*pt<TP) && (alive[*pt]!=0);
                (*pt)++);
                *pt=min(*pt,TP-1);
        }
        itemno[*pt]=it;
        g[*pt]=gv;
        fade[*pt]=fadev[it];
        state[*pt]=statev;
        x[*pt]=rnd(xl[it],xh[it]);
        y[*pt]=rnd(yl[it],yh[it]);
        vel=rnd(vell[it],velh[it]);
        angle=rnd(angl[it],angh[it]);
        xvel[*pt]=vel*sina[180+angle];
        yvel[*pt]=-(vel*cosa[180+angle]);
        col[*pt]=rnd(coll[it],colh[it]);
```

```
        size[*pt]=rnd(sizel[it],sizeh[it]);
        if ((alive[*pt]=rnd(alivel[it],aliveh[it]))>0) release(*pt);
}

void move_points() /*Move all active points through 1 step*/
{
        int i,j;
        num_active=0;
        num_dormant=0;
        for (j=0;j<=scan;j++) {
                if (alive[j]<=0) {
                        if (j<sep) {
                                for (i=1;i<=slowdown;i++);
                        }

                        if (alive[j]<0) num_dormant++;
                }
                else {
                        if (noise>0)
                                if (rand()<noise) outportb(0x61,3);
                        if (state[j]>0) show(x[j],y[j],col[j],size[j]);
                        else if (state[j]==0) state[j]=1;
                        num_active++;
                        alive[j]--;
                        yvel[j]+=g[j];
                        x[j]+=xvel[j];
                        if ((y[j]+=yvel[j])>ymax) {
                                y[j]-=yvel[j];
                                xvel[j]=0;
                        }
                        if (alive[j]==0) {
                                if (g[j]==0) {
                                        g[j]=gv;
                                        alive[j]=10;
                                }
                                else if (size[j]>1) {
                                        size[j]--;
                                        alive[j]=fade[j];
                                }
                                else {
                                        col[j]=0;
                                        if (j<sep) {
                                                next[j]=freep;
                                                freep=j;
                                        }
                                }
                        }
                        show(x[j],y[j],col[j],size[j]);
                        outportb(0x61,0);
                }
        }
        while ((scan>=sep) && (alive[scan]<=0)) scan--;
        if ((noise=abs(noise))>0) noise-=300;
}
process(t,waiting)
        int t,waiting;
{
        int it,i,timer;
```

**2-6** Continued.

```
        for (timer=1;timer<=t;timer++) {
                for (it=0;it<NI;it++) {
                        if (item_alive[it] > 0)
                            item_alive[it]--;
                        else
                            devicetype[it]=0;
                        switch(devicetype[it]) {
                                case SPURT:
                                        if (wait[it]>130) create(it,
                                        &newpt);
                                        else if (wait[it]==0) {
                                                setrange(&coll[it]
                                                ,&colh[it],
                                                    rnd(9,15),rnd(9,15));
                                                wait[it]=NP+130;
                                        }
                                        break;
                                case FLARE:
                                        create(it,&newpt);
                                        if (wait[it]==0) {
                                                if (++coll[it]>=14)
                                                   coll[it]=9;
                                                colh[it]=coll[it]+1;
                                                wait[it]=50;
                                        }
                                        break;
                                case BURST:
                                        if (wait[it]>0)
                                            create(it,&master[it]);
                                        else if (wait[it]==0) {
                                                for (i=0;i<TP;i++) {
                                                    if ((alive[i]<0) &&
                                                    (itemno[i]==it))
                                                    release(i);
                                                }
                                                noise=-3000;
                                        }
                                        break;
                                case ROCKET:
                                        if (wait[it]==0) {
                                                release(master[it]);
                                                item_alive[it]=alive
                                                [master[it]]+fade[master
                                                [it]]*
                                                    (size[master[it]]-1);
                                        }
                                        if (alive[master[it]] > 0) {
                                                create(it,&newpt);
                                                x[newpt]=x[master[it]]+
                                                rnd(-64,64);
                                                y[newpt]=y[master[it]]+
                                                rnd(-64,64);
                                                release(newpt);
                                        }
                                        break;
                                case ROMANCANDLE:
```

```
                                    if ((wait[it]<=9) && (wait[it]>0)) {
                                            create(it,&newpt);
                                            x[newpt]=x[master[it]]+
                                                (3<<sh)*sina[180+(360
                                                *(wait[it]-5)/9)];
                                            y[newpt]=y[master[it]]-
                                                (3<<sh)*cosa[180+(360
                                                *(wait[it]-5)/9)];
                                            xvel[newpt]=xvel[master
                                            [it]];
                                            yvel[newpt]=yvel[master
                                            [it]];
                                            alive[newpt]=alive[master
                                            [it]];
                                            col[newpt]=col[master[it]];
                                    }
                                    else if (wait[it]==0) {
                                            limits(it,0,0,0,0,0,0,0,0,-
                                            10,-5,col[master[it]],
                                               col[master[it]],1,1,0);
                                            for (i=0;i<TP;i++) {
                                                    if ((alive[i]<0) &&
                                                    (itemno[i]==it))
                                                        release(i);
                                            }
                                            item_alive[it]=alive[master
                                            [it]]+fade[master[it]]*
                                                (size[master[it]]-1);
                                    }
                                    if (alive[master[it]]>0) {
                                            create(it,&newpt);
                                            x[newpt]=x[master[it]]+rnd
                                            (-256,256);
                                            y[newpt]=y[master[it]]+rnd
                                            (-64,64);
                                            release(newpt);
                                    }
                                    break;
                            }
                            if ((wait[it]>-1) && (it!=waiting)) wait[it]--;
                    }
                    if (kbhit()) terminate();
                    move_points();
            }
}

terminate() /*Terminate display*/
{
        union REGS r;
        int j;

        if(kbhit()) {
                if(getch()==27) {
                        r.x.ax=0x0003;
                        int86(0x10,&r,&r);
                        exit(0);
                }
        }
```

**2-6** Continued.

```
        for (j=1;(j<=800) && (num_active+num_dormant>0);j++) process(1,-1);

        gv=0;
        statev=0;

        clearscreen();
}

calc_end() /*Calculate endpoint for burst*/
{
        endpt=NP-wait[ci]+1;
        if((mastercol=col[master[ci]])==15) mastercol=14;
        alive[master[ci]]=-(endpt-(size[master[ci]]-1)*fade[master[ci]]);
        xend=x[master[ci]]+endpt*xvel[master[ci]];
        yend=y[master[ci]]+endpt*yvel[master[ci]]+(gv*endpt*endpt)/2;
}

startup(devtype,xi,yi,life,p1,p2,p3,p4,waiting)
        int devtype,xi,yi,life,p1,p2,p3,p4,waiting;
{
        ci=0;
        while (item_alive[ci]>0) {
                process(1,waiting);
                if (++ci>=NI) ci=0;
        }
        devicetype[ci]=devtype;
        item_alive[ci]=life;
        switch(devicetype[ci]) {
                case SPURT:
                        coll[ci]=rnd(9,15);
                        limits(ci,xi-5,xi+5,SCREENDEEP-10,SCREENDEEP-10, 3,8,
                            -20,20,120,160,coll[ci],rnd(coll[ci],15),2,2, 25);
                        wait[ci]=NP+130;
                        break;
                case FLARE:
                        coll[ci]=rnd(9,14);
                        limits(ci,xi-5,xi+5,SCREENDEEP-10,SCREENDEEP-10,4, 8,
                            -20,20,20,30,coll[ci],coll[ci]+1,2,2,2);
                        wait[ci]=50;
                        break;
                case BURST:
                        if (waiting<0)
                            coll[ci]=rnd(9,14);
                        else
                            coll[ci]=mastercol;
                        limits(ci,xi-5,xi+5,yi-5,yi+5,rnd(p1,p2),
                            rnd(p3,p4),-180,180,-2*burstlife,-burstlife,
                            coll[ci],coll[ci]+1,2,2,
                            rnd(burstlife,3*burstlife));
                        wait[ci]=NP;
                        break;
                case ROCKET:
                        limits(ci,xi,xi,SCREENDEEP-10,SCREENDEEP-10,
                            5,10,p1,p2,-90,-80,9,15,3,4,3);
                        wait[ci]=20;
```

```
                    create(ci,&master[ci]);
                    limits(ci,xi,xi,SCREENDEEP-10,SCREENDEEP-10,
                        -2,2,90,90,-6,-7,
                        col[master[ci]],col[master[ci]],2,2,20);
                    vell[ci]=vell[ci]>>1;
                    velh[ci]=velh[ci]>>1;
                    calc_end();
                    break;
                case ROMANCANDLE:
                    limits(ci,xi,xi,SCREENDEEP-10,SCREENDEEP-10,
                        6,11,-10,10,-70,-100,9,15,3,3,1);
                    wait[ci]=30;
                    create(ci,&master[ci]);
                    calc_end();
                    break;
        }
}

multiple(int typ,int n,int rep,int life,int gap,int pause)
{
        int i,j;
        for (j=1;j<=rep;j++) for (i=1;i<=n;i++) {
                switch(typ) {
                    case ROCKET:
                        startup(rocket,320+100*rnd(-1,1),
                            SCREENDEEP-10,100,-45,45,0,0,-1);
                        if (rand()<25000)
                            startup(burst,xend>>sh,yend>>sh,100,1,
                            3,5,12,ci);
                        break;
                    case ROMANCANDLE:
                        startup(roman,i*(640/(n+1)),
                            SCREENDEEP-10,100,0,0,0,0,-1);
                        startup(burst,xend>>sh,yend>>sh,100,8,8,10,
                        12,ci);
                        break;
                    default:
                        if (typ==burst)
                            startup(burst,rnd(150,540),rnd(50,200),
                                life,1,3,5,12,-1);
                        else
                           startup(typ,i*(640/(n+1)),SCREENDEEP-10,
                                life,0,0,0,0,-1);
                }
                process(gap,-1);
        }
        process(pause,-1);
}
```

There are two principal issues of interest in FIREWORK. The first, actually animating the ballistics of the fireworks themselves, is illustrated fairly readily by the FIREWORK.C source code, should you care to dig through it. Somewhat less obvious is how the actual graphics work, as FIREWORK makes no calls to a graphics library. In fact, graphics at this level can be handled fairly simply by the application of some arcane magic and cheating.

The FIREWORK program runs on a VGA card in screen mode 12H. This is a graphics mode that supports 16 colors at 640-×-480 pixels. In this application, I'll use the default VGA 16-color palette.

Sixteen-color graphics are extremely peculiar, as the display memory is set up in planes rather than in pixels. The actual mechanism for addressing screen memory of this sort is somewhat beyond the scope of this book, and for practical purposes, you need not deal with it just to set a few pixels.

To set a screen pixel in mode 12H you must begin by setting up for write mode 2. This tells the display card that you want to set pixels rather than whole image planes—the latter was what happened when I wrote PCX images to the screen earlier in this chapter. In this case, I'd like to XOR the pixels with the current screen contents, such that XORing them a second time will return the screen to its former state. This is the code to set up the proper mode:

```
outp(0x3ce,3);
outp(0x3cf,0x18);
```

These calls toggle some of the latches in a VGA card's video controller.

On a VGA card, the screen in mode 12H lives at segment A000H. As such, if `screen` is a far pointer, `screen=MK_FP(0xa000,0x0000)` will assign it to point to the first byte of the video display. Each line of the display is 640 pixels across, or 80 bytes. The byte that contains the pixel at `(x,y)` would be at `screen[(y*80)+(x>>3)]`.

To write a pixel to the screen, you would calculate which bit of the aforementioned bytes the pixel would reside in, and create a mask that had a bit set for the position of the pixel in question. This can be calculated as `0x80 >> (x & 7)`. You must then tell the VGA card that you're interested in setting this particular bit:

```
outp(0x3ce,8);
outp(0x3cf,mask);
```

Finally, you must write the palette color number you want the pixel to show up as to the byte of screen memory where the pixel resides. Actually this is almost true. For reasons too unfathomable to discuss here, this only works if you've read a byte from this location first, a procedure called a *dummy read*.

Having completed a pixel write, you should always set the bit mask to FFH so that any subsequent writes will appear as they should. You should also switch off the XOR mode:

```
outp(0x3ce,3);
outp(0x3cf,0);
```

The mechanics of writing to a 16-color graphics screen are a bit ineffable. My book *Super VGA Graphics*, published by Windcrest, gets into it in considerably greater detail. However, if all you're interested in is seeing a few fireworks, this program is probably sufficiently deep.

## Use bitmaps in Windows dialogs

The About dialog for Graphic Workshop for Windows is illustrated in 2-7. The salient thing about this dialog is that it contains not only text, but a unicorn. Good unicorns are hard to find.

As with much of Windows programming, displaying a bitmap in a dialog isn't particularly difficult, but it's not really documented anywhere. It would be exceedingly handy if it could all be done with resource script manipulation—sadly, the largest bitmap you can install using nothing more than a dialog editor is 32 pixels on a side, in the form of an icon.

The basic structure of the dialog in 2-7 is somewhat fragmented. The unicorn itself is stored as a resource and the code to make it appear is in the WM_PAINT case of the message handler for the dialog. The resource script statement is fairly undemanding:

```
Unicorn BITMAP unicorn.bmp
```

This line causes the file UNICORN.BMP to be added to the RES file for the Graphic Workshop for Windows application. It will have the resource type BITMAP and the name "Unicorn." You can add a line like this to the RC resource script for your application.

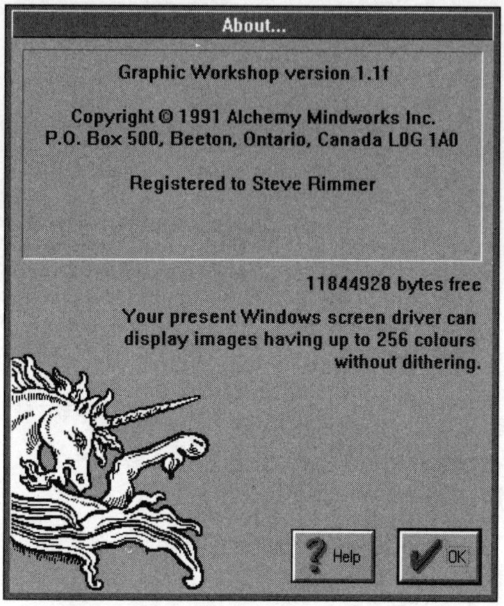


**2-7** The About dialog of Graphic Workshop for Windows, complete with a unicorn.

The message handler for this dialog is also pretty unremarkable, except for the bit that handles the unicorn, which is illustrated in 2-8.

**2-8** The About box message handler.

```
DWORD FAR PASCAL AboutDlgProc(HWND hwnd,WORD message,WORD wParam,LONG lParam)
{
        HDC hMemoryDC;
        HBITMAP hBitmap,hOldBitmap;
        HDC hdc;
        PAINTSTRUCT ps;
        RECT rect;
        BITMAP bitmap;
        POINT point;

        switch(message) {
                case WM_INITDIALOG:
                        return(TRUE);
                case WM_CTLCOLOR:
                        if(HIWORD(lParam)==CTLCOLOR_STATIC ||
                           HIWORD(lParam)==CTLCOLOR_DLG ||
                           HIWORD(lParam)==CTLCOLOR_BTN) {
                                SetBkColor(wParam,RGB(192,192,192));
                                SetTextColor(wParam,RGB(0,0,0));

                                ClientToScreen(hwnd,&point);
                                UnrealizeObject(GetStockObject(LTGRAY_BRUSH));
                                SetBrushOrg(wParam,point.x,point.y);
                                return((DWORD)GetStockObject(LTGRAY_BRUSH));
                        }
                        break;
                case WM_COMMAND:
                        switch(wParam) {
                                case IDOK:
                                        EndDialog(hwnd,wParam);
                                        return(TRUE);
                        }
                        break;
                case WM_PAINT:
                        hdc=BeginPaint(hwnd,&ps);
                        GetClientRect(hwnd,&rect);
                        if((hBitmap=LoadBitmap(hInst,"Unicorn")) != NULL) {
                                if((hMemoryDC=CreateCompatibleDC(hdc)) != NULL) {
                                        hOldBitmap=SelectObject(hMemoryDC,hBitmap);
                                        if(hOldBitmap) {
                                       GetObject(hBitmap,sizeof(BITMAP),(LPSTR)
                                       &bitmap);
                                                BitBlt(hdc,
                                                        0,
                                                        rect.bottom-bitmap.bmHeight,
                                                        bitmap.bmWidth,
                                                        bitmap.bmHeight,
                                                     hMemoryDC,
                                                        0,
                                                        0,
                                                        SRCCOPY);
                                                SelectObject(hMemoryDC,hOldBitmap);
```

```
                                    }
                                    DeleteDC(hMemoryDC);
                            }
                            DeleteObject(hBitmap);
                    }

                    EndPaint(hwnd,&ps);
                    return(0);
            }

        return(FALSE);
}
```

Two cases in 2-8 are important to the final appearance of the dialog in 2-7. The first is WM_CTLCOLOR. A WM_CTLCOLOR message is sent to the message handler for any dialog each time something is to be initially drawn in the dialog window. If the message handler returns a brush handle as a result of processing the message, the thing being drawn will use that brush as its background. This allows a message handler to control the colors of things in the dialog it supports. In this case, it causes the background of the dialog to be light gray rather than white.

This is not essential in using a bitmapped element in a dialog, of course. You can have the background any color you like, including white.

The WM_PAINT case handles fetching and displaying the bitmap. It first must locate and load the BITMAP resource called "Unicorn." The call to `LoadBitmap` will return a handle to the loaded bitmap, assuming that all went well. The `hInst` argument is the instance handle passed to your `WinMain` function when your application first started up. It's important to keep in mind that resource handles behave similarly to memory handles, but they aren't interchangeable.

The `CreateCompatibleDC` call returns a device context handle to the device surface of your display suitable for selecting a bitmap into.

While `hBitmap` is a handle to the unicorn bitmap, the program doesn't actually know the dimensions of the image, which is important if you want to display it and in this case, if you want to position it as well. A bitmap like this one will always be preceded by a BITMAP object, a header that defines the bitmap's dimensions and color depth. The call to `GetObject` copies the first bit of the contents of the buffer referenced by `hBitmap` into the object `bitmap`, which can thereafter be used to work out the image dimensions.

The `BitBlt` function moves bitmaps between device contexts. Finally, the `SelectObject` call selects the bitmap into the display device context, actually making it visible.

You can use any bitmap you like in a dialog like this, although you should keep a few practical considerations in mind. Sixteen-color images can be displayed correctly on devices having 16 or more colors, which defines almost all systems running Windows. Bitmaps with more colors, such as photorealistic 256-color bitmaps, won't look very good on 16-color systems. In addition, they'll require a significant time to load on slower systems and will add quite a bit of space to the EXE file for your application.

## Plot recursive graphics

*Recursion*, the technique of having a function call itself multiple times, has a number of exotic applications in writing sneaky programs. None is more illustrative of the art than the creation of recursive graphics. It might well be argued that such pictures aren't useful for much—and so they aren't—but they're interesting to watch and a good exploration of recursive programming. Mostly they're just interesting to watch. Three recursive graphics are illustrated in 2-9.

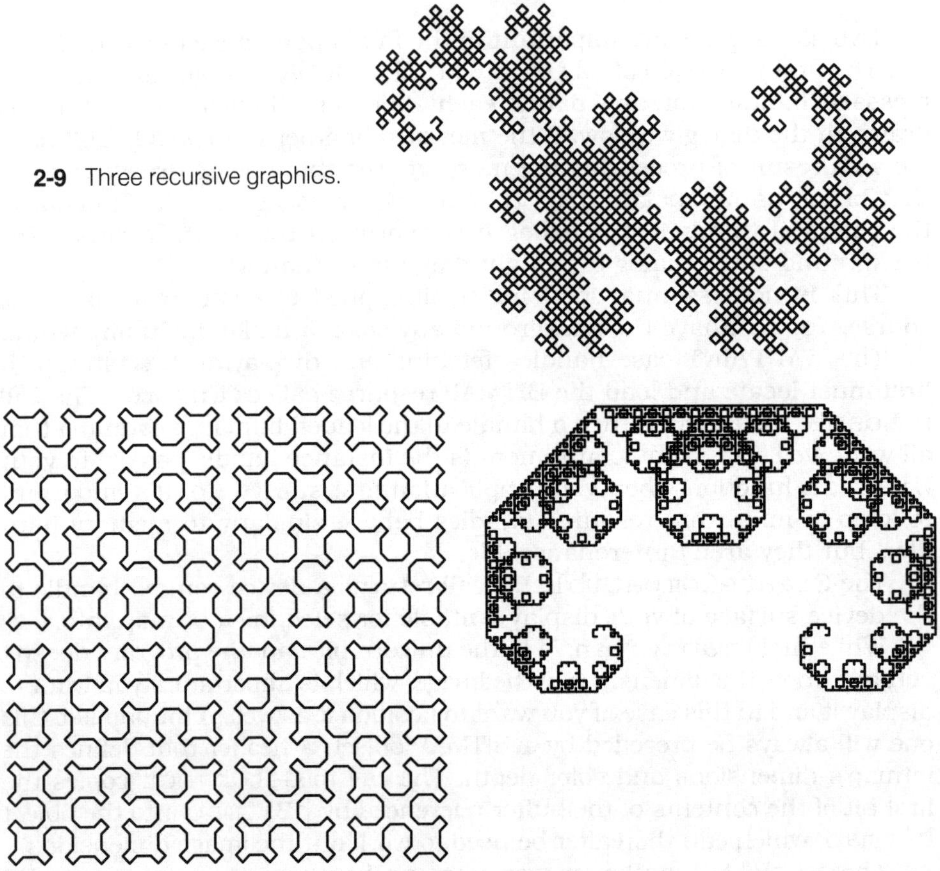

**2-9** Three recursive graphics.

The graphics in 2-9 were created by designing a function that will draw part of a shape and then call itself to draw the same shape again, and so on, until an arbitrary limit of complexity is reached. The C curve and dragon curves are handled using almost the same function, with periodic changes of direction in the latter case. Seirpinski's curve is somewhat different. It's an interesting artifact in that the closer it gets to being infinitely complex, the closer it gets to enclosing a space equal to half the area of the rectangle that encompasses it.

Despite the complexity of the recursive graphics in 2-9, the program to generate them is pretty short. In fact, it could be shorter still, except that it has a secondary function. It's called CURVES.C and can be found in 2-10.

**2-10** The CURVES.C source code.

```
#include "stdio.h"
#include "math.h"
#include "graphics.h"

#define HPLOUTPUT               0

#define DRAGONCURVE             1
#define SIERPINSKICURVE         1
#define CCURVE                  1

#define HPLEXP                  10
#define HPLOFFX                 2500
#define HPLOFFY                 1500

#define ANGLE   45

#define SQUARE(n)       (n*n)
#define PAUSE()                 {int n; for(n=0;n<5000 && !kbhit();++n) delay(1); }

#if !HPLOUTPUT
#define DRAWLINE(x1,y1,x2,y2)     line((int)x1,(int)y1,(int)x2,(int)y2);
#else
#define DRAWLINE(x1,y1,x2,y2)     plotline((double)x1,(double)y1,(double)x2,(double)y2);
#endif

CCurve(double x1,double y1,double x2,double y2);
DragonCurve(double x1,double y1,double x2,double y2,double th);
SierpinskiCurve(int n);

double prm[5];
double tmp_angle,sin_angle,cos_angle,posit;
double ox,oy;

#if HPLOUTPUT
FILE *fp=NULL;
int graphicindex=0;
#endif

main()
{
        init();

        do {
                #if DRAGONCURVE
                for(prm[4]=8;prm[4]>=3 && !kbhit();prm[4]-=1) {
                        NewScreen();
                        prm[0]=200;
                        prm[1]=240;
                        prm[2]=450;
                        prm[3]=240;
                        cos_angle=cos(ANGLE*M_PI/180);
```

**2-10** Continued.

```
                tmp_angle=sin(ANGLE*M_PI/180);

                DragonCurve(prm[0],prm[1],prm[2],prm[3],-1 * ANGLE);
                PAUSE()
        }
        if(kbhit()) break;
        #endif

        #if SIERPINSKICURVE
        prm[0]=32;
        prm[1]=32;

        for(prm[2]=1;prm[2] < 7 && !kbhit();prm[2]+=1) {
                NewScreen();
                posit=ceil(128/(pow(2,prm[2]-1)*4+2));
                SierpinskiCurve(prm[2]);
                PAUSE();
        }
        #endif

        #if CCURVE
        for(prm[4]=5;prm[4] >=2 && ! kbhit();prm[4]-=1) {
                NewScreen();
                prm[0]=225;
                prm[1]=112;
                prm[2]=412;
                prm[3]=112;

                cos_angle=cos(ANGLE*M_PI/180);
                sin_angle=sin(ANGLE*M_PI/180);

                CCurve(prm[0],prm[1],prm[2],prm[3]);
        }
        #endif

        #if HPLOUTPUT
        break;
        #endif
    } while(!kbhit());

    getch();

    deinit();
}

CCurve(x1,y1,x2,y2)
    double x1,y1,x2,y2;
{
    double xd,yd;
    double mx,my;
    double xdr,ydr;

    xd=x2-x1;
    yd=y2-y1;

    if((SQUARE(xd)+SQUARE(yd)) <= SQUARE(prm[4]) || kbhit()) {
```

```
                DRAWLINE(x1,y1,x2,y2);
        }
        else {
                xdr=xd/2/cos_angle;
                ydr=yd/2/cos_angle;
                mx=x1+xdr*cos_angle-ydr*sin_angle;
                my=y1+xdr*sin_angle+ydr*cos_angle;
                CCurve(x1,y1,mx,my);
                CCurve(mx,my,x2,y2);
        }
}

SierpinskiCurve(n)
        int n;
{
        left(n);
        DRAWLINE(prm[0],prm[1],prm[0]+posit,prm[1]+posit);
        prm[0]+=posit;
        prm[1]+=posit;

        top(n);
        DRAWLINE(prm[0],prm[1],prm[0]+posit,prm[1]-posit);
        prm[0]+=posit;
        prm[1]-=posit;

        right(n);
        DRAWLINE(prm[0],prm[1],prm[0]-posit,prm[1]-posit);
        prm[0]-=posit;
        prm[1]-=posit;

        bottom(n);
        DRAWLINE(prm[0],prm[1],prm[0]-posit,prm[1]+posit);
        prm[0]-=posit;
        prm[1]+=posit;
}

left(n)
        int n;
{
        if(n && !kbhit()) {
                --n;
                left(n);
                DRAWLINE(prm[0],prm[1],prm[0]+posit,prm[1]+posit);
                prm[0]+=posit;
                prm[1]+=posit;

                top(n);
                DRAWLINE(prm[0],prm[1],prm[0],prm[1]+posit*2);
                prm[1]+=floor(posit*2);

                bottom(n);
                DRAWLINE(prm[0],prm[1],prm[0]-posit,prm[1]+posit);
                prm[0]-=posit;
                prm[1]+=posit;

                left(n);
        }
```

**2-10** Continued.

```
}

top(n)
        int n;
{
        if(n && !kbhit()) {
                --n;
                top(n);
                DRAWLINE(prm[0],prm[1],prm[0]+posit,prm[1]-posit);
                prm[0]+=posit;
                prm[1]-=posit;

                right(n);
                DRAWLINE(prm[0],prm[1],prm[0]+posit*2,prm[1]);
                prm[0]+=floor(posit*2);

                left(n);
                DRAWLINE(prm[0],prm[1],prm[0]+posit,prm[1]+posit);
                prm[0]+=posit;
                prm[1]+=posit;

                top(n);
        }
}

right(n)
        int n;
{
        if(n && !kbhit()) {
                --n;
                right(n);
                DRAWLINE(prm[0],prm[1],prm[0]-posit,prm[1]-posit);
                prm[0]-=posit;
                prm[1]-=posit;

                bottom(n);
                DRAWLINE(prm[0],prm[1],prm[0],prm[1]-posit*2);
                prm[1]-=floor(posit*2);

                top(n);
                DRAWLINE(prm[0],prm[1],prm[0]+posit,prm[1]-posit);
                prm[0]+=posit;
                prm[1]-=posit;

                right(n);
        }
}

bottom(n)
        int n;
{
        if(n && !kbhit()) {
                --n;
                bottom(n);
                DRAWLINE(prm[0],prm[1],prm[0]-posit,prm[1]+posit);
                prm[0]-=posit;
```

```
                prm[1]+=posit;

                left(n);
                DRAWLINE(prm[0],prm[1],prm[0]-posit*2,prm[1]);
                prm[0]-=floor(posit*2);

                right(n);
                DRAWLINE(prm[0],prm[1],prm[0]-posit,prm[1]-posit);
                prm[0]-=posit;
                prm[1]-=posit;

                bottom(n);
        }
}

DragonCurve(x1,y1,x2,y2,th)
        double x1,y1,x2,y2,th;
{
        double xd,yd;
        double mx,my;
        double xdr,ydr;

        if(th > 0) sin_angle=tmp_angle;
        else sin_angle=-tmp_angle;

        xd=x2-x1;
        yd=y2-y1;

        if((SQUARE(xd)+SQUARE(yd)) <= SQUARE(prm[4]) || kbhit()) {
                DRAWLINE(x1,y1,x2,y2);
        }
        else {
                xdr=xd/2/cos_angle;
                ydr=yd/2/cos_angle;
                mx=x1+xdr*cos_angle-ydr*sin_angle;
                my=y1+xdr*sin_angle+ydr*cos_angle;
                DragonCurve(x1,y1,mx,my,ANGLE);
                DragonCurve(mx,my,x2,y2,-1*ANGLE);
        }
}

deinit()
{
        #if HPLOUTPUT
        if(fp != NULL) {
                fprintf(fp,"PU; SP0;");
                fclose(fp);
        }
        #else
        closegraph();
        #endif
}

init()
{
        #if !HPLOUTPUT
        int d,m;
```

**2-10** Continued.

```
        detectgraph(&d,&m);

        if(d<0) {
                puts("Error initializing graphics");
                exit(1);
        }
        initgraph(&d,&m,"");
        if(graphresult() < 0) {
                puts("Error initializing graphics");
                exit(1);
        }
        setcolor(getmaxcolor());
        #endif
}

NewScreen()
{
        #if HPLOUTPUT
        char b[24];
        if(fp != NULL) {
                fprintf(fp,"PU; SP0;");
                fclose(fp);
        }
        fp=NULL;
        sprintf(b,"CURVE%02.2u.PLT",++graphicindex);
        if((fp=fopen(b,"wa"))==NULL) {
                printf("Error creating %s\n",b);
                exit(1);
        }
        printf("Writing %s\n",b);
        ox=oy=0;
        #else
        cleardevice();
        #endif
}

#if HPLOUTPUT
plotline(x1,y1,x2,y2)
        double x1,y1,x2,y2;
{
        if(x1 != ox || y1 != oy)
            fprintf(fp,"PU, PA, %g, %g; PD, PA, %g, %g;\n",
                (double)HPLOFFX+x1*HPLEXP,
                (double)HPLOFFY+y1*HPLEXP,
                (double)HPLOFFX+x2*HPLEXP,
                (double)HPLOFFY+y2*HPLEXP);
        else
            fprintf(fp,"PA, %g, %g; PD, PA, %g, %g;\n",
                (double)HPLOFFX+x1*HPLEXP,
                (double)HPLOFFY+y1*HPLEXP,
                (double)HPLOFFX+x2*HPLEXP,
                (double)HPLOFFY+y2*HPLEXP);
}
#endif
```

Note that CURVES uses the Borland BGI graphics and it expects to be able to find a suitable BGI driver in the directory where it runs. It has been designed under the assumption that it will have a VGA card to draw on—it might require some fine-tuning if you intend to use it on a display device with different screen dimensions.

Each of the recursive curve graphics is drawn by CURVES in successively greater complexity. Perhaps not surprisingly, the curves take exponentially more time to create as they become more involved. Hitting any key on your keyboard will immediately halt the meanderings of CURVES and return you to the DOS prompt.

Note that the algorithm that generates the lines that form the curves is capable of much greater precision than your screen is capable of supporting. In the more detailed curves, rounding errors cause checkerboard patterns to appear in the curves.

If you look carefully at 2-9, you'll observe that it hasn't been created as a screen capture, but rather appears to be a line drawing. In fact, that's what it is. The secondary function of CURVES is that it will plot its curves to a PLT file rather than your screen. A PLT file is a list of HPGL plotter commands, as used to drive a Hewlett-Packard plotter. However, quite a few PC applications will import PLT files and use them as vector graphics. The art in 2-9 was created by importing PLT files generated by CURVES into Corel Draw.

If you set the HPLOUTPUT define at the top of the CURVES.C listing true, the program will compile to generate PLT files rather than screen output. When you run it, it will create files called CURVE00.PLT, CURVE01.PLT, and so on. Each file will contain one iteration of one of the three curve generation functions. Allowing CURVES to complete its cycle in this manifestation will generate several megabytes of PLT files—be warned.

A complete discussion of how to write PLT files is well beyond the scope of this book. However, you can see how to draw lines in the HPGL language if you look at the `plotline` function at the bottom of the CURVES.C listing.

If you attempt to import some of the more complex curves generated by this program into an application that reads HPGL.PLT files, plan on long waits and the use of a lot of free memory. While the fairly coarse resolution of a monitor doesn't really do justice to the complexity of some of these objects, they can entail a huge number of lines when you create them as vector graphics.

# 3
# Meddling with data

*"Stealing a rhinoceros should not be attempted lightly."*
—Graffiti

In the beginning, before VGA cards, microfloppies, 16-bit processors, and bidirectional parallel ports, data was all computers thought about. Actually, they also thought about moths. Original computers didn't use transistors, they used mechanical relays. Every so often, a moth would get stuck in one, and the program in question wouldn't run until somebody went into the computer with a screwdriver and scraped the moth out. This is the origin of the expression "programming bug." No foolin'.

Being able to manipulate data remains a very important element in creating software that actually does something rather than that which just looks good doing it. This chapter looks at a number of fairly elemental things you might want to incorporate in your applications.

## Verify credit card numbers

The somewhat meaningless-looking clumps of digits on credit cards aren't actually meaningless at all. Credit card numbers are very clever in that they contain checksums. If you're presented with a credit card for payment, you can ascertain whether it's valid without even having to call a bank. While this won't tell you whether the card has been stolen or overdrawn, it's a handy check to make sure that the number has been transcribed correctly and that it isn't just any 16 digits picked at random.

To begin with, the first digit of a credit card number will tell you what kind of card the number applies to:

- 3—American Express
- 4—Visa
- 5—MasterCard

The source code for PLASTIC.C is illustrated in 3-1. This is a program that, when given a credit card number, will check authenticity and tell you what it finds.

**3-1** The PLASTIC.C source code.

```
/*
        Credit card verification program
        Copyright (c) 1992 Alchemy Mindworks Inc.
*/

#include "stdio.h"
#include "ctype.h"

#define MASTERCARD          '5'
#define VISA                '4'
#define AMEX                '3'

main(argc,argv)
        int argc;
        char *argv[];
{
        char b[128];
        int i;

        printf("Alchemy Mindworks Inc. credit card verification program version 1.0\n");

        if(argc > 1) {
                for(i=1;i<argc;++i) {
                        cleanString(b,argv[i]);
                        printf("Card %-30.30s - ",argv[i]);
                        verify(b);
                        printf("\r\n");

                }
        } else printf("\r\nI need one or more credit card numbers to verify");
}

verify(s)
        char *s;
{
        int i,len,x=0,y=0,v=0;

        if(strlen(s) < 12) v=0;
        else {
```

```
                len = strlen(s);
                if(odd(len)) {
                        for(i=(len-2);i>=0;--i) {
                                if(odd(i)) y=((s[i]-'0')*2);
                                else y=(s[i]-'0');
                                if(y>=10) y=((y-10)+1);
                                x+=y;
                        }
                }
                else {
                        for(i=(len-2);i>=0;--i) {
                                if(odd(i)) y=(s[i]-'0');
                                else y=((s[i]-'0')*2);
                                if(y >= 10) y=((y-10)+1);
                                x+=y;
                        }
                }
                x=(10-(x % 10));
                if(x==10) x=0;
                if(x==(s[strlen(s)-1]-'0')) v=s[0];
                else v=0;
        }
        switch(v) {
                case VISA:
                        printf("verifies as a Visa card.");
                        break;
                case MASTERCARD:
                        printf("verifies as a MasterCard.");
                        break;
                case AMEX:
                        printf("verifies as an American Express card.");
                        break;
                default:
                        printf("is not a good credit card number.");
                        break;
        }
}

odd(n)          /* return true if n is an odd number */
        int n;
{
        if(n & 0x0001) return(1);
        else return(0);
}

cleanString(dest,source)
        char *dest,*source;
{
        while(*source) {
                if(isdigit(*source)) *dest++=*source;
                ++source;
        }
        *dest=0;
}
```

The smart bits of PLASTIC are in the `verify` function, which illustrates how to perform the checksum for a credit card. You'd invoke the program like this:

```
PLASTIC 5037-021-021-487
```

and the program would return with

```
Card 5037-021-021-487—verifies as a MasterCard
```

Incidentally, this number will verify as being a MasterCard, but it isn't. It's the number for a bank cash machine card, in this case, for a bank that no longer exists. It turns out that bank machines use the same system of checksums as credit cards do.

## Manage a fixed record database

Databases are a subject of considerable depth, and database managers such as dBASE and FoxPro are something that few software authors ever get involved with willingly. The distinction between interesting graphics, for example, and an interesting database is similar to the distinction between a Rolls Royce Silver Shadow and a beige '73 Ford. Both are arguably fine cars in their own right, but if you found the former vehicle in your driveway with a red ribbon around it, you'd probably have a pretty good day. The same might not be true of the latter. I'll return to both dBASE files and Rolls Royce Silver Shadows later in this chapter.

Simple databases are neither particularly complex nor all that hard to write applications for. A simple database is one in which the structure of each record in the database is hard-wired into the code that works with the data. Simple databases allow for very fast data access, albeit with a considerable flexibility penalty. This is arguably not the way to manage large databases for business applications, but it's the intelligent approach to dealing with private databases, ones in which you know the structure of the data won't change.

You might find that you have a need for a fixed record database in an application if you want to store records in which the structure of the records is fixed, and when getting at your data quickly is important. As an example, let's look at the code to manage a database of cars. You can adapt this code to manage a database of anything you like. A car will be defined as the following information:

- Manufacturer—24 characters
- Model—24 characters
- Year—unsigned integer
- Engine displacement—double
- Number made—long

You can define this information as a data structure. The text fields are one byte longer than they're defined above to allow for the null byte at the end of a C language string.

```
typedef struct {
        char manufacturer[25];
        char model[25];
        unsigned int year;
        double displacement;
        long quantity;
        } RECORD;
```

Each record in the file of cars, then, will be `sizeof(RECORD)` long.

It's also useful to have a header at the beginning of a database. This can be used to assure software that is to access the database that the database file is what it purports to be, as well as to keep count of the number of records in the file. I'll define the header like this:

```
typedef struct {
        char sig[8];
        unsigned long count;
        } HEADER;
```

The `sig` element can contain any eight-character string you like to serve as a key that identifies the database. Let's define it like this:

```
#define DATABASE_SIG  "DATABASE"
```

Having defined the objects that comprise a database—and allowing that a database of this sort does actually exist—you could locate record *n* in the database as

```
(long)sizeof(HEADER)+(long)n*(long)sizeof(RECORD);
```

Note that everything has been cast to a long integer in this calculation. This is very important, as it doesn't take much data to make a database file exceed 65,535 bytes, and hence, the range of short integers.

There are two elemental problems in working with any database: getting data into a database file and accessing the records in the database. The first problem will probably be defined somewhat by the nature of the data.

In this example, I'll start with some example data in a form that database gurus seem to like, this being comma-delimited fields. This means that the data for each record in the database is stored as a single line of text with a comma between each field. Here's some example data for the database of cars:

```
Jaguar,XKE roadster,1961,3.781,7827
Jaguar,XK150 roadster,1958,3.781,78
Jaguar,XKSS,1957,3.442,16
```

```
Rolls Royce,Silver Cloud 1,1955,4.887,2357
Rolls Royce,Silver Shadow 1,1965,6.320,20604
```

For the first record, then, the first field is the manufacturer. It would have the data "Jaguar." The second field is the model. It would have the data "XKE roadster," and so on.

The source code for the MAKE-DB program is shown in 3-2. It will read in as many lines of comma-delimited field data as exists in the source file and write it to database records. It assumes, of course, that the data will be for cars and structured in the previous format—the MAKE-DB program has error-checking that's just this side of nonexistent.

**3-2** The MAKE-DB.C source code.

```
/*
        fixed record database creator
        Copyright (c) 1993 Alchemy Mindworks Inc.
*/

#include "stdio.h"
#include "fcntl.h"
#include "io.h"
#include "math.h"
#include <sys/stat.h>

typedef struct {
        char manufacturer[25];
        char model[25];
        unsigned int year;
        double displacement;
        long quantity;
        } RECORD;

typedef struct {
        char sig[8];
        unsigned long count;
        } HEADER;

#define DATABASE_SIG        "DATABASE"

main(argc,argv)
        int argc;
        char *argv[];
{
        HEADER header;
        RECORD record;
        FILE *in;
        char b[129],*p;
        int out;

        puts("Automotive database creator");

        if(argc <= 2) error("Arguments:          path to a source file\n"
                            "                    database to create");
```

```
	if((in=fopen(argv[1],"ra"))==NULL) error("Can't open the source file");

	if((out=open(argv[2],O_WRONLY | O_CREAT | O_TRUNC | O_BINARY,S_IWRITE))==NULL)
	    error("Can't create the destination file");

	memset((char *)&header,0,sizeof(HEADER));

	if(!writeheader(out,&header)) error("Can't write header");

	do {
		if((p=fgets(b,128,in)) != NULL) {
			parserecord(&record,b);
			if(!writerecord(out,&record,header.count))
			    error("Can't write record");
			++header.count;
		}
	} while(p != NULL);

	if(!writeheader(out,&header)) error("Can't write header");

	close(out);

	fclose(in);
}

parserecord(r,b)
	RECORD *r;
	char *b;
{
	int i;
	char s[129];
	memset((char *)r,0,sizeof(RECORD));

	/* get the manufacturer */
	for(i=0;*b != 0 && *b != ',' && *b != '\n';++b,++i) {
		if(i < 24) r->manufacturer[i]=*b;
	}
	r->manufacturer[i]=0;
	while(*b==',')++b;

	/* get the model */
	for(i=0;*b != 0 && *b != ',' && *b != '\n';++b,++i) {
		if(i < 24) r->model[i]=*b;
	}
	r->model[i]=0;
	while(*b==',')++b;

	/* get the year*/
	for(i=0;*b != 0 && *b != ',' && *b != '\n';++b,++i) {
		if(i < 24) s[i]=*b;
	}
	s[i]=0;
	while(*b==',')++b;
	r->year=atoi(s);

	/* get the displacement */
	for(i=0;*b != 0 && *b != ',' && *b != '\n';++b,++i) {
```

**3-2** Continued.

```
                if(i < 24) s[i]=*b;
        }
        s[i]=0;
        while(*b==',')++b;
        r->displacement=atof(s);

        /* get the quantity */
        for(i=0;*b != 0 && *b != ',' && *b != '\n';++b,++i) {
                if(i < 24) s[i]=*b;
        }
        s[i]=0;
        while(*b==',')++b;
        r->quantity=atol(s);
}

writerecord(fh,r,n)
        int fh;
        RECORD *r;
        unsigned long n;
{
        lseek(fh,(long)sizeof(HEADER)+n*(long)sizeof(RECORD),SEEK_SET);
        if(write(fh,(char *)r,sizeof(RECORD))==sizeof(RECORD)) return(1);
        else return(0);
}

writeheader(fh,h)
        int fh;
        HEADER *h;
{
        memcpy(h->sig,DATABASE_SIG,8);
        lseek(fh,0L,SEEK_SET);
        if(write(fh,(char *)h,sizeof(HEADER))==sizeof(HEADER)) return(1);
        else return(0);
}

error(s)
        char *s;
{
        puts(s);
        exit(1);
}
```

The MAKE-DB program expects two command line arguments. The first argument should be the path to a file of comma-delimited source data, and the second argument the path to the database file you want to create. In this application, I used the extension FDB, for "fixed database."

It's not hard to see what MAKE-DB is up to. It uses the C language streamed file functions to read the source file and the block file functions to write the database; the latter being ill-equipped to read variable-length lines of text but very much faster at dealing with fixed blocks of data. The only fairly complex element of the program is the code to parse a comma-delimited line into a RECORD object.

A browse program for the database of cars, called VIEW-DB, is illustrated in 3-3. Much of its code should be familiar, as it's just screen handling functions from chapter 1.

**3-3** The VIEW-DB.C source code.

```
/*
        fixed record database viewer
        Copyright (c) 1993 Alchemy Mindworks Inc.
*/

#include "stdio.h"
#include "fcntl.h"
#include "io.h"
#include "math.h"
#include "conio.h"
#include "dos.h"
#include <sys/stat.h>

#define SCREENWIDE          80
#define SCREENDEEP          25

#define TEXTCOLOUR(foreground,background) (foreground | (background << 4))

#define BACKGROUND          TEXTCOLOUR(WHITE,BLUE)
#define BANNER              TEXTCOLOUR(BLACK,RED)
#define TEXT                TEXTCOLOUR(WHITE,BLUE)

#define HOME                0x4700
#define CURSOR_UP           0x4800
#define END                 0x4f00
#define CURSOR_DOWN         0x5000
#define PG_UP               0x4900
#define PG_DOWN             0x5100

#define LEFT                2
#define TOP                 2

typedef struct {
        char manufacturer[25];
        char model[25];
        unsigned int year;
        double displacement;
        long quantity;
        } RECORD;

typedef struct {
        char sig[8];
        unsigned long count;
        } HEADER;

#define DATABASE_SIG        "DATABASE"

char *screenPtr();
```

**3-3** Continued.

```
char *screen;

main(argc,argv)
        int argc;
        char *argv[];
{
        HEADER header;
        RECORD record;
        long page=0L,oldpage=-1L;
        int c,fh;

        screen=screenPtr();

        if(argc <= 1) error("Arguments:          path to a database");

        if((fh=open(argv[1],O_RDONLY | O_BINARY,S_IREAD))==NULL)
            error("Can't open the database");

        if(!readheader(fh,&header)) error("Can't read header");

        do {
                if(page != oldpage) showbanner();
                oldpage=page;

                if(!readrecord(fh,&record,page))
                    DrawString(LEFT,TOP,"Error reading record",TEXT);
                else
                    showrecord(&record,page,LEFT,TOP);

                switch(c=GetKey()) {
                        case HOME:
                                page=0L;
                                break;
                        case END:
                                page=header.count-1L;
                                break;
                        case CURSOR_UP:
                                if(page > 0L) --page;
                                break;
                        case CURSOR_DOWN:
                                if((page+1L) <= (header.count-1L)) ++page;
                                break;
                        case PG_UP:
                                if((page -10L) > 0L) page-=10L;
                                else page=0L;
                                break;
                        case PG_DOWN:
                                if((page+10L) <= (header.count-1L)) page+=10L;
                                else page=header.count-1L;
                                break;
                }
        } while(c != 27);

        close(fh);
}
```

```
showrecord(r,page,x,y)
        RECORD *r;
        long page;
        unsigned int x,y;
{
        char b[129];

        sprintf(b,"RECORD:       %lu",page+1L);
        DrawString(x,y++,b,TEXT);

        ++y;

        sprintf(b,"MANUFACTURER: %s",r->manufacturer);
        DrawString(x,y++,b,TEXT);

        sprintf(b,"MODEL:        %s",r->model);
        DrawString(x,y++,b,TEXT);

        sprintf(b,"YEAR:         %u",r->year);
        DrawString(x,y++,b,TEXT);

        sprintf(b,"DISPLACEMENT: %g litres",r->displacement);
        DrawString(x,y++,b,TEXT);

        sprintf(b,"QUANTITY:     %lu",r->quantity);
        DrawString(x,y++,b,TEXT);
}

readrecord(fh,r,n)
        int fh;
        RECORD *r;
        unsigned long n;
{
        lseek(fh,(long)sizeof(HEADER)+n*(long)sizeof(RECORD),SEEK_SET);
        if(read(fh,(char *)r,sizeof(RECORD))==sizeof(RECORD)) return(1);
        else return(0);
}

readheader(fh,h)
        int fh;
        HEADER *h;
{
        lseek(fh,0L,SEEK_SET);
        if(read(fh,(char *)h,sizeof(HEADER))==sizeof(HEADER)) {
                if(memcmp(h->sig,DATABASE_SIG,8))
                    return(0);
                else
                    return(1);
        }
        else return(0);
}

showbanner()
{
        ClearScreen(BACKGROUND);
        ClearLine(0,BANNER);
        HideCursor();
```

**3-3** Continued.

```
        DrawString(LEFT,0,"Database viewer copyright (c) 1993 Alchemy Mindworks Inc.",
            BANNER);
}

DrawString(x,y,text,attr)
        int x,y;
        char *text;
        int attr;
{
        unsigned int a,*ip,n=0;

        ip=(unsigned int *)(screen+(y*160+x*2));
        a=attr << 8;

        while(*text) ip[n++]=*text++ | a;
        return(n);
}

HideCursor()
{
        union REGS r;

        r.x.ax=0x0f00;
        int86(0x10,&r,&r);

        r.x.ax=0x0200;
        r.x.dx=(SCREENDEEP+1)<8;
        int86(0x10,&r,&r);
}

char *screenPtr()
{
        union REGS r;

        r.x.ax=0x0f00;
        int86(0x10,&r,&r);

        if(r.h.al==0x07) return(MK_FP(0xb000,r.h.bh*0x1000));
        else return(MK_FP(0xb800,r.h.bh*0x1000));
}

ClearScreen(attr)
        int attr;
{
        unsigned int i,a,*ip;

        ip=(unsigned int *)screen;
        a=attr << 8;

        for(i=0;i<SCREENWIDE*SCREENDEEP;++i) *ip++=32 | a;
}

ClearLine(y,attr)
        int y,attr;
{
        unsigned int a,i,*ip;
```

```
        ip=(unsigned int *)(screen+(y*160));
        a=(attr << 8) | 32;

        for(i=0;i<SCREENWIDE;++i) *ip++=a;
}

error(s)
        char *s;
{
        puts(s);
        exit(1);
}

GetKey()
{
        int c;

        c = getch();
        if(!(c & 0x00ff)) c = getch() << 8;
        return(c);
}
```

The VIEW-DB program illustrates how to fetch and display records from the database. It begins by reading the HEADER object at the beginning of the database to make sure the file it's been given really is a database. It then reads the first record and displays it on the screen. The `do` loop in its `main` function will wait for keyboard activity and step through the records. The up and down arrow keys move by one record. The Home and End keys move to the extremes of the database. The PgUp and PgDn keys move in jumps of 10 records—which won't mean much in this example because the database only has five records in total. Hitting Esc will return you to DOS.

A database manager like this one can deal with large databases reliably and surprisingly quickly, as long as you can accept its limitations. It can be both more space efficient and faster than a dBASE database of the sort I'll look at in the next section. However, if you create a database of several thousand records and realize you need an extra field in each of them, plan on a fair bit of cursing and head-bashing to get it there.

The example database files from this section, CARS.TXT and CARS.FDB, are included on the companion disk for this book.

## Work with dBASE DBF files

The dBASE application and its descendants, such as FoxBase, are actually dedicated programming languages designed to manipulate data records. The native file format of dBASE is DBF. The dBASE package is now a product of Borland, who also probably made the C compiler you're using to work with the code in this book.

The thing that makes dBASE fairly remarkable is that it allows its database files to define the structure of the data in the file. It also includes the internal smarts to swab the data in databases—you can add or remove fields from the record structure of a database relatively easily, which was clearly not the case for the fixed-record database manager discussed in the previous section.

The drawback to DBF files is that they're typically slower to access than a fixed-record database would be. In addition, if your application for a database includes getting data into DBF files you'll probably require dBASE or one of its competitors, as well as some knowledge of the dBASE programming language. Anyone who's relatively comfortable with C will likely find dBASE to be an uncomfortable fusion of BASIC and Klingon pig latin.

Despite its lexical shortcomings, dBASE is a useful front end for applications that deal with a lot of data. While you might not want to work in dBASE itself, you probably will find yourself confronted with reading data from DBF files that have originated with other sources. In fact, there's a lot of fairly interesting data in this form.

Unlike the fixed-record database manager in the previous section, an application to read DBF files need not be written with a particular record structure in mind. The header of a DBF file will define the structure of the records that comprise the rest of the file. This includes specifying the number of fields in each record, the size of each field, and the type of data each field can be expected to contain.

The source code VIEW-DBF, a DBF file browser, is illustrated in 3-4. It works very much like the VIEW-DB program in the previous section, except that it will display the data of any version 3 DBF file, rather than just one specific hard-wired database.

**3-4** The VIEW-DBF.C source code.

```
/*
        dBASE DBF file viewer
        Copyright (c) 1993 Alchemy Mindworks Inc.

        Based in part on code by M.C. Mason,
        which was based on code by R. Ragsell
*/
#include "stdio.h"
#include "stdlib.h"
#include "string.h"
#include "alloc.h"
#include "conio.h"
#include "dos.h"

#define TRUE    1
#define FALSE   0

#define SCREENWIDE      80
#define SCREENDEEP      25

#define TEXTCOLOUR(foreground,background) (foreground | (background << 4))
```

```
#define BACKGROUND      TEXTCOLOUR(WHITE,BLUE)
#define BANNER          TEXTCOLOUR(BLACK,RED)
#define TEXT            TEXTCOLOUR(WHITE,BLUE)

#define HOME            0x4700
#define CURSOR_UP       0x4800
#define END             0x4f00
#define CURSOR_DOWN     0x5000
#define PG_UP           0x4900
#define PG_DOWN         0x5100

#define LEFT            2
#define TOP             2

typedef struct {
        char Name[12];                  /* Name of field        */
        char Type;                      /* Field type           */
        int Length;                     /* Field length         */
        int Dec;                        /* Decimal location     */
        } DBFIELD;

typedef struct {
        int Version;                    /* File struct version  */
        char update[3];                 /* Date last updated    */
        long NumRex;                    /* # records in file    */
        int HdrLen;                     /* Header length        */
        int RecLen;                     /* Record length        */
        int NumFlds;                    /* # of fields in recs  */
        long FileSize;                  /* # of bytes in file   */
        FILE *file;                     /* File holding data    */
        DBFIELD (*fld)[];               /* fld data array ptr   */
        } DBFILE;

typedef struct {
        char Version;
        char update[3];
        long NumRex;
        int HdrLen;
        int RecLen;
        char Reserved[20];
        } DBHEADERMASK;

typedef struct {
        char Name[11];
        char Type;
        char Reserved1[4];
        unsigned char Length;
        unsigned char Dec;
        char Reserved2[14];
        } DBFIELDMASK;

char *screenPtr();
DBFILE *dbfOpen(char *fname);

#define Day_upd update[2]               /*Last update: day   */
#define Mon_upd update[1]               /*Last update: month */
#define Yr_upd  update[0]               /*Last update: year  */
```

**3-4** Continued.

```
#define F(x) (*x->fld)

char *screen;

main(argc,argv)
        int argc;
        char *argv[];
{
        DBFILE *dbf;
        char *buf;
        long page=0L,oldpage=-1L;
        int c;

        screen=screenPtr();

        if(argc <= 1) error("Argument:      path to a DBF file");

        if((dbf=dbfOpen(argv[1]))==NULL)
            error("Can't open the DBF file");

        do  {
                if(page != oldpage) showbanner(page);
                oldpage=page;

                if(page==0L) dbfShowHeader(dbf,LEFT,TOP);
                else if(page==1L) dbfShowStructure(dbf,LEFT,TOP);
                else {
                        if((buf=malloc(dbf->RecLen+2)) == NULL )
                            error("Can't allocate memory");

                        if(!dbfReadRec(dbf,page-1,buf))
                            DrawString(LEFT,TOP,"Error reading record",TEXT);
                        else dbfShowRecord(dbf,page-1,buf,LEFT,TOP);
                        free(buf);
                }

                switch(c=GetKey()) {
                        case HOME:
                                page=0L;
                                break;
                        case END:
                                page=dbf->NumRex+1L;
                                break;
                        case CURSOR_UP:
                                if(page > 0L) --page;
                                break;
                        case CURSOR_DOWN:
                                if((page+1L) <=(dbf->NumRex+1L)) ++page;
                                break;
                        case PG_UP:
                                if((page -10L) > 0L) page-=10L;
                                else page=0L;
                                break;
                        case PG_DOWN:
                                if((page+10L) <= (dbf->NumRex+1L)) page+=10L;
                                else page=dbf->NumRex+1L;
```

```
                                break;
                }
        } while(c != 27);
}

DBFILE *dbfOpen(fname)
        char *fname;
{
        int i;
        DBFILE *r;
        DBHEADERMASK h;
        DBFIELDMASK FldTmp;

        if((r=(DBFILE *)malloc(sizeof(DBFILE)))==NULL) return(NULL);

        if((r->file = fopen(fname,"rb"))==NULL) {
                free((char *)r);
                return(NULL);
        }

        if(fread((char *)&h,1,sizeof(DBHEADERMASK),r->file) != sizeof(DBHEADERMASK)) {
                free((char *)r);
                return(NULL);
        }
        r->Version = h.Version & 0x07;
        r->Day_upd = h.Day_upd;
        r->Mon_upd = h.Mon_upd;
        r->Yr_upd  = h.Yr_upd;
        r->NumRex  = h.NumRex;
        r->HdrLen  = h.HdrLen;
        r->RecLen  = h.RecLen;
        r->NumFlds = (h.HdrLen - 33)/32;
        r->FileSize= (long)h.HdrLen+(long)h.RecLen*(long)h.NumRex+1L;

        if (r->Version != 3) {
                free((char *)r);
                return(NULL);
        }

        if((r->fld=malloc(sizeof(DBFIELD)*r->NumFlds))==NULL) {
                free((char *)r);
                return(NULL);
        }

        for(i=0;i<r->NumFlds;i++) {
                if(fread((char *)&FldTmp,1,sizeof(DBFIELDMASK),r->file) !=
                    sizeof(DBFIELDMASK)) {
                        free((char *)r);
                        return(NULL);
                    }
                strncpy(F(r)[i].Name,FldTmp.Name,11);
                F(r)[i].Type = FldTmp.Type;
                F(r)[i].Length = FldTmp.Length;
                F(r)[i].Dec = FldTmp.Dec;
        }

        return(r);
}
```

**3-4** Continued.

```
dbfClose(dbf)
        DBFILE *dbf;
{
        fclose(dbf->file);
        if(dbf->fld != NULL) free(dbf->fld);
        if(dbf != NULL) free(dbf);
}

dbfShowHeader(hdr,x,y)
        DBFILE *hdr;
        int x,y;
{
        char b[129],buf[129];

        sprintf(b,"dBASE Version          :%8.8s",itoa(hdr->Version,buf,10));
        DrawString(x,y++,b,TEXT);

        sprintf(b,"Number of data records:%8.8s",ltoa(hdr->NumRex,buf,10));
        DrawString(x,y++,b,TEXT);

        sprintf(b,"Date of last update   : %2.2s/"
                 "%s/%s",itoa(hdr->Mon_upd,buf,10),
            itoa(hdr->Day_upd,buf+10,10),
            itoa(hdr->Yr_upd, buf+20,10));
        DrawString(x,y++,b,TEXT);

        sprintf(b,"Header length          :%8.8s",
            itoa(hdr->HdrLen,buf,10));
        DrawString(x,y++,b,TEXT);

        sprintf(b,"Record length          :%8.8s",
            itoa(hdr->RecLen,buf,10));
        DrawString(x,y++,b,TEXT);

        sprintf(b,"Number of fields       :%8.8s",
            itoa(hdr->NumFlds,buf,10));
        DrawString(x,y++,b,TEXT);

        sprintf(b,"File size              :%8.8s",
            ltoa(hdr->FileSize,buf,10));
        DrawString(x,y++,b,TEXT);
}

dbfShowStructure(hdr,x,y)
        DBFILE *hdr;
        int x,y;
{
        char *Ty,b[129],buf[129];
        int i;

        DrawString(x,y++,"Field  Field Name  Type        Width"
         "     Dec",TEXT);

        for(i=0;i<hdr->NumFlds;i++) {
                switch(F(hdr)[i].Type) {
                        case 'C':
```

```
                                        Ty = "Character  ";
                                        break;
                                case 'L':
                                        Ty = "Logical    ";
                                        break;
                                case 'N':
                                        Ty = "Number     ";
                                        break;
                                case 'F':
                                        Ty = "Floating Pt";
                                        break;
                                case 'D':
                                        Ty = "Date       ";
                                        break;
                                case 'M':
                                        Ty = "Memo       ";
                                        break;
                                default:
                                        Ty = "Unknown    ";
                                        break;
                        }
                        sprintf(b,"%5d  %-11.11s%11.11s  %3d"
                            "      %2d",i+1,F(hdr)[i].Name,Ty,
                           F(hdr)[i].Length,F(hdr)[i].Dec);
                        DrawString(x,y++,b,TEXT);
                }
                itoa(hdr->RecLen,buf,10);
                sprintf(b,"   ** Total **                   %4s",buf);
                DrawString(x,y++,b,TEXT);
}

dbfReadRec(hdr,Rec,b)
        DBFILE *hdr;
        long Rec;
        char *b;
{
        long CurrentPos;

        CurrentPos=(Rec-1)*(long)hdr->RecLen+(long)hdr->HdrLen;
        fseek(hdr->file,CurrentPos,SEEK_SET);
        if(fread(b,1,hdr->RecLen,hdr->file) == hdr->RecLen) return(1);
        return(0);
}

dbfShowRecord(hdr,Rec,bf,x,y)
        DBFILE *hdr;
        long Rec;
        char *bf;
        int x,y;
{
        char b[129],buf[129];
        int FPos,i,n=20;

        sprintf(b,"RECORD %3d  %c",Rec,*bf);
        DrawString(x,y++,b,TEXT);

        ++y;
```

**3-4** Continued.

```
        FPos=1;
        for(i=0;i<hdr->NumFlds;i++) {
                sprintf(b,"%-11.11s",F(hdr)[i].Name);
                DrawString(x,y,b,TEXT);

                switch (F(hdr)[i].Type) {
                        case 'D':
                                sprintf(b,"%2.2s/%2.2s/%4.4s ",
                                    bf+FPos+4,bf+FPos+6,bf+FPos);
                                DrawString(x+n,y++,b,TEXT);
                                break;
                        case 'L':
                                switch (bf[FPos]) {
                                        case 'Y':
                                        case 'T':
                                                DrawString(x+n,y++,"TRUE ",TEXT);
                                                break;
                                        case 'N':
                                        case 'F':
                                                DrawString(x+n,y++,"FALSE ",TEXT);
                                                break;
                                        default:
                                                DrawString(x+n,y++,"UNKNOWN ",TEXT);
                                }
                                break;
                        case 'M':    /* Ignore MEMO fields */
                                break;
                        default:
                                sprintf(buf,"%%%d.%ds",
                                    F(hdr)[i].Length,F(hdr)[i].Length);
                                sprintf(b,buf,bf+FPos);
                                DrawString(x+n,y++,b,TEXT);
                }
                FPos += F(hdr)[i].Length;
        }
}

showbanner(page)
        unsigned long page;
{
        char b[64];

        ClearScreen(BACKGROUND);
        ClearLine(0,BANNER);
        HideCursor();
        DrawString(LEFT,0,"DBF viewer copyright (c) 1993 Alchemy Mindworks Inc.",
            BANNER);

        if(page==0L) strcpy(b,"HEADER");
        else if(page==1L) strcpy(b,"STRUCTURE");
        else strcpy(b,"RECORD");

        DrawString(60,0,b,BANNER);
}

DrawString(x,y,text,attr)
```

```
        int x,y;
        char *text;
        int attr;
{
        unsigned int a,*ip,n=0;

        ip=(unsigned int *)(screen+(y*160+x*2));
        a=attr << 8;

        while(*text) ip[n++]=*text++ | a;
        return(n);
}

HideCursor()
{
        union REGS r;

        r.x.ax=0x0f00;
        int86(0x10,&r,&r);

        r.x.ax=0x0200;
        r.x.dx=(SCREENDEEP+1)<<8;
        int86(0x10,&r,&r);
}

char *screenPtr()
{
        union REGS r;

        r.x.ax=0x0f00;
        int86(0x10,&r,&r);

        if(r.h.al==0x07) return(MK_FP(0xb000,r.h.bh*0x1000));
        else return(MK_FP(0xb800,r.h.bh*0x1000));
}

ClearScreen(attr)
        int attr;
{
        unsigned int i,a,*ip;

        ip=(unsigned int *)screen;
        a=attr << 8;

        for(i=0;i<SCREENWIDE*SCREENDEEP;++i) *ip++=32 | a;
}

ClearLine(y,attr)
        int y,attr;
{
        unsigned int a,i,*ip;

        ip=(unsigned int *)(screen+(y*160));
        a=(attr << 8) | 32;

        for(i=0;i<SCREENWIDE;++i) *ip++=a;
}
```

**3-4** Continued.

```
error(s)
        char *s;
{
        puts(s);
        exit(1);
}

GetKey()
{
        int c;

        c = getch();
        if(!(c & 0x00ff)) c = getch() < 8;
        return(c);
}
```

The VIEW-DBF program shows the header structure of a DBF file as its first page, the record structure as its second page, and then the first record of the file as its third page, working forward from there. The page movement of VIEW-DBF works just as it did in VIEW-DB in the previous section.

A DBF file begins with the following header:

```
typedef struct {
        int Version;          /* File struct version */
        char update[3];       /* Date last updated   */
        long NumRex;          /* # records in file   */
        int HdrLen;           /* Header length       */
        int RecLen;           /* Record length       */
        int NumFlds;          /* # of fields in recs */
        long FileSize;        /* # of bytes in file  */
        FILE *file;           /* File holding data   */
        DBFIELD(*fld)[];      /*ld data array ptr    */
        } DBFILE;
```

The DBFILE structure is, in fact, a variable-length object. The number of entries in the `fld` array will be determined by the value of the `Num flds` element of the header. A DBFIELD object looks like this:

```
typedef struct {
        char Name[12];        /* Name of field    */
        char Type;            /* Field type       */
        int Length;           /* Field length     */
        int Dec;              /* Decimal location */
        } DBFIELD;
```

The actual data, as it's stored in a DBF file, is structured like this:

```
typedef struct {
        char Name[11];
        char Type;
```

```
        char Reserved1[4];
        unsigned char Length;
        unsigned char Dec;
        char Reserved2[14];
        } DBFIELDMASK;
```

The dbfOpen function in VIEW-DBF illustrates how to open a DBF file and read its header. It returns a pointer to a DBFILE object if the DBF file passed to it has been opened successfully.

Reading a DBF file record is simple once you've got a pointer to a DB-FILE object that defines the database.

```
long CurrentPos;
CurrentPos=(Rec-1)*(long)hdr->RecLen+(long)hdr->HdrLen;
fseek(hdr->file,CurrentPos,SEEK_SET);
fread(b,1,hdr->RecLen,hdr->file;
```

In this example, the value of Rec is the record number—beginning with record one—and b is a buffer large enough to contain one record worth of data. This is defined by the RecLen field of a DBFILE object. The hdr object is a pointer to the DBFILE object for the DBF file being read.

Reading the data out of a DBF record is a bit more involved—you can see how it's handled in the dbfReadRecord function in 3-4.

While a fairly useful application in its own right, the functions in VIEW-DBF can be readily excised for your own software. One of the decided advantages of maintaining your data as DBF files rather than in a proprietary fixed-record database structure like the database of cars in the previous section, is that other dBASE-compatible software can get at it as well. At least this is usually an advantage. The portability of data in the DBF format offers a limited degree of protection if you find that you'd like to keep some of your files secret.

The DBF reader functions are based in part on code by M. C. Mason, which was based on code by R. Ragsell.

## Display a calendar in Windows

Our current calendar is properly called the Gregorian calendar—I'll get to who Gregory was in a moment. It's based on a starting year that's ostensibly the year that Jesus Christ was born. In fact, there's all sorts of historical evidence to suggest that this date is inaccurate by as much as four years either way—our year 1 is perhaps more of an agreed-upon convenience. The year 1 only began being widely regarded as the year 1 around the year 384.

Most civilized cultures have had calendars of one sort or another—and most have been inaccurate. The problem in devising a workable calendar is that the earth's rotation around the sun doesn't take an even number of days. One calendar year should be 365.2422 days. A calendar that rounds this off to, for example, 365 days, will be out by one day four years after its inception, and by almost a month within a century of its start. Early calendars are said to have "slipped" for this reason. The start of the year might be in mid-winter when such a calendar is instigated, but it will gradually drift as time passes.

All calendars that work correctly deal with this problem by inserting "leap" days into the cycle, such that when the cumulative errors in a calendar have made it inaccurate by a full day, the slack is taken up by adding a day to the year.

Five hundred years before our year 1, Chinese astronomers had calculated the length of one year as 365.2444 days, and the Chinese calendar based on this value represents one of the first calendars to keep its accuracy over a reasonable period of time. It was arranged in a complex cycle of 12-year periods, with suitable leap days inserted to keep the calendar on track.

The Roman calendar was, in fact, borrowed from Egyptian astronomers who had calculated the period of the earth extremely poorly. Rome dealt with this by adding leap days—or occasionally leap weeks—whenever the calendar had grown measurably different from the position of the sun. The old Roman calendar had 12 months with 30 days in them and then 5 extra days tacked onto the end.

Julius Caesar is credited with creating the first workable Roman calendar. His calendar had months of varying lengths, and it included leap days every four years. It assumed, in effect, that the earth circles the sun every 365.25 days, which is slightly incorrect.

Our current calendar, the Gregorian calendar, was created from the Julian calendar by Pope Gregory XXIII in 1582. It works just like the Julian calendar except there is no leap day added in leap years evenly divisible by 100 unless they're also evenly divisible by 400. By Gregory's time, the Julian calendar was inaccurate by about 11 days.

In fact, Gregory's calendar isn't perfect—its errors will begin to be obvious around the beginning of the fortieth century. Perhaps we'll all be using star dates by then.

It's possible to calculate the start of any month for any year accurately—at least until the year 4046—by beginning at the inception of the Gregorian calendar and counting forward, using the aforementioned rules. January 1, 1583, was a Saturday. Inasmuch as 1583 was not a leap year, you can calculate the day that January 1, 1584 fell on by adding 365 to this day and taking the result MOD seven. In the numbering system used in the program in this section, Saturday is day six. January 1, 1584, then, was a Sunday.

You can also work out the starting day of any month in a year this way as well. You have to keep in mind that the length of February changes, of course.

The application window for CALENDAR is illustrated in 3-5. When it first pops up, CALENDAR displays the calendar page for the current month and year, as read from your system clock. Moving the vertical scroll bar of the window changes the year—it ranges from 1583 to 4046. Moving the horizontal scroll bar changes the month.

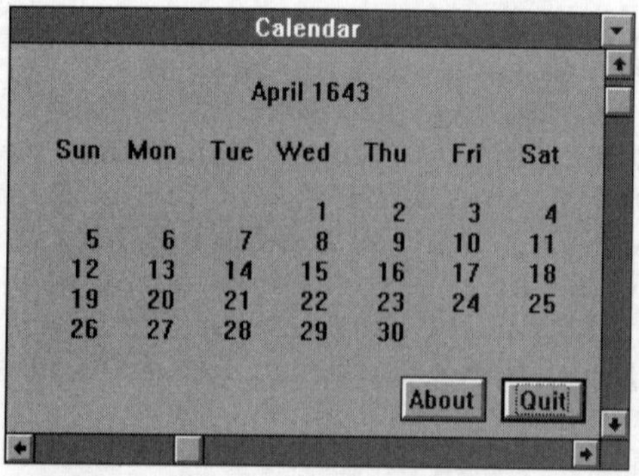


**3-5** The Windows CALENDAR program.

Understanding how CALENDAR works is fairly elementary if you followed the previous discussion of calendar theory. To find out what day of the week a particular date falls on this year, all you need do is begin with the day that January 1 fell on for this year and count forward by the intervening number of days. This, in turn, requires that you know how many days occur in each of the intervening months. Because the lengths of the months in the Gregorian calendar vary, I'll use a lookup table to keep track of them:

```
int number_days[2][12} = {
        { 31,28,31,30,31,30,31,31,30,31,30,31 },
        { 31,29,31,30,31,30,31,31,30,31,30,31 },
};
```

There are two sets of entries in the `number days` table because some years have an extra day added to February. The number of days in a month, then, can be defined as `numberdays[isleap(year)][month]`, where `year` is the year in question, `month` is the number of the month, beginning with zero for January, and `isleap` is the following function:

```
int isleap(int n)
{
        int r=0;

        if(!(n % 4)) r = 1;
        if(!(n % 100)) {
               r = 0;
               if(!(n % 400)) r = 1;
        }
        return(r);
}
```

This implements Gregory's formula for adding leap years.

Because you know how long every month from the beginning of the calendar in 1583 to the present is—and because we know the day on which the calendar began—it's possible to work out what day any month thereafter will begin on by just tallying up the days involved. This is the sort of thing computers are good at.

The C language source code, CALENDAR.CPP, for the CALENDAR application is illustrated in 3-6. In addition, you'll need CALENDAR.RC, CALENDAR.PRJ, and CALENDAR.DEF, as illustrated in 3-7.

The CALENDAR application is thick with opportunities for expansion if you feel like making something more of it. For example, you might want to have it display the dates of particular annual events. This would be exceedingly handy if you needed to know at a glance what day Michaelmas fell on in the year that Queen Victoria was crowned, or whether old midsummer's day happens to occur on a weekend this year, or other bits of trivia vital to life in the 1990s.

**3-6** The CALENDAR.CPP source code.

```
/*
        Calendar
        Copyright (c) 1993 Alchemy Mindworks Inc.

*/

#include <windows.h>
#include <dir.h>
#include <alloc.h>
#include <stdio.h>
#include <dos.h>

#define QUIT     101
#define ABOUT    102

#define STARTYEAR       1583      /* year after Gregory hiccuped */
#define STARTMONTH      0         /* january of that year... */
#define STARTDAY        6         /* ...was a saturday */
#define ENDYEAR         4046      /* no more calendars aftr this date */
#define LEFT            50        /* left margin of window */
#define YEARJUMP        10        /* jump by decades */
#define MONTHJUMP       3         /* jump by seasons */
#define DAYSPACE        6         /* space between days */

int PASCAL WinMain(HANDLE hInstance,HANDLE hPrevInstance,LPSTR lpszCmdParam,int nCmdShow);
DWORD FAR PASCAL CalendarProc(HWND hwnd,WORD message,WORD wParam,LONG lParam);
DWORD FAR PASCAL AboutDlgProc(HWND hwnd,WORD message,WORD wParam,LONG lParam);
int firstday(int year,int month);
void showmonth(HDC hdc,int year,int month,RECT *r);
int isleap(int n);

HANDLE hInst;

/* array to work out month sizes */
int number_days[2][12] = {
        { 31,28,31,30,31,30,31,31,30,31,30,31 },
        { 31,29,31,30,31,30,31,31,30,31,30,31 },
};

/* names of months */
```

```
char months[12][10] = {
"January","February","March","April","May","June","July","August","September",
        "October","November","December"
};

/* names of days */
char days[7][4] = { "Sun","Mon","Tue","Wed","Thu","Fri","Sat" };

#pragma warn -par
int PASCAL WinMain(HANDLE hInstance,HANDLE hPrevInstance,
                   LPSTR lpszCmdParam,int nCmdShow)
{
        FARPROC dlgProc;
        int r=0;

        hInst=hInstance;

        dlgProc=MakeProcInstance((FARPROC)CalendarProc,hInst);
        r=DialogBox(hInst,"CalendarBox",NULL,dlgProc);

        FreeProcInstance(dlgProc);

        return(r);
}

/* handle message to main window */
DWORD FAR PASCAL CalendarProc(HWND hwnd,WORD message,WORD wParam,LONG lParam)
{
        HDC hdc;
        PAINTSTRUCT ps;
        FARPROC lpfnDlgProc;
        RECT rect;
        POINT point;
        struct date d;
        static int year,month;

        switch(message) {
                case WM_INITDIALOG:
                        SetClassWord(hwnd,GCW_HICON,
                                     (WORD)LoadIcon(hInst,"Calendar"));
                        SetScrollRange(hwnd,SB_VERT,STARTYEAR,ENDYEAR,FALSE);
                        SetScrollRange(hwnd,SB_HORZ,0,11,FALSE);
                        getdate(&d);
                        year=d.da_year;
                        month=d.da_mon-1;
                        SetScrollPos(hwnd,SB_HORZ,month,TRUE);
                        SetScrollPos(hwnd,SB_VERT,year,TRUE);
                        InvalidateRect(hwnd,NULL,TRUE);
                        break;
                case WM_CTLCOLOR:
                        if(HIWORD(lParam)==CTLCOLOR_STATIC ||
                           HIWORD(lParam)==CTLCOLOR_DLG) {
                                SetBkColor(wParam,RGB(192,192,192));
                                SetTextColor(wParam,RGB(0,0,0));

                                ClientToScreen(hwnd,&point);
                                UnrealizeObject(GetStockObject(LTGRAY_BRUSH));
                                SetBrushOrg(wParam,point.x,point.y);
```

**3-6** Continued.

```
                return((DWORD)GetStockObject(LTGRAY_BRUSH));

            }
            if(HIWORD(lParam)==CTLCOLOR_BTN) {
                SetBkColor(wParam,RGB(192,192,192));
                SetTextColor(wParam,RGB(0,0,0));

                ClientToScreen(hwnd,&point);
                UnrealizeObject(GetStockObject(BLACK_BRUSH));
                SetBrushOrg(wParam,point.x,point.y);

                return((DWORD)GetStockObject(BLACK_BRUSH));
            }
            break;
        case WM_VSCROLL:
            switch(wParam) {
                case SB_LINEUP:
                    year-=1;
                    break;
                case SB_LINEDOWN:
                    year+=1;
                    break;
                case SB_PAGEUP:
                    year-=YEARJUMP;
                    break;
                case SB_PAGEDOWN:
                    year+=YEARJUMP;
                    break;
                case SB_THUMBPOSITION:
                    year=LOWORD(lParam);
                    break;
            }

            if(year < STARTYEAR ) year=STARTYEAR;
            else if(year >= ENDYEAR ) year=ENDYEAR-1;

            if(year != GetScrollPos(hwnd,SB_VERT)) {
                SetScrollPos(hwnd,SB_VERT,year,TRUE);
                InvalidateRect(hwnd,NULL,TRUE);
            }
            break;
        case WM_HSCROLL:
            switch(wParam) {
                case SB_LINEUP:
                    month-=1;
                    break;
                case SB_LINEDOWN:
                    month+=1;
                    break;
                case SB_PAGEUP:
                    month-=MONTHJUMP;
                    break;
                case SB_PAGEDOWN:
                    month+=MONTHJUMP;
                    break;
                case SB_THUMBPOSITION:
```

```
                        month=LOWORD(lParam);
                        break;
                }

                if(month < 0) month=0;
                else if(month >= 12) month=11;

                if(month != GetScrollPos(hwnd,SB_HORZ)) {
                        SetScrollPos(hwnd,SB_HORZ,month,TRUE);
                        InvalidateRect(hwnd,NULL,TRUE);
                }
                break;
        case WM_PAINT:
                hdc=BeginPaint(hwnd,&ps);
                GetClientRect(hwnd,&rect);
                showmonth(hdc,year,month,&rect);
                EndPaint(hwnd,&ps);
                break;
        case WM_COMMAND:
                switch(wParam) {
                        case QUIT:
                                PostQuitMessage(0);
                                break;
                        case ABOUT:
                                if((lpfnDlgProc=MakeProcInstance((FARPROC)About
                                DlgProc,hInst)) != NULL) {
                                        DialogBox(hInst,"AboutBox",hwnd,lpfnDlg
                                        Proc);
                                        FreeProcInstance(lpfnDlgProc);
                                }
                                return(0);

                }
                break;
        case WM_DESTROY:
                PostQuitMessage(0);
                break;
        }
        return(FALSE);
}


/* find the first day in a month */
int firstday(int year,int month)
{
        int i,d=0;

        for(i=STARTYEAR;i<year;++i) {
                if(isleap(i)) d += 366;
                else d += 365;
                d %= 7;
        }
        for(i=STARTMONTH;i<month;++i) {
                d += number_days[isleap(year)][i];
                d %= 7;
        }
        if(d==0) d=7;
        return(d-1);
```

**3-6** Continued.

```
}

void showmonth(HDC hdc,int year,int month,RECT *r)
{
        TEXTMETRIC tm;
        char b[128];
        int i,n,y,cx,cy,day,thisday;

        SetBkColor(hdc,RGB(192,192,192));
        GetTextMetrics(hdc,&tm);
        cx=tm.tmAveCharWidth;
        cy=tm.tmHeight+tm.tmExternalLeading;

        SetTextAlign(hdc,TA_CENTER);
        n=wsprintf((LPSTR)b,(LPSTR)"%s %u",(LPSTR)months[month],year);
        TextOut(hdc,r->left+((r->right-r->left)/2),r->top+cy,b,n);

        thisday=day=firstday(year,month);

        y=r->top+cy*3;

        SetTextAlign(hdc,TA_RIGHT);

        for(i=0;i<7;++i)
            TextOut(hdc,r->left+LEFT+i*(cx*DAYSPACE),y,days[i],3);

        y+=(cy*2);

        for(i=0;i < number_days[isleap(year)][month];++i,++day,++thisday) {
                if(thisday >= 7) {
                        y+=cy;
                        thisday=0;
                }
                n=wsprintf(b,"%u",i+1);
                TextOut(hdc,r->left+LEFT+thisday*(cx*DAYSPACE),y,b,n);
        }
}

/* return true if n is a leap year */
int isleap(int n)
{
        int r=0;

        if(!(n % 4)) r=1;
        if(!(n % 100)) {
                r = 0;
                if(!(n % 400)) r = 1;
        }
        return(r);
}

DWORD FAR PASCAL AboutDlgProc(HWND hwnd,WORD message,WORD wParam,LONG lParam)
{
        POINT point;

        switch(message) {
```

```
        case WM_INITDIALOG:
                return(TRUE);
        case WM_CTLCOLOR:
                if(HIWORD(lParam)==CTLCOLOR_STATIC ||
                   HIWORD(lParam)==CTLCOLOR_DLG) {
                        SetBkColor(wParam,RGB(192,192,192));
                        SetTextColor(wParam,RGB(0,0,0));

                        ClientToScreen(hwnd,&point);
                        UnrealizeObject(GetStockObject(LTGRAY_BRUSH));
                        SetBrushOrg(wParam,point.x,point.y);

                        return((DWORD)GetStockObject(LTGRAY_BRUSH));

                }
                if(HIWORD(lParam)==CTLCOLOR_BTN) {
                        SetBkColor(wParam,RGB(192,192,192));
                        SetTextColor(wParam,RGB(0,0,0));

                        ClientToScreen(hwnd,&point);
                        UnrealizeObject(GetStockObject(BLACK_BRUSH));
                        SetBrushOrg(wParam,point.x,point.y);

                        return((DWORD)GetStockObject(BLACK_BRUSH));
                }
                break;
        case WM_COMMAND:
                switch(wParam) {
                        case IDOK:
                                EndDialog(hwnd,wParam);
                                return(TRUE);
                }
                break;
        }

        return(FALSE);
}

/* that's it... */
```

**3-7(a)** The CALENDAR.RC file.

```
CalendarBox DIALOG 19, 19, 172, 112
STYLE WS_POPUP | WS_CAPTION | WS_VSCROLL | WS_HSCROLL | WS_MINIMIZEBOX
CAPTION "Calendar"
BEGIN
        DEFPUSHBUTTON "Quit", 101, 136, 88, 24, 12, WS_CHILD | WS_VISIBLE | WS_TABSTOP
        PUSHBUTTON "About", 102, 108, 88, 24, 12, WS_CHILD | WS_VISIBLE | WS_TABSTOP
END

Calendar ICON
BEGIN
        '00 00 01 00 01 00 20 20 10 00 00 00 00 00 E8 02'
        '00 00 16 00 00 00 28 00 00 00 20 00 00 00 40 00'
        '00 00 01 00 04 00 00 00 00 00 80 02 00 00 00 00'
        '00 00 00 00 00 00 00 00 00 00 00 00 00 00 00 00'
        '00 00 00 00 80 00 00 80 00 00 00 80 80 00 80 00'
```

**3-7(a)** Continued.

```
        '00 00 80 00 80 00 80 80 00 00 80 80 80 00 C0 C0'
        'C0 00 00 00 FF 00 00 FF 00 00 00 FF FF 00 FF 00'
        '00 00 FF 00 FF 00 FF FF 00 00 FF FF FF 00 00 00'
        '00 00 77 70 00 00 00 00 00 00 00 07 77 00 00'
        '77 7B BB 70 00 77 70 00 77 70 00 00 CC C7 00 09'
        '99 7B BB 70 0A AA 70 0E EE 70 00 00 CC C7 00 09'
        '99 7B BB 00 0A AA 70 0E EE 70 00 00 CC C0 00 09'
        '99 00 00 00 0A AA 00 0E EE 00 77 70 00 00 00 00'
        '00 00 00 00 00 00 00 00 0C CC 70 00 00 00 00'
        '00 00 00 00 00 00 00 00 0C CC 70 00 00 00 07'
        '77 77 70 00 00 07 77 00 00 0C CC 00 00 00 00 99'
        '9B BB 70 77 70 EE E7 77 70 00 00 00 07 77 00 99'
        '9B BB 7A AA 70 EE EC CC 70 00 77 70 DD D7 00 99'
        '9B BB 0A AA 70 EE EC CC 70 0D DD 70 DD D7 00 77'
        '70 00 0A AA 00 00 0C CC 00 0D DD 70 DD D0 09 99'
        '77 77 00 07 77 00 00 07 77 0D DD 00 00 00 09 99'
        'BB B7 00 EE E7 77 70 DD D7 00 00 00 00 00 99 99'
        'BB B7 77 EE EC CC 70 DD D7 00 00 00 00 00 99 97'
        'BB BA AA EE EC CC 77 DD D0 00 00 00 00 00 99 9B'
        'BB 7A AA 70 0C CC DD D7 00 00 00 00 00 00 99 9B'
        'BB AA AA 77 CC C7 DD D7 00 00 00 00 00 00 99 9B'
        'BB AA AE EE CC C7 DD D0 00 00 00 00 00 00 99 9B'
        'BB AA AE EE CC CD DD 70 00 00 00 00 00 00 99 9B'
        'BB AA AE EE CC CD DD 70 00 00 00 00 00 00 99 9B'
        'BB AA AE EE CC CD DD 70 00 00 00 00 00 00 99 9B'
        'BB AA AE EE CC CD DD 70 00 00 00 00 00 00 99 9B'
        'BB AA AE EE CC CD DD 70 00 00 00 00 00 00 99 9B'
        'BB AA AE EE CC CD DD 70 00 00 00 00 00 00 99 9B'
        'BB AA AE EE CC CD DD 70 00 00 00 00 00 00 99 9B'
        'BB AA AE EE CC CD DD 70 00 00 00 00 00 00 99 9B'
        'BB AA AE EE CC CD DD 70 00 00 00 00 00 00 99 9B'
        'BB AA AE EE CC CD DD 70 00 00 00 00 00 00 99 9B'
        'BB AA AE EE CC CD DD 70 00 00 00 00 00 00 99 9B'
        'BB AA AE EE CC CD DD 70 00 00 00 00 00 00 99 9B'
        'BB AA AE EE CC CD DD 00 00 00 00 00 00 00 FF 1F'
        'FF F8 F0 1C 71 F0 E0 18 61 F0 E0 38 61 F1 E3 F8'
        'E3 1F FF FF FE 1F FF FF FE 1F E0 7E 3E 3F C0 44'
        '07 F8 C0 04 07 10 C0 84 06 10 C7 8F 8E 11 80 E3'
        'E2 3F 80 C0 43 FF 00 00 43 FF 00 00 07 FF 00 18'
        '0F FF 00 00 0F FF 00 00 1F FF 00 00 1F FF 00 00'
        '1F FF 00 00 1F FF 00 00 1F FF 00 00 1F FF 00 00'
        '1F FF 00 00 1F FF 00 00 1F FF 00 00 1F FF 00 00'
        '1F FF 00 00 1F FF 00 00 1F FF 00 00 3F FF'
END

AboutBox DIALOG 86, 56, 200, 116
STYLE WS_POPUP | WS_CAPTION
CAPTION "About..."
BEGIN
        DEFPUSHBUTTON "Ok", IDOK, 88, 96, 24, 12, WS_CHILD | WS_VISIBLE | WS_TABSTOP
        CTEXT "Copyright \251 1993 Alchemy Mindworks Inc.", 102, 8, 40, 184, 8, WS
        _CHILD | WS_VISIBLE | WS_GROUP
        CTEXT "Calendar version 1.0", 101, 8, 8, 184, 8, WS_CHILD | WS_VISIBLE | WS
        _GROUP
        ICON "Calendar", -1, 92, 20, 16, 16, WS_CHILD | WS_VISIBLE
        CONTROL "The source code for this application... and numerous others... can be
```

```
        found in the book Canned Code, by Steve Rimmer, published by Windcrest/McGraw
        Hill (ISBN 0-8306-4512-8)", 103, "STATIC", SS_CENTER | WS_CHILD | WS_VISIBLE |
        WS_BORDER | WS_GROUP, 8, 52, 184, 36
END
```

**3-7(b)** The CALENDAR.PRJ file.

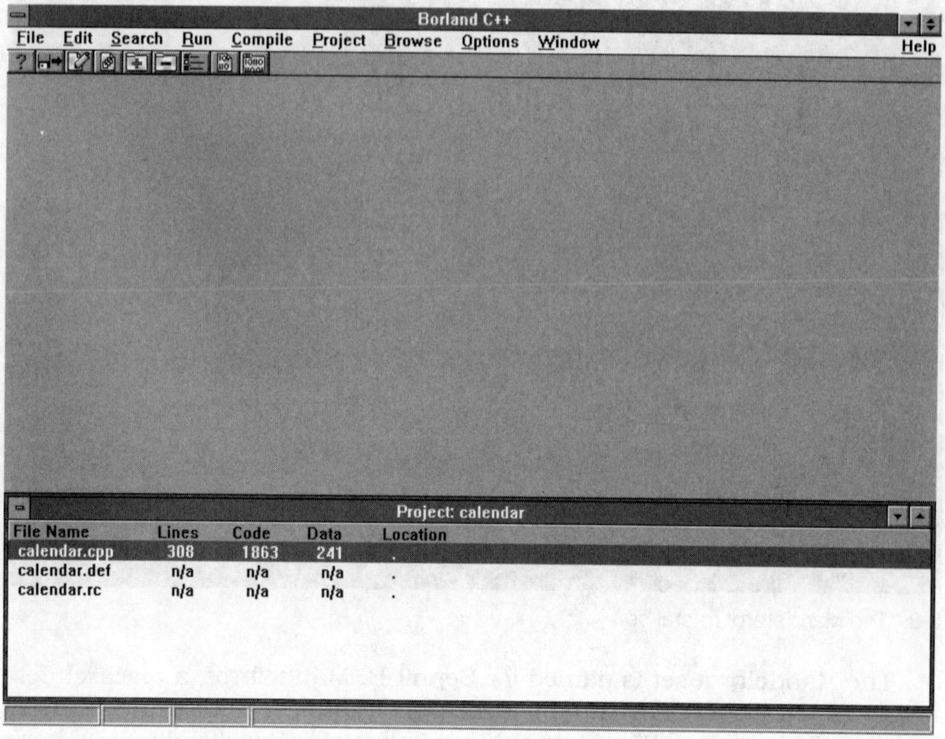


**3-7(c)** The CALENDAR.DEF file.

```
NAME            EXIT
DESCRIPTION     'Calendar'
EXETYPE         WINDOWS
CODE            PRELOAD MOVEABLE
DATA            PRELOAD MOVEABLE MULTIPLE
HEAPSIZE        1024
STACKSIZE       5120
```

# Plot a Mandelbrot fractal

Fractal geometry is one of the peculiarities to grow from the widespread availability of personal computers. While it certainly existed before there were computers to play with it, the intense calculation required to appreciate fractals is something that human mathematicians would have been unlikely to undertake in the absence of a machine.

Fractals such as the Mandelbrot set provide us with a surreal glimpse of the complex world of imaginary numbers. A plot of the Mandelbrot set is illustrated in 3-8.

**3-8** The Mandelbrot fractal set.

The Mandelbrot set is named for Benoit B. Mandelbrot, a research fellow at IBM's Thomas J. Watson Research Center. It's an exploration of some odd characteristics of imaginary numbers. Specifically, numbers with imaginary components in the range of 1.25 to −1.25 and real components in the range of −2 through 0.50 behave unpredictably if they're iterated through a particular calculation. The calculation is $z^2+c$, where *z* is a complex number beginning with zero and *c* is a complex number in the previous set. Here's the iterative process in pseudocode:

```
COMPLEX z=0,c;

for(n=0;n<MAX;++n) {
        if(z >= 2) break;
        z=z*z+c
}
```

Of course, there is no COMPLEX data type in C, and as you'll see in a moment, the real and imaginary components of a complex number must be handled as discrete entities to make a workable program.

If MAX in the foregoing bit of code is relatively large—approaching infinity in theory—it will be found that most complex numbers will simply increase indefinitely as they're iterated. Numbers in the range of the Mandelbrot set will behave differently. If you plot the result of iterating them on your screen, with the number of iterations required to drive $z$ to two or more displayed as different colors, you'll find yourself looking at 3-8.

The thing that makes the Mandelbrot set so fascinating is that the details along the edges of the bulbous figure that rests at its center are infinitely complex. You can "zoom in" on them to whatever degree you like, limited only by the accuracy of the floating point math your computer is capable of. Zooming in, in terms of the complex number plane, means reducing the range of numbers to be plotted and moving the initial point to somewhere other than $(-2r, 1.25i)$, the origin of the entire plot.

The catch to plotting the Mandelbrot set is that doing so is tremendously processor intensive. Each point in the interesting part of the set might require many thousands of floating point calculations, and there are more than 300,000 points to plot on a 640-×-480-pixel screen.

Mandelbrot "microscopes" far more sophisticated than the one discussed in this section have appeared to explore the Mandelbrot set using some clever cheating, or doing approximate calculations with integer mathematics. This is possible to a degree, although it places finite limits on the depth to which one can zoom in on the Mandelbrot set. Several close-up sections of the Mandelbrot set are illustrated in 3-9.

With all this fairly exotic number theory behind it, you'll probably find the actual source code for the Mandelbrot set program to be disappointingly short. In fact, calculating the values of the Mandelbrot set doesn't take a lot of code—just a lot of time. The MANDELB program, shown in 3-10, is all there is to creating simple fractals. Note that a good third of it handles setting up the display palette.

My version of MANDELB displays the Mandelbrot set in increasing densities of gray, mostly because it was used to create the figures for this section, which are in black and white. You can modify it if you like and substitute a more interesting palette. The colors originally assigned to Mandelbrot plots are wholly arbitrary, of course.

The MANDELB program, as it stands, will only run on a VGA card—you can certainly modify it for other display devices if you like. Unlike some of the other graphic applications discussed in this book, this one uses hard-wired code to drive mode 12H of a VGA card. The `setpixel` macro that does the actual plotting uses some complex VGA card manipulation to set points. For a complete discussion of how to work with 16-color VGA graphics, you might want to have a look at my book *Super VGA Graphics*, published by Windcrest.

As you'll unquestionably notice when you run it, MANDELB is slow. If you are using it on a system with a math coprocessor installed, be sure you set your compiler to use math chip floating point numbers. Note that the 80486DX and 80586 Pentium processors have on-chip floating point processors. A math coprocessor won't really make MANDELB run quickly, but it will improve its speed to some degree.

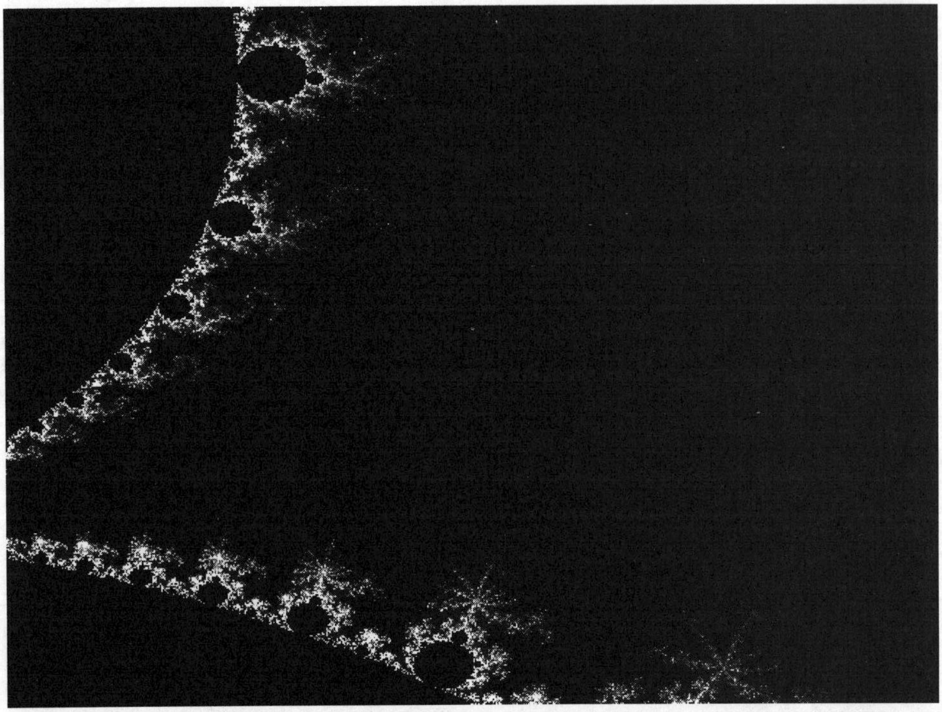

(a)

**3-9** Several close-up sections of the Mandelbrot set. Image (a) is at 0.15*i*, –1.05*r*, range 0.40; (b) is at 0.15*i*, –0.85*r*, range 0.40; (c) is at 0.15*i*, –0.25*r*, range 0.80; (d) is at 0.00*i*, –1.35*r*, range 0.80; (e) is at –1.05*i*, –0.15*r*, range 0.25; (f) is at –1.00*i*, –0.05*r*, range 0.05; and (g) is at –0.75*i*, –0.25*r*, range 0.25.

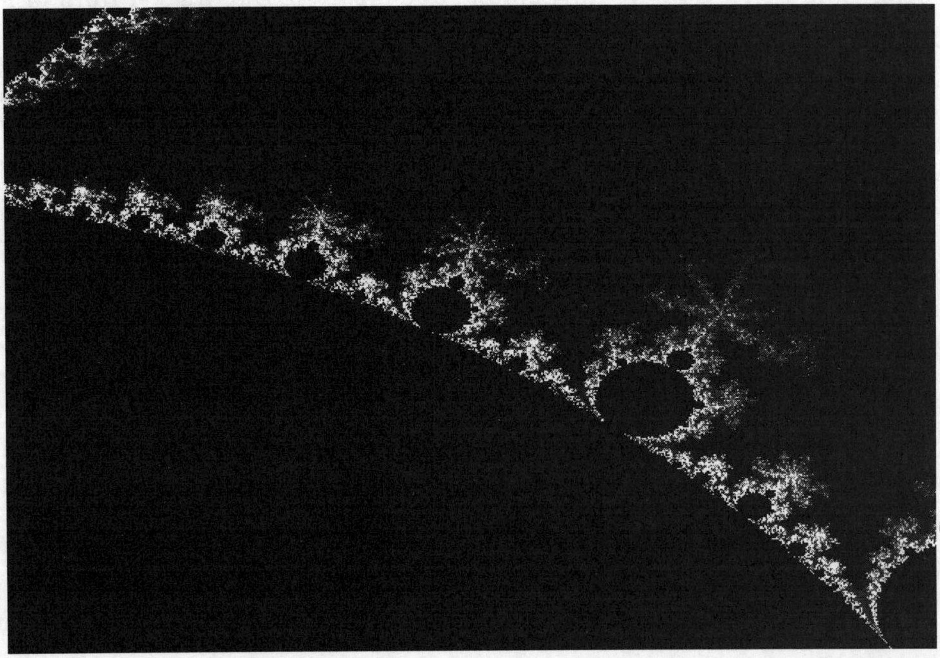

(b)

(c)

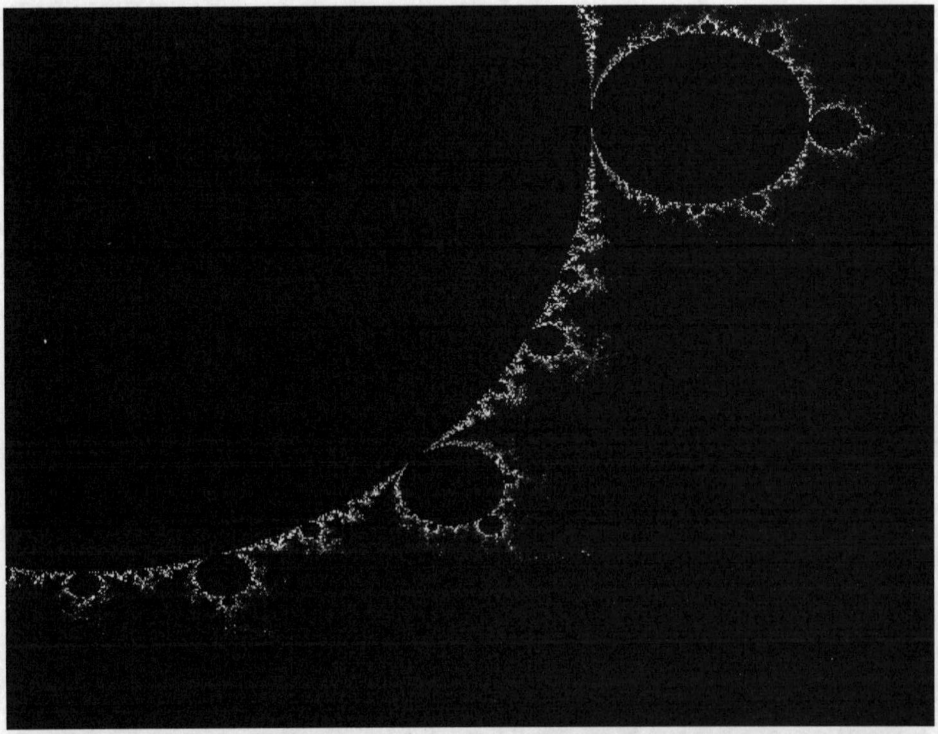

(d)

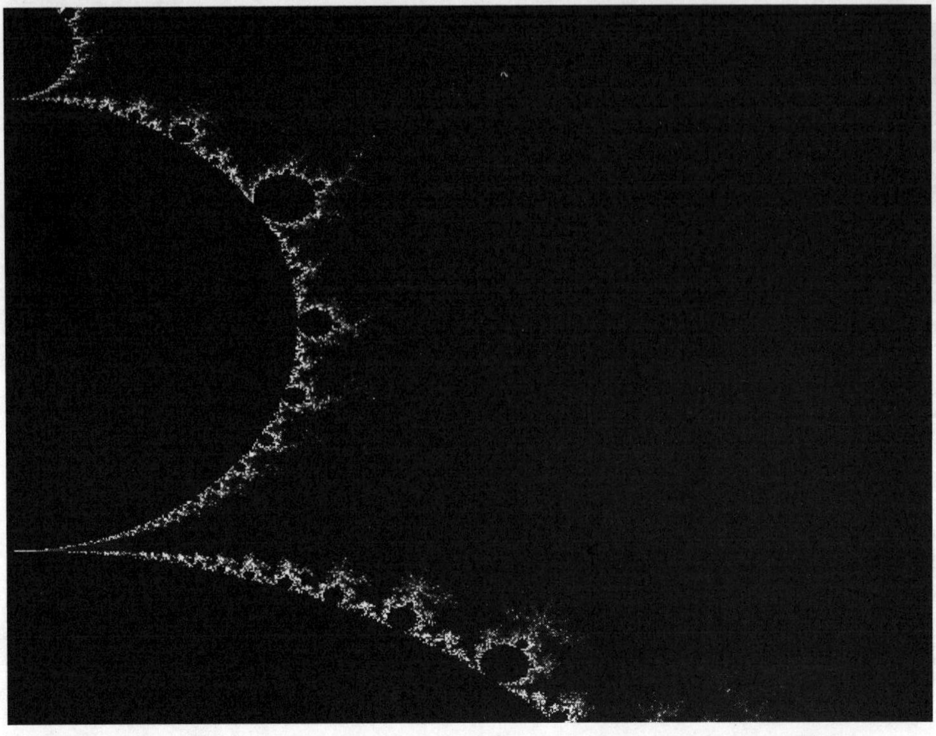

3-9 Continued.

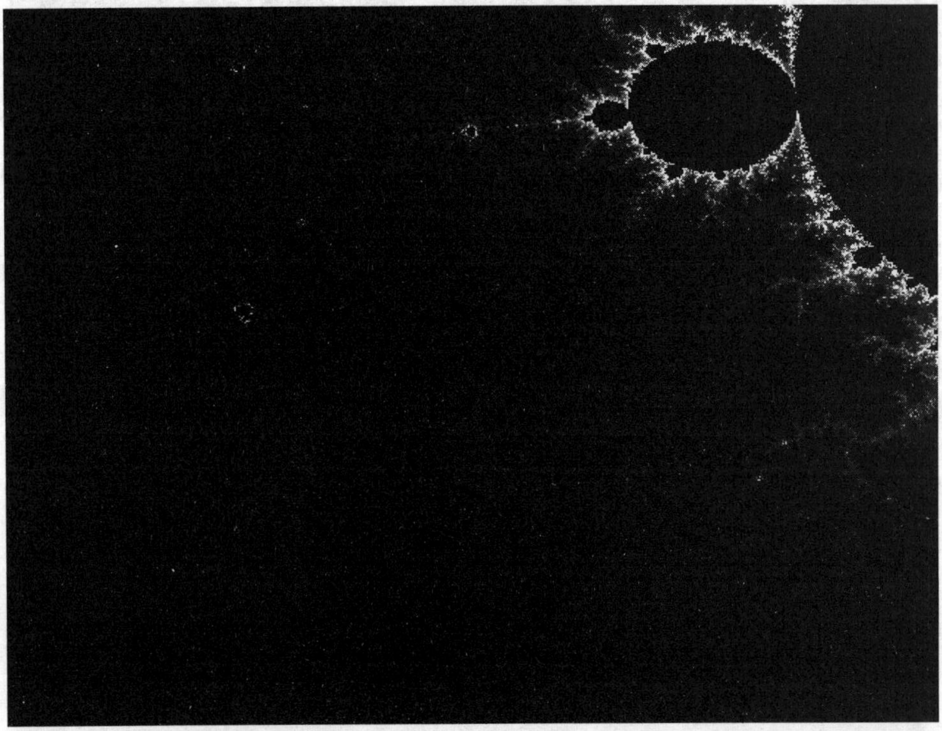

(e)

(f)

(g)

3-10 The MANDELB.C source code.

```
/*
        Mandelbrot fractal generator
        Copyright (c) 1993 Alchemy Mindworks Inc.
*/

#include "stdio.h"
#include "dos.h"
#include "math.h"

#define setpixel(x,y,c) { char *p; \
                          p=MK_FP(0xa000,SCREENTBL[(y)]+((x)>>3)); \
                          outp(0x3ce,8); outp(0x3cf,masktable[(x) & 0x0007]); \
                          outp(0x3ce,5); outp(0x3cf,2); \
                          *p=*p; *p=(c); \
                          outp(0x3ce,5); outp(0x3cf,0); \
                          outp(0x3ce,8); outp(0x3cf,255); }

#define MAXRANGE        512
#define COLOURS         16
#define SCREENWIDE      640
#define SCREENDEEP      480
#define SQUARE(n)       (n*n)

char masktable[8]={0x80,0x40,0x20,0x10,0x08,0x04,0x02,0x01};
```

**3-10** Continued.

```
unsigned int SCREENTBL[SCREENDEEP];

main(argc,argv)
	int argc;
	char *argv[];
{
	union REGS r;
	int x,y,z;
	double xfac,yfac;
	double xstart=-1.250;
	double ystart=-2.000;
	double range=2.500;
	double ca,cb,za,zb,sizefac,temp1,temp2;

	for(x=0;x<480;++x) SCREENTBL[x]=x*80;

	for(x=1;x<argc;++x) {
		switch(x) {
			case 1:
				xstart=atof(argv[x]);
				break;
			case 2:
				ystart=atof(argv[x]);
				break;
			case 3:
				range=atof(argv[x]);
				break;
		}
	}

	r.x.ax=0x0012;
	int86(0x10,&r,&r);

	makepalette();

	xfac=range / (double)SCREENWIDE;
	yfac=range / (double)SCREENDEEP;

	for(y=0;y < SCREENDEEP && !kbhit(); ++y) {
		ca=yfac*y+ystart;
		for(x=0;x < SCREENWIDE && !kbhit();++x) {
			za = 0.0 ;
			zb = 0.0 ;
			cb = xfac * (double)x + xstart;
			sizefac = sqrt(SQUARE(ca)+SQUARE(cb)) ;
			for(z=0;(sizefac < 2) && (z <= MAXRANGE) && !kbhit();++z) {
				temp1=SQUARE(za)-SQUARE(zb)+ca;
				temp2=(2*za*zb)+cb;
				sizefac=sqrt(SQUARE(temp1)+SQUARE(temp2));
				za=temp1;
				zb=temp2;
			}
			setpixel(x,y,z/(MAXRANGE/COLOURS));
		}
	}
	getch();
```

```
        r.x.ax=0x0003;
        int86(0x10,&r,&r);
}

makepalette()
{
        union REGS r;
        int i;

        for(i=0;i<16;++i) {
                r.x.ax=0x1000;
                r.h.bh=i;
                r.h.bl=i;
                int86(0x10,&r,&r);
        }

        outp(0x3c6,0xff);
        for(i=0;i<16;++i) {
                outp(0x3c8,i);
                outp(0x3c9,i<<2);
                outp(0x3c9,i<<2);
                outp(0x3c9,i<<2);
        }
}
```

Running on a 50-megahertz 80486 system compiled with floating point math enabled, MANDELB can take up to two hours per plot. Note that smaller values of MAXRANGE will produce less interesting plots, but ones that can be completed in minutes rather than hours. You might want to modify the program to include a command line parameter to set this. Low values of MAXRANGE are useful for scouting around the Mandelbrot set before you decide to tie up your computer for a couple of hours with a detailed plot.

If you execute MANDELB without any command line arguments it will plot the entire Mandelbrot set. You can zoom in on a specific area of the set by including three command line arguments: the imaginary start value first, the real start value second, and the range of points on the imaginary number plane to plot third. You might want to try the coordinates given in 3-8 to begin with, although there's an infinite universe of places to explore in the Mandelbrot set.

For a more complete discussion of Mandelbrot fractals, have a look at A. K. Dewdney's "Computer Recreations" column in the August 1985 edition of *Scientific American*.

# 4

# Programmers' toys

*"The price of purity is purists."*
—Graffiti

There are a lot of programs users never get to see. Some programs only exist to make the creation of other programs possible—or at least a bit easier. This is probably as it should be. Confronted with a document preprocessor, a recursion function, or a keyboard interrupt, most nonprogrammers will look around their desks for some paper clips to bend and hope the phone rings soon.

This chapter discusses a few gadgets to help you write better software, even if little of it is likely to make it to the real world in its present form.

## Use configuration blocks

Software configuration under DOS is a serious nuisance because no real mechanism for handling it exists in the operating system. There are several obvious ways to tell a DOS application how it's to behave when it runs, all of which have their drawbacks.

Under Windows, of course, applications can find your \WINDOWS directory in software, and hence can store things there with every hope of finding them again. A DOS application has no comparable facility.

The obvious way to store configuration options for a DOS application would be to write a configuration file to disk in the same subdirectory as the application it pertains to. This works admirably until someone attempts to run the application from another subdirectory, perhaps as a result of its being on the DOS command path. In this instance, the application will think it's starting up in the current directory, rather than on its own, and will as such be unable to locate its configuration file.

The way around this is to use a configuration block and write configuration changes to that. A *configuration block* is a data structure in the executable code for your application that contains all its configuration options and which can be modified by a configuration utility external to your application.

The procedure for setting all this up is a tad funky, because DOS wasn't written to allow for it. However, it does work, and it will provide you with a way to configure your software so that it never loses its configuration information. The configuration block becomes a part of your application's EXE file.

Let's begin by defining an example configuration block.

```
typedef struct {
        char sig[4];
        int textcolour;
        int boxcolour;
        int warningcolour;
        int screenlines;
        int printerport;
        char startup_directory[144];
        } CONFIG;
```

The actual data in the CONFIG structure is irrelevant, except that it's the information that's pertinent to setting up your application. Except for the `sig` element, you can store whatever fields you require in a CONFIG structure.

The `sig` element is a four-byte string that makes it possible to locate the configuration block in your EXE file. Make this a string that will not occur elsewhere in your application.

Having defined the information that you want to be configurable in your application, define a configuration block:

```
CONFIG theConfig = {
        "APP_",         /* the signature string */
        GREEN,          /* the text color */
        BLUE,           /* the box color */
        RED,            /* the warning color */
        50,             /* the number of lines on the screen */
        LPT1,           /* the printer port */
        "C:\\"          /* the startup directory */
        };
```

When your application is compiled, this data structure will exist somewhere in its EXE file.

In order for an external configuration utility to modify the data in `theConfig`, it must open your EXE file as if it were a normal binary file, seek to where this structure resides, read into a CONFIG object, change the relevant fields, and write the structure back to disk. None of this is all that tricky because an EXE file really is just a binary data file.

The only hard part is knowing where in the trackless expanse of a DOS EXE file your configuration block resides. Specifically, you must know the absolute offset into the file so you can program your configuration utility to seek to the correct location.

You can locate the configuration block easily with DEBUG. The catch to this is that when DEBUG is asked to load a file having the extension EXE, it does a real EXE load, splitting the file up into segments, initializing its fix-up tables, and so on, on the assumption that you might attempt to execute it under DEBUG. To force DEBUG to treat your EXE file like a simple binary file, do this:

```
COPY PROGRAM.EXE SCRAP
DEBUG SCRAP
```

You now want to search for the `sig` string in your configuration block. In this example it contains the bytes "APP_". To begin with, type `R` and hit Enter at the DEBUG dash prompt to have a look at the current register contents. Here's an example register display.

```
AX=0000  BX=0000  CX=0000  DX=0000  SP=FFEE  BP=0000  SI=0000  DI=0000
DS=1835  ES=1835  SS=1835  CS=1835  IP=0100  NV UP EI PL NZ NA PO NC
1835:0100 A4      MOVSB
```

Your DS segment value will probably be different than the one shown here. In this example I'd begin searching for the configuration block at location 1835:0000, like this:

```
S1835:0000,FFFF,"APP_"
```

This has instructed DEBUG to search from location 0000H to location FFFFH in memory segment 1835 for the string "APP_". If it doesn't find it, search the next 64 kilobytes of memory:

```
S2835:0000,FFFF,"APP_"
```

Continue doing this until the configuration block appears, as evidenced by DEBUG returning its location in memory. For example, it might come back with:

```
3835:8B42
```

You can now create an external configuration program to locate and modify the configuration block in your application's EXE file. Let's begin by defining where in the file the CONFIG object is to be found:

```
#define CONFIGSEG    0x2000    /* 2000H above the base segment */
#define CONFIGOFF    0x8a42    /* 0100H below the located string */
```

The CONFIGSEG value should be the difference between the segment at which DEBUG found your configuration block and the base segment at which your binary EXE file was loaded. In this case it's 3835H–1835H, for a difference of 2000H.

The CONFIGOFF value should be the offset into the segment where DEBUG found your configuration block, minus 0100H. For historical reasons, DEBUG loads binary files beginning at memory location 0100H rather than at 0000H.

Finally, here's how to actually load the configuration block into memory:

```
CONFIG theConfig;
FILE *fp;
long l;

if((fp-fopen("PROGRAM.EXE","rb+"))!=NULL) {
        l=((long)CONFIGSEG * 16L)+ CONFIGOFF;
        fseek(fp,l,SEEK_SET);
        fread((char *)&theConfig,1,sizeof(CONFIG),fp);
        if(!memcmp(theConfig.sig,"APP_",4)) {
                /* do the configuration */
                fseek(fp,l,SEEK_SET);
                fwrite((char *)&theConfig,1,sizeof(CONFIG),fp);
        }
        else puts("Can't find the configuration block");
        fclose(fp);
}
```

Using configuration blocks this way allows users of your applications to run them from anywhere on their systems. It makes the prospect of losing a configuration file cosmically unlikely, even in unusual environments such as networks.

In fairness, it's worth noting that there are three potential drawbacks to the system of configuration blocks. None are crippling, but they're worth being aware of.

The first is that the configuration block in your application's EXE file will tend to move around as you change your code, necessitating that you locate it and recompile your configuration utility each time you create a new version of your software.

The second is that because the configuration block in your application's EXE file is located by your configuration utility based on its offset relative to the beginning of the file, this whole procedure will fail if the block moves after you've compiled your application. While this might seem like an unlikely occurrence, it will happen if someone applies a run time file compressor to your EXE file, such as PKLITE. Once compressed, your application might run correctly but it will no longer be configurable.

Finally, this procedure actually modifies the contents of your application's EXE file. Some virus checking packages ostensibly catch viruses by watching for just this occurrence. In this case, users of your software who also have a virus checker installed in their systems might think that your application's EXE file has been infected with a virus, when in fact, it's only had its configuration block modified. A warning to this effect in your documentation is probably worth considering.

False-positive returns from virus checkers are a nuisance not to be lightly underestimated. A recent version of Norton Antivirus decided that the PKUNZIP file uncompressor contained the Maltese Amoeba virus, which in fact, it did not. Norton didn't inform its users of this directly, but rather issued a few press releases about the confusion and hoped the faux pas would go away quietly. One of my earlier books for Windcrest, *Super VGA Graphics*, included PKUNZIP on its companion disk. I still hear from a few readers every week who are certain that the disk in the back of the book contains a virus that will infect their hard drives if they attempt to read it.

## See if a drive is on-line

Having an application attempt to access an off-line disk drive, such as a floppy drive with its door open, can be a bit embarrassing. Far from doing something civilized, such as returning an error code, DOS will display its "Abort, Retry, Ignore" message and drop your users back to the command line. Beyond being inconvenient and highly unprofessional, this can convince your users that their computers have hung up. If you use the high-speed text mode screen function discussed earlier in this book, including the `HideCursor` call to dispatch the conventional text mode cursor, the "Abort, Retry, Ignore" message will be displayed beginning one line below the visible area of your screen. In this case, most users don't realize what has happened and that hitting A will get them back to DOS.

Prior to your software attempting to access a new drive, it should check to make sure that the drive in question is on-line and paying attention. This would seem to be a problem, however, inasmuch as any attempt to access an off-line drive—even if you just want to see if it's off-line—will provoke the DOS "Abort, Retry, Ignore" message.

In order to deal with this problem, it's necessary to understand the mechanism by which DOS gets at this message. In fact, it's generated by the default interrupt handler for INT 24H. This is the interrupt that DOS throws any time it encounters a disk error.

Knowing this bit of esoterica, you can devise a way around the "Abort, Retry, Ignore" message fairly easily. To test the status of the drive, you must redirect the vector for INT 24H to something a bit less destructive, attempt to access the drive, see what happened, and then restore the INT 24 vector to its former state. There's little more to a reliable drive status tester than this, except for a clearer vision of what "something a bit less destructive" might be.

When DOS throws an INT 24H to indicate that a disk error has occurred, it pushes an error code onto the stack, as well as the current AX, BP, and SI registers. A new INT 24H handler should check the error condition and set a flag if an error has returned. It should then issue a C language hardretn call to return to whatever your software was doing when the disk error occurred.

A program called ISDRIVE is illustrated in 4-1. It accepts a drive letter as a command line argument and tests the specified drive status.

This ISDRIVE program is useful as it stands in batch files because it returns a DOS error level based on the drive status. You can excise the test Disk function and its attendant code from it for your own applications.

**4-1** The ISDRIVE.C source code.

```
/*
Drive status checker
        Copyright (c) 1993 Alchemy Mindworks Inc.
*/

#include "stdio.h"
#include "dos.h"
#include "dir.h"
#include "process.h"
#include "ctype.h"
#include "stdlib.h"

int diskErrorHandler(int errval,int ax,int bp,int si);
char tempdir[144];
int diskErr;

main(argc,argv)
        int argc;
        char *argv[];
{
        int c;

        if(argc <= 1) error("Argument:            Letter of drive to check");

        c=toupper(argv[1][0]);
        if(c < 'A' || c > 'Z') error("Illegal argument");

        if(!testDisk(c-'A')) {
                printf("Drive %c: is on line.\n",c);
                exit(0);
        }
        else {
                printf("Drive %c: is off line or does not exist.\n",c);
                exit(1);
        }
}

/* critical error handler for drive change - not working yet */
testDisk(n)
        int n;
{
        void interrupt (*oldHarderr)();
        FILE *fp;
        char b[32];

        oldHarderr=getvect(0x24);
```

```
        harderr(diskErrorHandler);
        diskErr=0;
        getcwd(tempdir,80);
        sprintf(b,"%c:\\TEMP.DAT",n+'A');
        if((fp=fopen(b,"r")) != NULL) fclose(fp);
        setvect(0x24,oldHarderr);
        return(diskErr);
}

#pragma warn -par
int diskErrorHandler(errval,ax,bp,si)
        int errval,ax,bp,si;
{
        if(ax >=0) {
                diskErr=1;
                restoreDir(tempdir);
        }
        hardretn(2);
}

restoreDir(s)    /* restore a saved directory path */
        char *s;
{
        strupr(s);
        if(isalpha(s[0]) && s[1]==':') setdisk(s[0]-'A');
        chdir(s);
}


error(s)
        char *s;
{
        puts(s);
        exit(1);
}
```

## Shell to COMMAND.COM

No matter how sophisticated an application is, there are times when it's essential to get back to DOS. In many cases, the only way to arrange this is to exit the application, which is frequently time-consuming and invariably a nuisance. Any software whose architecture doesn't predate the fall of Rome should include a DOS shell option, such that one can quickly pop out to DOS, kill a few files or do some other light housekeeping, and then return to the application in question.

One of the few civilized aspects of DOS is that it's quite prepared to let you do this. An application having been spawned by DOS can in turn spawn other applications, a second copy of DOS being among them.

The only catch to running DOS shelled from another application is that some of your system memory will be tied up by the application in memory, making it impractical to run large or particularly memory-hungry applications in this condition.

Having a DOS prompt appear from within your application requires that you be able to do two things: locate COMMAND.COM and then subsequently run it. Locating it is fairly easy, as there will be an entry in your system environment table called COMPSEC that defines where it is. A call like this:

```
getenv("COMSPEC");
```

will return a pointer to the path to COMMAND.COM.

The C language `spawnl` function can be used to run COMMAND.COM as a child task of your current application. You will probably want to do some housekeeping before and after executing this function to clear the screen.

Here's a function that puts the whole works together. Call `dosShell` and a second copy of COMMAND.COM will run and begin accepting DOS commands until someone types `EXIT`. When `dosShell` returns, your application can get on with whatever it was doing.

```
dosShell()
{
        char b[144];
        strcpy(b,getenv("COMSPEC"));

        if(strlen(b)) {
                clrscr();
                printf("Type EXIT to return to...");
                if(spawnl(P_WAIT,b,NULL) == -1)
                        printf("Error: can't run COMMAND.COM");
        } else printf("Error: can't find COMMAND.COM");
}
```

The `dosShell` function should not be used in applications written in the tiny memory model; that is, ones that are ultimately to be converted to COM files. By definition, a COM file "owns" all the memory in your system while it's running. As COMMAND.COM must load into free memory to run, the `spawnl` function will always fail if it's running from a COM file.

## Find the processor type

There are a number of good reasons for knowing which generation of processor your software is running under. It can provide you with an approximate determination of the speed at which certain functions can be expected to run, possibly allowing you to calibrate delay loops. If you really want to optimize the way your applications perform, you might choose to have several versions of time-critical functions—one version written in 8086 code, one in the more efficient 80286 code, and so on.

The `CpuType` assembly language function in 4-2 will return the processor type as one of the following constants:

- 86—The processor is an 8088 or an 8086.
- 286—The processor is an 80286.

- 386—The processor is an 80386.
- 486—The processor is an 80486.

The CpuType function figures out the processor type by attempting to execute instructions that are valid on newer processors and illegal on older ones.

Honesty bids me to say that I've no idea who came up with this. It was discovered some while back on a bulletin board. It's deviously clever, though, and as nearly as I've been able to tell, utterly reliable.

**4-2** THE CPUTYPE.ASM source code.

```
; GET THE PROCESSOR TYPE - RETURNS        086 = 8088 OR 8086
;                                          286 = 80286
;                                          386 = 80386
;                                          486 = 80486
            PUBLIC _CpuType
_CpuType    PROC    FAR
            PUSHF                           ;SAVE OLD FLAGS

            MOV     DX,86                   ;TEST FOR 8086
            PUSH    SP                      ;IF SP DECREMENTS BEFORE
            POP     AX                      ;A VALUE IS PUSHED
            CMP     SP,AX                   ;IT'S A REAL-MODE CHIP
            JNE     CPUT_X                  ;8088,8086,80188,80186,NECV20/V30

            MOV     DX,286                  ;TEST FOR 286
            PUSHF                           ;IF NT (NESTED TASK)
            POP     AX                      ;BIT (BIT 14) IN THE
            OR      AX,4000H                ;FLAGS REGISTER
            PUSH    AX                      ;CAN'T BE SET (IN REAL MODE)
            POPF                            ;THEN IT'S A 286
            PUSHF
            POP     AX
            TEST    AX,4000H
            JZ      CPUT_X

            MOV     DX,386                  ;TEST FOR 386/486
            .386                            ;DO SOME 32-BIT STUFF
            MOV     EBX,ESP                 ;ZERO LOWER 2 BITS OF ESP
            AND     ESP,0FFFFFFFCH          ;TO AVOID AC FAULT ON 486
            PUSHFD                          ;PUSH EFLAGS REGISTER
            POP     EAX                     ;EAX = EFLAGS
            MOV     ECX,EAX                 ;ECX = EFLAGS
            XOR     EAX,40000H              ;TOGGLE AC BIT(BIT 18)
                                            ;IN EFLAGS REGISTER
            PUSH    EAX                     ;PUSH NEW VALUE
            POPFD                           ;PUT IT IN EFLAGS
            PUSHFD                          ;PUSH EFLAGS
            POP     EAX                     ;EAX = EFLAGS
            AND     EAX,40000H              ;ISOLATE BIT 18 IN EAX
            AND     ECX,40000H              ;ISOLATE BIT 18 IN ECX
            CMP     EAX,ECX                 ;IS EAX AND ECX EQUAL?
            JE      A_386                   ;YUP, IT'S A 386
            MOV     DX,486                  ;NOPE,IT'S A 486
```

**4-2** Continued.

```
A_386:
                PUSH    ECX                 ;RESTORE
                POPFD                       ;EFLAGS
                MOV     ESP,EBX             ;RESTORE ESP
                .8086
CPUT_X:         MOV     AX,DX               ;PUT CPU TYPE IN AX
                POPF                        ;RESTORE OLD FLAGS
                RET
_CpuType        ENDP
```

# Play background music

Being able to play mindless little tunes while your software is otherwise engaged is a feature of questionable worth, and one that you might want to apply sparingly if you apply it at all. It has the singular advantage of indicating that your application hasn't crashed if it's otherwise engaged in some deep inner thought, but it will make most people want to shoot their computers after a while. While long-term warranties are growing more and more comprehensive as the competition for hardware market share heats up, almost all of them can be successfully violated with a 12-gauge shotgun.

As with so many other things that a PC can do if you only knew how, DOS doesn't provide you with an easily accessible hook to handle background tasks. You can set one up for yourself, however, if you understand a bit about what a PC does when you aren't looking. In this case, it will require some understanding of the hardware interrupts PCs have available and how to hook into them.

About 18 times a second your computer throws the hardware equivalent of INT 1CH. In most cases, this has the effect of tying up a minute amount of your processor's time to do absolutely nothing—this interrupt leaps to an IRET statement lodged somewhere in your system BIOS and immediately returns. However, interrupt vectors can be changed, and you can have this interrupt leap to some other code if you like.

Unlike timing loops, the 1CH interrupt will run at the same speed on all computers, no matter how antediluvian and glacially slow they may be.

You can write a C language handler for the 1CH interrupt, with the result that your C code can be called 18 times a second to perform brief tasks. There are whole classes of things you should not attempt to do from within such a function—DOS calls, for example, would be a very bad idea—but things like manipulating data or playing music is well within the purview of an interrupt handler.

A background music player is fairly easy to envision under these circumstances. It would have to keep track of a list of instructions to play notes. If no note was currently playing when the 1CH interrupt called the music playing function, it would turn on the next note in the list and set a counter for the number of 1CH clock ticks the note is to play for. On each subsequent call to the music player the counter would be decremented until it reached zero, when the current note would be switched off and the process repeated.

Playing notes is fairly easy under Borland and Turbo C. The `sound` function will cause a tone of any frequency you like to emerge from your speaker, and `nosound` will switch it off. The pitch values passed to `sound` have to be integral, which makes a perfectly tuned scale impossible, but then the fidelity of a PC's speaker probably makes this a bit irrelevant.

Coming up with a convenient way to define the music to be played is the largest problem. While the program discussed in this chapter would probably make any one of a number of famous classical composers rise from the dead just to be able to die all over again, it represents a reasonable way to define music in a singularly limited environment.

The bit of music that the PLAYTUNE program in this section will play is illustrated in 4-3. You can ignore this if you don't sight-read music. This is a hornpipe called "Blue Peter"—you might also recognize it as being the very last bit of Mike Oldfield's first tubular Bells album. You'll know it when you hear it.

**4-3** Blue Peter—musical source code.

The music encoding system used by PLAYTUNE is pretty easy to understand. There are three types of musical events it can recognize: notes, rests, and octave changes. Notes are coded as the letter of the note, an optional sharp symbol, and then the duration of the note to be played. The duration value can be 1, 2, 4, 8, 16, or 32, for whole, half, quarter, eighth, sixteenth, and thirty-second notes. For example, "c#16" would be C-sharp, played as a sixteenth note.

Rests are encoded as "r" followed by the duration of the rest, as with notes. Octave changes are coded as "o" followed by an octave number. It's important to keep in mind that octave changes occur at C rather than at A. Each event must be followed by a space character.

This is the coding for the first few measures of "Blue Peter":

```
o3 c16 o2 b16 o3 c16 r16 o2 c8 c8 g16 f16 e16 g16 o3 c8 c16 e16
```

The beNoisy function in PLAYTUNE parses the current song string and plays it. It's set up by the setvect call in the main function of PLAYTUNE. Note that a call to getvect is used to fetch the old contents of the 1CH interrupt vector prior to calling setvect, and that this vector is restored before PLAYTUNE quits. This is very important, lest the 1CH interrupt find itself leaping into the blackness of space and taking your computer with it.

The source code for PLAYTUNE.C is illustrated in 4-4.

In order to illustrate that PLAYTUNE is actually doing something while it's playing music, it draws some graphics as it plays, all handled by the DoSomething function. These have absolutely nothing to do with playing music.

**4-4** The PLAYTUNE.C source code.

```
    /*
        Background music
        Copyright (c) 1993 Alchemy Mindworks

        Run this thing for half an hour and you'll
        start listing to port.
*/

#include "stdio.h"
#include "stdlib.h"
#include "dos.h"
#include "graphics.h"

typedef struct {
        int pitch;
        char name[3];
        } NOTE;

/* this is blue peter, a tradional hornpipe */
char song[]="o3 c16 o2 b16 o3 c16 r16 o2 c8 c8 g16 f16 e16 g16 o3 c8 c16 e16 "
            "d16 c16 d16 r16 o2 d8 d8 d16 c16 o1 b16 o2 d16 g8 g8 "
            "o2 a16 b16 o3 c16 o2 b16 "
            "a16 g16 a16 g16 "
            "f16 e16 f16 e16 "
            "d16 c16 d16 c16 "
            "o1 b16 a16 g16 a16 "
            "b16 o2 c16 d16 e16 "
            "f16 g16 e8 c8 c8 "
            "o3 c16 o2 b16 o3 c16 r16 c8 c8 "
            "c16 o2 b16 a16 r16 f8 f8 "
            "b16 o3 c16 d16 r16 d8 d8 d16 c16 o2 b16 r16 o2 g8 g8 "
            "o2 a16 b16 o3 c16 o2 b16 "
            "a16 o2 g16 a16 g16 "
            "f16 e16 f16 e16 "
            "d16 c16 d16 c16 "
            "o1 b16 a16 g16 a16 b16 o2 "
            "c16 d16 e16 f16 g16 e8 c8 c8"
            ;

NOTE scale[]={  262,"c",
                278,"c#",
```

```
                    294,"d",
                    312,"d#",
                    330,"e",
                    349,"f",
                    371,"f#",
                    392,"g",
                    416,"g#",
                    440,"a",
                    468,"a#",
                    494,"b"
                    };

#define SCALESIZE       (sizeof(scale)/sizeof(NOTE))

char *songpointer=NULL;
int octave=1;
int duration=4;
int pitch=-1;
int songindex=0;

void interrupt beNoisy(); /* little music function */

main()
{
        void interrupt (*oldTimer)();

        oldTimer=getvect(0x1c);
        setvect(0x1c,beNoisy);

        playtune(song);

        DoSomething();

        setvect(0x1c,oldTimer);
        nosound();
}

playtune(song)
        char *song;
{
        disable();
        songindex=0;
        songpointer=song;
        enable();
}

void interrupt beNoisy()
{
        static int count,busy;
        int i,n,gotnote=0;

        if(busy) return;

        if(songpointer == NULL) return;

        if(count > 1) {
                --count;
                return;
```

**4-4** Continued.

```
}

busy=1;

do {
        while(songpointer[songindex]==32) ++songindex;

        switch(n=tolower(songpointer[songindex])) {
                case 'a':
                case 'b':
                case 'c':
                case 'd':
                case 'e':
                case 'f':
                case 'g':
                        for(i=0;i<SCALESIZE;++i) {
                                if(n==scale[i].name[0]) {
                                        ++songindex;
                                        if(songpointer[songindex]=='#') {
                                                ++i;
                                                ++songindex;
                                        }
                                        pitch=scale[i].pitch;
                                        break;
                                }
                        }

                        n=atoi(songpointer+songindex);
                        if(n >= 1 && n <= 32) duration=32/n;
                        ++songindex;
                        gotnote=1;
                        break;
                case 'r':
                        ++songindex;
                        n=atoi(songpointer+songindex);
                        if(n >= 1 && n <= 32) duration=32/n;
                        pitch=-1;
                        ++songindex;
                        gotnote=1;
                        break;
                case 'o':
                        ++songindex;
                        n=atoi(songpointer+songindex);
                        if(n >= 1 && n <= 4) octave=n;
                        pitch=-1;
                        ++songindex;
                        break;
                case 0:
                        songindex=0;
                        pitch=-1;
                        duration=1;
                        octave=1;
                        gotnote=1;
                        break;
                default:
                        while(songpointer[songindex] != 32 &&
```

```
                                songpointer[songindex] != 0) ++songindex;
                        break;
                }
        } while (!gotnote);

        if(pitch==-1) nosound();
        else {
                nosound();
                sound(pitch*(1<<(octave-1)));
        }
        count=duration;
        busy=0;
}

DoSomething()
{
        int screenwide,screendeep;
        int d,m,i,n=0;

        detectgraph(&d,&m);

        if(d<0) return(0);
        initgraph(&d,&m,"");
        if(graphresult() < 0) return(0);
        setcolor(getmaxcolor());
        screenwide=getmaxx();
        screendeep=getmaxy();

        do {
                setcolor(n++);
                for(i=0;i<screenwide;i+=4) {
                        line(screenwide/2,screendeep/2,i,0);
                        line(screenwide/2,screendeep/2,i,screendeep-1);
                }
                for(i=0;i<screendeep;i+=4) {
                        line(screenwide/2,screendeep/2,0,i);
                        line(screenwide/2,screendeep/2,screenwide-1,i);
                }
        } while(!kbhit());
        getch();

        closegraph();
}
```

## Change the volume label of a disk

While in many cases the DOS volume name function is more of a nuisance than anything useful, you might have cause to change the volume name of a disk under software control if you choose to implement volume names for disk identification. The procedure for handling this is highly peculiar. The volume name for a disk is actually stored as a file with an odd attribute. The file itself contains nothing—only its name is important.

In principal, you'd change the volume name of a disk by deleting the old volume name file and writing a new one. The DOS file renaming function won't work on volume names. Unfortunately, the DOS path-based file functions won't work on them either. To delete and subsequently re-create a volume name file, you must use the old DOS 1.0 file block functions. The code for the function `setVolume` is illustrated in 4-5.

**4-5** The `setVolume` function source code.

```
setVolume(drive,name)
        int drive;
        char *name;
{
        union REGS r;
        struct SREGS sr;
        struct xfcb f;
        char *dta,b[64],s[16];

        if(testdisk(drive)) return(1);

        dta=getdta();
        setdta(b);

        sprintf(s,"%-11.11s",name);

        memset((char *)&r,0,sizeof(struct xfcb));

        f.xfcb_flag=0xff;
        f.xfcb_attr=0x08;
        f.xfcb_fcb.fcb_drive=drive+1;
        memset(f.xfcb_fcb.fcb_name,'?',11);

        r.x.ax=0x1100;
        r.x.dx=FP_OFF((char *)&f);
        sr.ds=FP_SEG((char *)&f);
        int86x(0x21,&r,&r,&sr);
        if(r.h.al==0x00) {
                memcpy(f.xfcb_fcb.fcb_ext+8,s,11);
                r.x.ax=0x1700;
                r.x.dx=FP_OFF((char *)&f);
                sr.ds=FP_SEG((char *)&f);
                int86x(0x21,&r,&r,&sr);
        }
        else {
                memcpy(f.xfcb_fcb.fcb_name,s,11);
                r.x.ax=0x1600;
                r.x.dx=FP_OFF((char *)&f);
                sr.ds=FP_SEG((char *)&f);
                int86x(0x21,&r,&r,&sr);
                r.x.ax=0x1000;
                r.x.dx=FP_OFF((char *)&f);
                sr.ds=FP_SEG((char *)&f);
                int86x(0x21,&r,&r,&sr);
        }
        setdta(dta);
        return((int)r.h.al & 0x00ff);
}
```

To use `setVolume`, pass the drive you want to change the volume of as it's first argument, where zero is drive A, one is drive B, and so on. Pass the new name for the volume as the second argument. Like conventional file names, volume names are limited to 11 characters.

Remember that `setVolume` makes a call to `testDisk` to make sure that the volume you're about to change the name of actually exists. You can remove this call if you like.

## Exit Windows quickly

One of the less dignified aspects of Windows is that it grovels and pleads for its life every time you attempt to terminate it. One can imagine future versions of it asking, "Do you want to end your Windows session?", "Do you *really* want to end your Windows session?", "Do you want to reconsider ending your Windows session?", "Have you given this matter sufficient reflection?", and so on.

The program in 4-6 is EXIT, a quicker way out of Windows. It creates a very small dialog that lives in the lower right corner of your screen. It has a button called "Exit." Click on it and you'll be back to DOS with no complaints, whining, questions about your intentions, or petitions for mercy.

**4-6** The EXIT.CPP source code.

```
/*
        Exit to DOS
        Copyright (c) 1993 Alchemy Mindworks Inc.
*/

#include <windows.h>
#include <dir.h>
#include <alloc.h>
#include <stdio.h>
#include <ctype.h>

int PASCAL WinMain(HANDLE hInstance,HANDLE hPrevInstance,LPSTR lpszCmdParam,int nCmdShow);
BOOL FAR PASCAL ExitProc(HWND hwnd,WORD message,WORD wParam,LONG lParam);

#define         EXIT_BUTTON         101

HANDLE hInst;

#pragma warn -par
int PASCAL WinMain(HANDLE hInstance,HANDLE hPrevInstance,
                  LPSTR lpszCmdParam,int nCmdShow)
{
        FARPROC dlgProc;
        int r=0;

        hInst=hInstance;
```

**4-6** Continued.

```
        dlgProc=MakeProcInstance((FARPROC)ExitProc,hInst);
        r=DialogBox(hInst,"ExitBox",NULL,dlgProc);

        FreeProcInstance(dlgProc);

        return(r);
}

BOOL FAR PASCAL ExitProc(HWND hwnd,WORD message,
                         WORD wParam,LONG lParam)
{
        RECT r;
        int x,y;

        switch(message) {
                case WM_INITDIALOG:
                        GetWindowRect(hwnd,&r);
                        x=GetSystemMetrics(SM_CXSCREEN)-
                                (r.right-r.left);
                        y=GetSystemMetrics(SM_CYSCREEN)-
                                (r.bottom-r.top);
                        SetWindowPos(hwnd,NULL,x,y,0,0,SWP_NOSIZE);
                        return(FALSE);
                case WM_COMMAND:
                        if(wParam==EXIT_BUTTON) ExitWindows(0L,0);
                        return(TRUE);
        }
        return(FALSE);
}
/* that's it... */
```

In addition, you'll need EXIT.RC, EXIT.DEF, and EXIT.PRJ, as illustrated in 4-7. If you put EXIT.EXE in the Startup group of Program Manager, it will be ready to beam you back to Earth whenever you need it.

**4-7(a)** The EXIT.RC file.

```
ExitBox DIALOG 18, 18, 50, 14
CAPTION "Exit to DOS"
STYLE DS_MODALFRAME | WS_POPUP | WS_CAPTION
BEGIN
        PUSHBUTTON "Exit", 101, 0, 0, 50, 14, WS_CHILD | WS_VISIBLE | WS_TABSTOP
END
ExitIcon ICON
BEGIN
        '00 00 01 00 01 00 20 20 10 00 00 00 00 00 E8 02'
        '00 00 16 00 00 00 28 00 00 00 20 00 00 00 40 00'
        '00 00 01 00 04 00 00 00 00 00 80 02 00 00 00 00'
        '00 00 00 00 00 00 00 00 00 00 00 00 00 00 00 00'
        '00 00 00 00 80 00 00 80 00 00 00 80 80 00 80 00'
```

```
              '00 00 80 00 80 00 80 80 00 00 80 80 80 00 C0 C0'
              'C0 00 00 00 FF 00 00 FF 00 00 00 FF FF 00 FF 00'
              '00 00 FF 00 FF 00 FF FF 00 00 FF FF FF 00 00 00'
              '00 00 00 00 00 00 00 00 00 00 00 00 00 00 00 00'
              '00 00 00 00 00 00 00 00 00 00 00 00 00 00 00 00'
              '00 00 00 00 00 00 00 00 00 00 00 00 00 00 00 00'
              '00 00 00 00 00 00 00 00 00 00 00 00 00 00 00 00'
              '00 00 00 00 00 00 00 00 00 00 00 00 00 00 00 00'
              '00 00 00 00 00 00 00 00 00 00 00 00 00 00 00 00'
              '00 00 00 00 00 00 00 00 00 00 00 00 00 00 00 01'
              '11 11 11 11 11 11 11 11 11 11 11 11 11 00 00 99'
              '99 99 99 99 99 99 99 99 99 99 99 99 91 10 09 99'
              '99 99 99 99 99 99 99 99 99 99 99 99 99 10 09 99'
              '99 99 99 99 99 99 99 99 99 99 99 99 99 10 09 99'
              '99 33 33 39 39 99 99 39 39 99 93 99 99 10 09 99'
              '9B BB BB 9B 39 99 9B 3B 39 99 B3 99 99 10 09 99'
              '9B 39 99 9B 39 99 9B 3B 39 99 B3 99 99 10 09 99'
              '9B 39 99 99 B3 99 B3 9B 39 99 B3 99 99 10 09 99'
              '9B 33 33 99 9B 3B 39 9B 39 99 B3 99 99 10 09 99'
              '9B BB B9 99 99 B3 99 9B 39 99 B3 99 99 10 09 99'
              '9B 39 99 99 9B 3B 39 9B 39 99 B3 99 99 10 09 99'
              '9B 39 99 99 B3 99 B3 9B 39 99 B3 99 99 10 09 99'
              '9B 33 33 3B 39 99 9B 3B 39 99 B3 39 99 10 09 99'
              '9B BB BB 9B 39 99 9B 3B 99 BB BB B3 99 10 09 99'
              '99 99 99 99 99 99 99 99 99 99 99 99 99 10 09 99'
              '99 99 99 99 99 99 99 99 99 99 99 99 99 00 00 99'
              '99 99 99 99 99 99 99 99 99 99 99 99 90 00 00 00'
              '00 00 00 00 00 00 00 00 00 00 00 00 00 00 00 00'
              '00 00 00 00 00 00 00 00 00 00 00 00 00 00 00 00'
              '00 00 00 00 00 00 00 00 00 00 00 00 00 00 00 00'
              '00 00 00 00 00 00 00 00 00 00 00 00 00 00 00 00'
              '00 00 00 00 00 00 00 00 00 00 00 00 00 00 00 00'
              '00 00 00 00 00 00 00 00 00 00 00 00 00 00 00 00'
              '00 00 00 00 00 00 00 00 00 00 00 00 00 00 00 00'
              '00 00 00 00 00 00 00 00 00 00 00 00 00 00 FF FF'
              'FF FF FF FF FF FF FF FF FF FF FF FF FF FF FF FF'
              'FF FF FF FF FF FF FF FF FF FF E0 00 00 03 C0 00'
              '00 01 80 00 00 01 80 00 00 01 80 00 00 01 80 00'
              '00 01 80 00 00 01 80 00 00 01 80 00 00 01 80 00'
              '00 01 80 00 00 01 80 00 00 01 80 00 00 01 80 00'
              '00 01 80 00 00 01 80 00 00 03 C0 00 00 07 FF FF'
              'FF FF FF FF FF FF FF FF FF FF FF FF FF FF FF FF'
              'FF FF FF FF FF FF FF FF FF FF FF FF FF FF'
END
```

**4-7(b)** The EXIT.DEF file.

```
NAME            EXIT
DESCRIPTION     'Exit to DOS'
EXETYPE         WINDOWS
CODE            PRELOAD MOVEABLE
DATA            PRELOAD MOVEABLE MULTIPLE
HEAPSIZE        1024
STACKSIZE       5120
```

**4-7(c)** The EXIT.PRJ file.

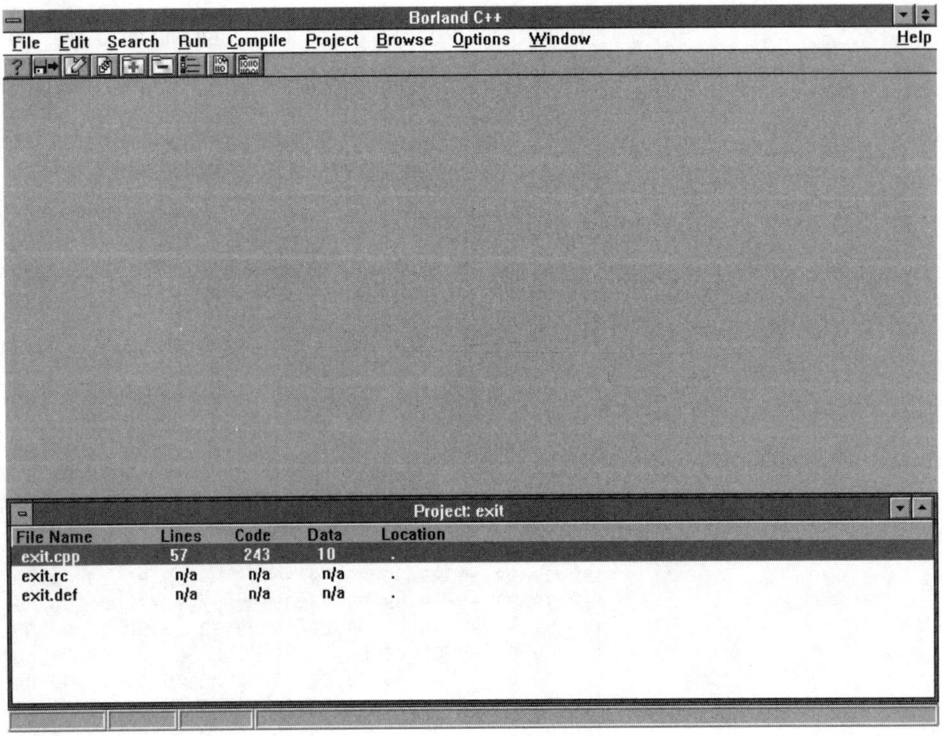


## Reboot your system

There are few software applications for doing a cold reboot of your computer—you might want to do so if you write a configuration program that modifies the CONFIG.SYS or AUTOEXEC.BAT files of the computers it runs on. The procedure for doing a cold reboot is pretty simple:

```
JMP FAR 0FFFFH:0F000H
```

There is no C language function to jump into oblivion, but if you find you have to do so from C, you can create one. Here's a very simple program to have your computer leap off a cliff and reincarnate itself:

```
#include "dos.h"

main()
{
        _emit_(0xea,0x00,0x00,0xff,0xff);
}
```

The `_emit_` macro inserts the bytes that define the preceding JMP instruction into the ultimate executable file that this program will generate.

# Create C or assembly language from binary data

There are uncountable applications for compiling or assembling large amounts of data into an application rather than reading it from a disk file or other repository. Large amounts of data can be defined as anything that would be inconvenient or potentially troublesome to type into your source code by hand.

You have two in-house gadgets that address this problem. While neither is all that elegant, they serve to sneak past a welter of keyboard bashing. The first, BIN2ASC, is discussed in this section. The other, PRELINK, appears in a moment.

The BIN2ASC utility accepts two or three command line arguments. The first is a path to some binary data. The second is a path to a file into which to write equivalent data statements. The third, if you use it, is a switch to define the target language for the data statements. This can be "/C" for C language data, "/A" for assembly language data, or "/W" for Windows resource script hexadecimal data.

The source code for BIN2ASC is illustrated in 4-8. Not a model of efficient software or lucid code, it has the advantage of having been around for ages, and hence of having all its wrinkles removed.

**4-8** The BIN2ASC.C source code.

```
#include "stdio.h"

main(argc,argv)
        int argc;
        char *argv[];
{
        FILE *src,*dest;
        int c,i=0,af=1,cf=0,wf=0,n=7,pnl=1;

        if((src=fopen(argv[1],"rb")) != NULL) {
                if((dest=fopen(argv[2],"wa")) != NULL) {
                        if(argc > 3 && !memicmp(argv[3],"/C",2)) {
                                af=0;
                                cf=1;
                        }
                        if(argc > 3 && !memicmp(argv[3],"/W",2)) {
                                af=0;
                                wf=1;
                                n=15;
                        }
                        /*
                        if(af) fprintf(dest,"\n\t\tDB\t");
                        if(cf) fprintf(dest,"\t");
                        if(wf) fprintf(dest,"\t'");
                        */
                        while((c=fgetc(src)) != EOF) {
                                if(pnl) {
                                        if(af) fprintf(dest,"\n\t\tDB\t");
```

**4-8** Continued.

```
                                        if(cf) fprintf(dest,",\n\t");
                                        if(wf) fprintf(dest,"'\n\t'");
                                        pnl=0;
                                }

                                if(af) fprintf(dest,"0%02.2XH",c & 0xff);
                                if(cf) fprintf(dest,"0x%02.2x",c & 0xff);
                                if(wf) fprintf(dest,"%02.2X",c & 0xff);
                                if(i++==n) {
                                        pnl=1;
                                        i=0;
                                }
                                else {
                                        if(af) fprintf(dest,",");
                                        if(cf) fprintf(dest,",");
                                        if(wf) fprintf(dest," ");
                                }
                        }
                        fprintf(dest,"\n");
                        fclose(dest);
                }
        }
}
```

You can, of course, convert any file of any type into text data using BIN2ASC. For example, this is how I got the COM file for the self-displaying text in chapter 1 into a C language array. Note, however, that huge data objects can slow down your compiler considerably and make your final applications slower to boot up.

## Create object modules from binary data

There's a considerably more elegant way to include data objects in your applications. Rather than turn them into source code, compile or assemble, and then link them back to binary files, you can turn them into object modules directly, linking them to your application. To link an object module to an application being created by your C compiler, simply add the name of the module to the project file for your program.

Addressing the data in an object module requires that you understand a bit about how Borland's C compilers actually name and link functions. Specifically, when a C language program attempts to reference a function or a data object in another module, your C compiler will add an underbar to the beginning of its name. As such, if you write a line like:

```
printf("Arrow velocity in furlongs per minute: %lu",arrowspeed);
```

the symbol that will actually get linked in your program will be `_printf`.

Knowing that C will expect to see an underbar at the beginning of an external symbol, you must make sure that one appears in the names you give data objects in your object modules.

The source code for another inelegant command line utility, PRELINK, is illustrated in 4-9. This version of PRELINK has been written to create object modules to link to Borland languages. However, you might have to modify it a bit if you want to use it with languages from other manufacturers, such as Microsoft. Several reference books published by Microsoft explain the object module format in exacting detail should you want to investigate it further. If you have a look through the source code for PRELINK you probably won't want to.

**4-9** The PRELINK.C source code.

```
/*
        prelink - binary data to Microsoft OBJ module
        converter copyright (c) 1990 Alchemy Mindworks Inc.
*/

#include "stdio.h"
#include "alloc.h"

#define         buffersize          0xfff0

FILE *infile, *outfile;
char *buffer;
unsigned int buffsize=0;
main(argc,argv)
        int argc;
        char *argv[];
{
        puts("Prelink version 1.0 copyright "
             "(c) 1990 Alchemy Mindworks Inc.");
        if(argc > 3) {
                if((buffer=malloc(buffersize))!=NULL) {
                        if((infile=fopen(argv[1],"rb")) != NULL) {
                                if((outfile=fopen(argv[2],"wb")) != NULL) {
                                        fillbuffer();
                                        trecord();
                                        lnames("\004DATA\006DGROUP\005_DATA");
                                        segmentdef();
                                        groupdef();
                                        drecord();
                                        pnames(argv[3]);
                                        endmodule();
                                        fclose(outfile);
                                }
                                fclose(infile);
                        } else printf("%s not found.\n",argv[1]);
                        free(buffer);
                } else puts("Memory allocation error");
        }
        else {
```

**4-9** Continued.

```
                puts("     PRELINK <source file> <destination file> <symbol>");
        }
}

fillbuffer()
{
        static char b[16]="\xa0\x04\x00\x01\x00\x00";
        char *p;
        int c;

        p=buffer+6;
        memcpy(buffer,b,6);
        do {
                c=fgetc(infile);
                if(c!=EOF) {
                        *p++=c;
                        ++buffsize;
                        ++buffer[1];
                        if(!buffer[1])++buffer[2];
                }
        } while(c !=EOF && p < buffer+buffersize);
}

endmodule()         /* write a module end record */
{
        static char b[16]="\x8a\x02\x00\x00";

        checksum(b);
        wrecord(b);
}

segmentdef()         /* write a segment deffinition record */
{
        static char b[16]="\x98\x07\x00\x48\x00\x00\x04\x02\x01";

        b[4]=buffsize & 0xff;
        b[5]=buffsize >> 8;
        checksum(b);
        wrecord(b);
}

groupdef()          /* write a group deffinition record */
{
        static char b[16]="\x9a\x04\x00\x03\xff\x01";

        checksum(b);
        wrecord(b);
}

pnames(s)         /* write a public names record */
        char *s;
{
        static char b[128]="\x90\x00\x00\x00\x01\x00";
        unsigned int i=6;

        while(*s) {
```

```
                b[i++]=*s++;
                ++b[5];
        }
        b[1]=i+1;
        checksum(b);
        wrecord(b);
}

drecord()           /* write a data record */
{
        checksum(buffer);
        wrecord(buffer);
}

trecord()           /* write a t record */
{
        static char b[16]="\x80\x03\x00\x01\x41\x3b";

        wrecord(b);
}

lnames(s)           /* write a list of names record */
        char *s;
{
        static char b[128]="\x96\x00\x00\x00";
        unsigned int i=4;

        while(*s) b[i++]=*s++;
        b[1]=i-2;
        checksum(b);
        wrecord(b);
}

wrecord(s)          /* write a record */
        char *s;
{
        unsigned int i;

        for(i=0;i<3;++i) fputc(s[i],outfile);
        for(i=0;i<(unsigned int)(s[1] + (s[2] <<8));++i) fputc(s[i+3],outfile);
}

checksum(p)         /* set the checksum for record p */
        char *p;
{
        unsigned int l,i,c = 0;

        l=(p[1]+(p[2]<<8))+2;

        for(i=0;i<l;++i) c = c + *p++;
        c = (c ^ 0xff)+1;
        *p=c;
        return(c);
}
```

The PRELINK program accepts three arguments: the name of the binary file you want to create an object module from, the name of the object module you want to create, and the symbol you want to assign to the data. The symbol should be in uppercase and begin with an underbar.

SHOWEYE, an example program that illustrates how to use a linked-in data object from an object module created by PRELINK is illustrated in 4-10. This program uses a graphic fragment of the sort expected by the Borland `putimage` function to draw a bitmap of a girl's eye on your screen. The bitmap can be found on the companion source code disk for this book as GIRLSEYE.BIN.

**4-10** The SHOWEYE.C source code.

```
/*
        Example of data linked as an object module
        Copyright (c) 1993 Alchemy Mindworks
*/

#include "stdio.h"
#include "graphics.h"
#include "alloc.h"

extern char GIRLSEYE[];                 /* in the GIRLSEYE.OBJ module */
char *mono2ega(char *source);

main()
{
        char *p;
        int d,m;

        detectgraph(&d,&m);

        if(d<0) return(0);
        initgraph(&d,&m,"");
        if(graphresult() < 0) exit(1);

        if(getmaxcolor()==2) putimage(10,10,GIRLSEYE,NOT_PUT);
        else {
                if((p=mono2ega(GIRLSEYE)) != NULL) {
                        putimage(10,10,p,NOT_PUT);
                        free(p);
                }
        }

        getch();

        closegraph();
}

char *mono2ega(source)
        char *source;
{
        char *p;
        int x,y,j,ls,sz;

        x=1+source[0]+(source[1] << 8);
        y=1+source[2]+(source[3] << 8);
```

```
        if((sz=imagesize(0,0,x,y)) != -1) {
                if((p=malloc(sz)) != NULL) {
                        memcpy(p,source,4);
                        ls=(x+7)/8;
                        for(j=0;j<y;++j) {
                                memcpy(p+4+((j*4)*ls),source+4+(j*ls),ls);
                                memcpy(p+4+ls+((j*4)*ls),source+4+(j*ls),ls);
                                memcpy(p+4+(ls*2)+((j*4)*ls),source+4+(j*ls),ls);
                                memcpy(p+4+(ls*3)+((j*4)*ls),source+4+(j*ls),ls);
                        }
                        return(p);
                }
        } else return(NULL);
}
```

To compile this program, you would begin by converting GIRLSEYE .BIN to GIRLSEYE.OBJ, like this:

```
PRELINK GIRLSEYE.BIN GIRLSEYE.OBJ _GIRLSEYE
```

Next, create a project for SHOWEYE that contains the following files:

```
SHOWEYE.C
GIRLSEYE.BIN
```

The `mono2ega` function in SHOWEYE allows the bitmap fragment in GIRLSEYE, essentially a monochrome picture, to be drawn correctly on a 16-color display. There are much more complete discussions of bitmaps, `putimage`, and related issues in my books *Graphical User Interface Programming* and *Super VGA Graphics*, both published by Windcrest.

Note that SHOWEYE expects to find a BGI driver for your display card when it runs.

The PRELINK program is a bear of very little brain, and as such it does have its limitations. One of these is that it's only useful for creating fairly small object modules. Feeding it source binary files in excess of about 4 kilobytes should be avoided.

## Use extended memory

The megabyte of memory space addressed directly by an 8086-series processor probably seemed like a lot of real estate once. However, even if about a third of it wasn't tied up with the system BIOS, video display, and other paraphernalia of a PC's memory-mapped system requirements, it would still be grossly inadequate for much of the application software that people run today. There might well be high-end microprocessor-controlled toasters and furnace controls that have more memory.

Later generations of processors, beginning with the 80286, were able to address more than a megabyte of memory space, but because the PC's BIOS and other immovable objects resided at the top of the original 1-megabyte address space, it was impractical to simply tack this extra memory onto the conventional system memory. Rather, the additional memory was placed beyond the 1-megabyte address range and accessed through a protocol called "extended" memory, or XMS. This is singularly inelegant. In real mode, the way DOS-based applications typically work, extended memory can't be used to run code, but only to store data.

Extended memory is accessed through an extended memory driver that loads through your CONFIG.SYS file. The most common of these is HIMEM.SYS, which is included with DOS and Windows. More sophisticated memory managers, such as 386$^{MAX}$ and Quarterdeck's QEMM offer more flexible use of extended memory, but for the sake of this discussion they all do effectively the same thing.

An extended memory manager serves as a central clearinghouse for requests to use high memory, as well as providing a convenient, relatively easy interface to it. Calling for extended memory through HIMEM.SYS both relieves you of the task of writing some fairly ugly looking 80286 assembly language code to deal with your extra memory directly, as well as making sure that your use of extended memory won't mangle that of another program—such as SMARTDRV or RAMDISK.

You can call your extended memory manager to allocate and free extended memory and to ascertain how much extended memory is available. Because of the way the extended memory manager is called, it's more practical to create the actual interface to it as an assembly language module, which can then be added to the project file of your application. The module, XMEM.ASM, is shown in 4-11.

**4-11** The XMEM.ASM source code.

```
;
;               Extended memory control functions
;               Copyright (c) 1989, 1993 Alchemy Mindworks Inc.
;
;

VERSION         EQU     1                       ;VERSION
SUBVERSION      EQU     0                       ;SUBVERSION

_AOFF           EQU     6                       ;FAR STACK OFFSET

;THIS MACRO FETCHES THE DATA SEGEMENT
LDATASEG        MACRO
                PUSH    AX
                MOV     AX,_DATA
                MOV     DS,AX
                POP     AX
                ENDM

ENABLE_A20      MACRO
                PUSH    AX
                PUSH    BX
                MOV     AH,5
                CALL    CS:[CONTROL]
```

```
                POP     BX
                POP     AX
                ENDM

DISABLE_A20     MACRO
                PUSH    AX
                PUSH    BX
                MOV     AH,4
                CALL    CS:[CONTROL]
                POP     BX
                POP     AX
                ENDM

XMEM_TEXT       SEGMENT BYTE PUBLIC 'CODE'
                ASSUME  CS:XMEM_TEXT,DS:_DATA

;THIS FUNCTION INITIALIZES THE DRIVER
;               CALLED AS
;               get_xmem();
;
;               Returns the version number or -1 if no driver
;
                PUBLIC  _get_xmem
_get_xmem       PROC    FAR
                PUSH    BP
                MOV     BP,SP
                PUSH    DS
                PUSH    ES
                MOV     AX,4300H
                INT     2FH
                CMP     AL,80H
                JE      GETX1

                MOV     AX,0FFFFH
                JMP     GETX2

GETX1:          MOV     AX,4310H

                INT     2FH
                MOV     WORD PTR CS:[_CONTOFF],BX
                MOV     WORD PTR CS:[_CONTSEG],ES

                MOV     AX,0000H
                CALL    CS:[CONTROL]

GETX2:          POP     ES
                POP     DS
                POP     BP
                RET
_get_xmem       ENDP

;THIS FUNCTION MOVES EXTENDED MEMORY
;               CALLED AS
;               move_xmem(p);
;               p = pointer to move structure
;                       /* returns true if successfull */
;
                PUBLIC  _move_xmem
```

**4-11** Continued.

```
_move_xmem      PROC    FAR
                PUSH    BP
                MOV     BP,SP
                PUSH    DS
                PUSH    ES

                ENABLE_A20

                MOV     SI,[BP + _AOFF + 0]     ;OFFSET OF STRUCTURE
                MOV     DS,[BP + _AOFF + 2]     ;SEGMENT OF STRUCTURE

                MOV     AH,11
                CALL    CS:[CONTROL]

                DISABLE_A20

                POP     ES
                POP     DS
                POP     BP
                RET
_move_xmem      ENDP

;THIS FUNCTION DEALLOCATES EXTENDED MEMORY
;               CALLED AS
;               dealloc_xmem(h);
;               int h;  /* handle to deallocate */
;                       /* returns true if successfull */
;
                PUBLIC  _dealloc_xmem
_dealloc_xmem   PROC    FAR
                PUSH    BP
                MOV     BP,SP
                PUSH    DS
                PUSH    ES

                ENABLE_A20

                MOV     DX,[BP + _AOFF + 0]
                MOV     AH,10
                CALL    CS:[CONTROL]

                DISABLE_A20

                POP     ES
                POP     DS
                POP     BP
                RET
_dealloc_xmem   ENDP

;THIS FUNCTION ALLOCATES EXTENDED MEMORY
;               CALLED AS
;               alloc_xmem(n);
;               int n; /* number of kilobytes to allocate */
;                      /* returns handle or -1 if error */
;
                PUBLIC  _alloc_xmem
```

```
_alloc_xmem     PROC    FAR
                PUSH    BP
                MOV     BP,SP
                PUSH    DS
                PUSH    ES

                ENABLE_A20

                MOV     AH,8
                CALL    CS:[CONTROL]
                CMP     AX,[BP + _AOFF + 0]
                JL      ALLOC1

                MOV     DX,[BP + _AOFF + 0]         ;ALLOCATE THE MEMORY
                MOV     AH,9
                CALL    CS:[CONTROL]

                OR      AX,AX
                JZ      ALLOC1

                MOV     AX,DX
                JMP     ALLOC2

ALLOC1:         MOV     AX,0FFFFH

                DISABLE_A20

ALLOC2:         POP     ES
                POP     DS
                POP     BP
                RET
_alloc_xmem     ENDP

;THIS FUNCTION RETURNS THE AMOUNT OF FREE XMS MEMORY
;               CALLED AS
;               coreleft_xmem();
;
                PUBLIC  _coreleft_xmem
_coreleft_xmem  PROC    FAR
                PUSH    BP
                MOV     BP,SP
                PUSH    DS
                PUSH    ES

                ENABLE_A20

                MOV     AH,8
                CALL    CS:[CONTROL]

                DISABLE_A20

                POP     ES
                POP     DS
                POP     BP
                RET
_coreleft_xmem  ENDP

;THIS FUNCTION CONVERTS A POINTER TO AN INTEL LONG
```

**4-11** Continued.

```
;               CALLED AS
;               long ptr2long(p);
;               char *p
;
                PUBLIC  _ptr2long
_ptr2long       PROC    FAR
                PUSH    BP
                MOV     BP,SP

                MOV     AX,[BP + _AOFF + 0]       ;OFFSET OF POINTER
                MOV     DX,[BP + _AOFF + 2]       ;SEGMENT OF POINTER

                POP     BP
                RET
_ptr2long       ENDP

;THIS FUNCTION IS A DUMMY RETURN FOR UNSET PROCEDURES
_DUMMY          PROC    FAR
                MOV     AX,0FFFFH
                RET
_DUMMY          ENDP

CONTROL         LABEL   DWORD
_CONTOFF        DW      _DUMMY
_CONTSEG        DW      XMEM_TEXT

XMEM_TEXT       ENDS
DGROUP          GROUP   _DATA,_BSS
_DATA           SEGMENT WORD PUBLIC 'DATA'

_DATA           ENDS

_BSS            SEGMENT WORD PUBLIC 'BSS'
_BSS            ENDS
                END
```

The XMEM module provides a number of new functions to whatever applications it's bolted onto. The first of these is the initialization call to make sure that an extended memory driver exists and thereafter to initialize it. Here's how it works:

```
if(get_xmem() < 0x0200) puts("No XMS driver");
```

The `get_xmem` function actually returns the version number of your extended memory driver, with the major version number in the high-order byte and the minor revision number in the low-order byte. It will return −1 if no extended memory manager can be found.

It's often useful to know how much free extended memory is available. Here's the call to do so:

```
coreleft_xmem();
```

The coreleft_xmem function returns the number of free kilobytes of extended memory as an unsigned integer. To work out the number of bytes, cast this value to long and multiply it by 1024L.

To allocate some extended memory:

```
int handle

if((handle=alloc_xmem(size))==-1
    puts("Can't allocate extended memory");
```

The alloc_xmem function expects to be passed an unsigned integer defining the number of kilobytes of memory you want to allocate. It will return a handle to an allocated memory block if the request was successful or –1 if it failed. There are several things to keep in mind about all this. To begin with, you can't allocate blocks of extended memory that are smaller than 1 kilobyte, and all requests for allocation should be rounded up to the nearest kilobyte.

Second, extended memory handles are a relatively scarce resource. In designing an application that will make use of multiple extended memory buffers it's a good idea to combine them into one, lest you find that there is more extended memory available than there are handles to access it.

Once you no longer need an extended memory buffer, you should pass its handle to dealloc _xmem. It's very important to keep in mind that unlike conventional DOS memory, extended memory is not automatically deallocated when your program terminates. It must be explicitly freed with a call to dealloc _xmem; otherwise, it will be orphaned, and subsequently inaccessible, until you reboot your computer.

To actually access extended memory, you must move all or part of an allocated extended memory buffer in or out of a conventional memory buffer. The buffers involved are specified by setting up fields in an XMOVE object. This is what one looks like:

```
typedef struct {
        unsigned long length;
        unsigned int sourceH;
        unsigned long sourceOff;
        unsigned int destH;
        unsigned long destOff;
        } XMOVE;
```

The length element of an XMOVE structure specifies the number of bytes to move. It's important that this value always be rounded up to the nearest 16 bytes. To this end, length values should always be specified with the following macro:

```
#define roundup(n)        (((n_+15L)>>4)<<4)
```

The sourceH element of an XMOVE object is the extended memory handle for the memory block you want to move data from, or zero if the source is in conventional memory. The `sourceOff` value is the offset into the extended memory buffer you want to access, or a far pointer to the conventional memory you'll be moving data to or from. In most cases, the former condition will be zero. You might want to use the `ptr2long` function in the XMEM module for the latter. Make sure you include a prototype in your programs to declare its return value as being a long integer.

The `destH` and `destOff` elements of an XMOVE object behave like the `sourceH` and `sourceOff` elements, save that they address the destination of the move. Unless you have cause to move data between two extended memory blocks, either `sourceH` or `destH` will always be zero.

This is how you would copy the contents of a conventional buffer to a previously allocated extended memory buffer:

```
XMOVE xmove;
xmove.length = (long)roundup(DATASIZE);
xmove.sourceH=0;
xmove.sourceOff=ptr2long(p);
xmove.destH=handle;
xmove.destOff=0L;
if(!move_xmem(&xmove)) puts("Can't write to extended memory");
```

In this example, `DATASIZE` is the size of the block to move, `p` is the conventional memory buffer where your data initially resides, and `handle` is an extended memory handle, as returned by `alloc xmem`. The `move xmem` function does the actual move—it will return a false value if the move was not successful. Calls to `move xmem` will fail if you pass it an invalid extended memory handle, or if you attempt to access more extended memory than you allocated.

The call to get data back from an extended memory buffer is similar to the previous one, except that the source and destination handles and offsets have been reversed.

```
xmove.length = (long)roundup(DATASIZE);
xmove.sourceH=handle;
xmove.sourceOff=0L;
xmove.destH=0;
xmove.destOff=ptr2long(p);
if(!move_xmem(&xmove)) puts("Can't read from extended memory");
```

A program called TESTXMEM to exercise the extended memory interface is illustrated in 4-12. It fills a large buffer with random numbers, derives a checksum of the buffer, writes the buffer to extended memory, and then fills it with zeros. On retrieving the data from extended memory, it calculates the checksum again. If all is well, the two checksums will be the same, indicating that the data in question has indeed made the trip to extended memory and is back safely.

**4-12** The TESTXMEM.C source code.

```
/*
        Extended memory exerciser
        Copyright (c) 1993 Alchemy Mindworks Inc.
*/

#include "stdio.h"
#include "stdlib.h"
#include "alloc.h"

#define         BLOCKSIZE        98307L

#define         roundup(n)        (((n+15L)>>4)<<4)

typedef struct {
        unsigned long length;
        unsigned int sourceH;
        unsigned long sourceOff;
        unsigned int destH;
        unsigned long destOff;
        } XMOVE;

unsigned long ptr2long(char *p);
unsigned int coreleft_xmem();

main()
{
        XMOVE xmove;
        char huge *p;
        long n;
        unsigned int size;
        int i,handle;
        puts("Exercise extended memory copyright (c) 1993 Alchemy Mindworks Inc.");

        if((p=farmalloc(BLOCKSIZE))==NULL)
            error("Can't allocate conventional memory");

        puts("Creating a block of random numbers");
        randomize();
        for(n=0;n<<BLOCKSIZE;++n) p[n]=random(256);

        printf("The source checksum is %u\n",checksum(p,BLOCKSIZE));

        if((i=get_xmem()) << 0x0200)
            error("Extended memory manager not found");

        printf("Extended memory version %u.%u\n",i>>8,i & 0x00ff);

        printf("There are %lu bytes of extended memory available\n",
           (long)coreleft_xmem()*1024L);

        size=(unsigned int)(roundup(BLOCKSIZE)/1024L);

        if((handle=alloc_xmem(size+1))==-1)
            error("Can't allocate extended memory");

        xmove.length = (long)roundup(BLOCKSIZE);
```

**4-12** Continued.

```
        xmove.sourceH=0;
        xmove.sourceOff=ptr2long((char *)p);
        xmove.destH=handle;
        xmove.destOff=0L;
        if(!move_xmem(&xmove)) {
                dealloc_xmem(handle);
                error("Can't write to extended memory");
        }

        for(n=0;n<BLOCKSIZE;++n) p[n]=0;

        xmove.length = (long)roundup(BLOCKSIZE);
        xmove.sourceH=handle;
        xmove.sourceOff=0L;
        xmove.destH=0;
        xmove.destOff=ptr2long((char *)p);
        if(!move_xmem(&xmove)) {
                dealloc_xmem(handle);
                error("Can't read from extended memory");
        }

        printf("The destination checksum is %u\n",checksum(p,BLOCKSIZE));

        dealloc_xmem(handle);
        farfree((char *)p);

        puts("All done");
}

checksum(p,size)
        char huge *p;
        long size;
{
        long n;
        unsigned int a=0;

        for(n=0;n<size;++n) a+=p[n];
        return(a);
}

error(s)
        char *s;
{
        puts(s);
        exit(1);
}
```

If you'll be writing applications that use a lot of storage, it's almost certain you'll want to access extended memory. While doing so involves somewhat more work than simply calling `malloc` would, it will avail you of vastly more storage. It's a major cheat around some initial shortsightedness in the architecture of PC systems, but it's one that will be here for some time to come.

# 5
# Disks and disk files

*"If you can't do it well, learn to enjoy doing it badly."*
—Graffiti

Disks can be whatever you want them to be—an alternate universe full of games, an ordered set of data mapping every known orbiting object bigger than a cat's brain, thousands of scanned pictures of questionable taste, and so on. The adaptable nature of disks, allowing them to store whatever you can think of putting in a file, offers a wealth of possibilities for disk gadgets.

Just as human beings have greatly developed visual senses, and as such have based a technology and a culture primarily on things they can see, personal computers are greatly dependent on mass storage and the idea that information can be stored as quantum units; that is, as files. One of the elemental aspects of making many sorts of applications work well is in creating workable ways to manipulate files.

This chapter looks at a number of things to make your software better able to handle the exigencies of a disk.

## Write-protect a hard drive

While hard drives began life as big floppies with better warranties, they're seethingly complex things now. Errant software—or errant viruses—writing unexpectedly to your hard drive can do some very nasty things to it. Despite the exhortations in DOS primers to do so, backing up a 200-megabyte hard drive is not a thing to be done lightly or often. Having the file allocation table of your hard drive scrambled will almost certainly spoil your whole day.

Unlike floppy disks, hard drives do not have write-protect notches. There is no mechanical way to keep one safe in the presence of potentially destructive beta software or applications that might have been infected with a virus. However, you can arrive at software write protection that is almost as effective.

Except in very exotic circumstances, all writing to a hard drive is handled through its system BIOS extension. The interrupt that speaks to hard drives is 13H. As with all PC interrupts, you can intercept INT 13H calls and do something with them other than what was intended for them.

For example, in order to write a track to your hard drive, INT 13H must be called with the AH register set to three. To write-protect a hard drive, then, you could watch for INT 13H with AH containing three and fail any such requests. In practice, there are several INT 13H calls you must deal with this way.

The source code for NOWRITE, a small resident program that will watch all the INT 13H calls issued by any software running on your machine and fail those that involve writing to your hard drive, is illustrated in 5-1. Calls that involve reading are unaffected.

**5-1** The NOWRITE.ASM source code.

```
;
;           Hard drive write protect
;           Copyright (c) 1993 Alchemy Mindworks Inc.
;
;           With code from various sources, originally
;           from PC magazine, I think.
;

CSEG        SEGMENT
            ASSUME  CS:CSEG
            ORG     100H

START:      JMP     INITIALIZE

SIG:        DB      "NOWRITE_"

OLDINT13    DD      ?           ; ORIGINAL INTERRUPT 13 VECTOR
SWITCH      DB      0FH         ; ON/OFF SWITCH FOR PROTECTION

NEWINT13    PROC    FAR
                                ;CHECK FOR
            CMP     AH,03H      ;... A DISK WRITE
            JZ      CHECKSTAT

            CMP     AH,05H      ;... A DISK FORMAT (VERY NASTY)
            JZ      CHECKSTAT

            CMP     AH,06H      ;... FORMAT TRACK AND SET BAD SECTOR
            JZ      CHECKSTAT

            CMP     AH,07H      ;... FORMAT DRIVE
            JZ      CHECKSTAT
```

```
                CMP     AH,0BH          ;... WRITE LONG
                JZ      CHECKSTAT

                CMP     AH,0FH          ;... WRITE SECTOR BUFFER
                JZ      CHECKSTAT

                CMP     AH,13H          ;... DRIVE DIAGNOSTIC
                JZ      CHECKSTAT

                CMP     AH,19H          ;... PARK HEADS ON A PS/2
                JZ      CHECKSTAT

                CMP     AH,1AH          ;... FORMAT ESDI DISK ON A PS/2
                JZ      CHECKSTAT

CONTINUE:       JMP     CS:[OLDINT13]   ;CALL THE REAL INT 13H HANDLER

CHECKSTAT:      CMP     SWITCH,00H      ; IS THE WRITE PROTECT ON?
                JNZ     CONTINUE
                CMP     DL,00H          ; IS THE A DRIVE SELECTED?
                JZ      CONTINUE
                CMP     DL,01H          ; IS THE B DRIVE SECLECTED
                JZ      CONTINUE

                MOV     AH,03H          ;MAKE THE REQUEST FAIL... WP ERROR
                STC                     ;SET CARRY FOR FAILURE
                RET     2

NEWINT13        ENDP

INITIALIZE:     MOV     DX,OFFSET SIG   ; OFFSET TO BEGIN CODE SEARCH
                MOV     AX,CS            ;... LOOK THROUGH THE PSPs TO
                MOV     ES,AX           ;... FIND A MATCH FOR OUR
                                        ;... SIGNATURE STRING
NEXTSEG:        DEC     AX
                MOV     DS,AX
                MOV     SI,DX
                MOV     DI,DX

                MOV     CX,0004H
                CLD
                REPE    CMPSW
                JNZ     NOTFOUND

                CMP     DS:SWITCH,0FH
                JNZ     TOGGLESW

NOTFOUND:       CMP     AX,0001H
                JNZ     NEXTSEG

                MOV     SWITCH,00H

                MOV     AX,3513H        ;GET THE OLD INT 13H VECTOR
                INT     21H             ;... AND SAVE IT

                MOV     WORD PTR CS:[OLDINT13],BX
                MOV     WORD PTR CS:[OLDINT13+2],ES
```

**5-1** Continued.

```
                PUSH    CS
                POP     DS

                MOV     DX, OFFSET PROTECT_ON
                MOV     AH,09H
                INT     21H             ; SAY THAT WRITE PROTECTION IS ON

                MOV     DX,OFFSET NEWINT13
                MOV     AX,2513H
                INT     21H             ; POINT TO OUR NEW INTERRUPT

                LEA     DX,INITIALIZE
                ADD     DX,15
                MOV     CL,4
                SHR     DX,CL

                MOV     AX,3100H        ;BE A TSR
                INT     21H

; TOGGLE THE SWITCH IF NOWRITE HAS BEEN LOADED BEFORE
TOGGLESW:       NOT     DS:SWITCH
                CMP     DS:SWITCH,00H   ; IS SWITCH ON?
                JZ      ON
                MOV     DX, OFFSET PROTECT_OFF
                JMP     EXIT
ON:             MOV     DX, OFFSET PROTECT_ON

EXIT:           MOV     AH,09H
                PUSH    CS
                POP     DS
                INT     21H             ; PRINT THE STATUS
                INT     20H

PROTECT_ON      DB      "Your hard drive is write-protected$"
PROTECT_OFF     DB      "Your hard drive is NOT write protected$"

CSEG            ENDS

                END     START
```

The NOWRITE program is fairly easy to use. The first time you run it, NOWRITE loads itself into memory and starts protecting your hard drive. Running it a second time toggles it off, and then on again, and so on. Note that for invocations subsequent to the first, NOWRITE doesn't actually reload itself, but merely finds the first copy of itself in memory and toggles a flag.

The NOWRITE program is a fairly typical DOS TSR; that is, a program that loads itself into memory, hooks some vectors, and remains resident. It consists of two sections: the handler and the installer. The handler, the NEWINT13 procedure, is what does all the work. It watches all the calls to INT 13H and if the SWITCH flag is set, it fails those that involve writing.

Any calls that don't involve writing are passed along to the real INT 13H handler by calling OLDINT13.

The installer, INITIALIZE, begins by trolling through the program segment prefixes in memory looking for the signature string of NOWRITE. If it finds a copy in memory it merely toggles the SWITCH flag and prints a message as to whether your hard drive is currently write-protected or not. If NOWRITE has not been loaded, it hooks the INT 13H vector and uses an INT 21H call to make the NEWINT13 code resident. Note that when NEWINT13 is resident, the INITIALIZE code will be discarded.

You can test NOWRITE by invoking it and attempting to copy a file to your hard drive. When NOWRITE is working, you should encounter a write-protect error.

While NOWRITE offers a considerable degree of protection for your hard drive, it's by no means infallible. A sufficiently clever virus might figure a way around it, possibly by sneaking past your BIOS and manipulating your hard drive controller directly. An up-to-date virus detection program, such as McAfee's SCAN, is a useful thing to have.

## Do optimal file copying

Being confronted with lots of files to copy onto lots of floppies can be a challenge of cosmic proportions. It can also be intensely frustrating, because DOS does not provide a way to arrange the order of files being copied such that they fill multiple disks efficiently. Nor does it provide a way to copy such that when one destination floppy is full you can pause and replace it with a fresh disk. Rather, it tells you that your target disk is full and aborts.

In fact, optimal file copying is fairly easy to arrange. Here's how it works in theory:

```
ReadAllFiles();
SortFilesBySize();

do {
        GetFreeSpace();
        CopyLargestFile();
        DeleteFileFromList();
} while(FilesAreLeft());
```

In practice this bit of pseudocode has some fairly cavernous holes in it, but it will serve to explain the premise of the program discussed in this section.

To begin with, you must fetch all the file names and file sizes from the source directory for the files to be copied and store them as elements in an array. This array should be sorted, such that the entries for the largest files are first.

The do loop in the previous example handles copying the files. Each iteration begins by seeing how much free space is left on the destination drive and selecting the largest file that will fit on it. This is fairly easy to do, as the largest file in the array will always be the first one. If the first file won't fit, it will skip to the next, and so on, until it finds one that will. If none of the files in the array will fit on the destination disk, the destination disk is full—or at least it's as full as it's likely to get.

Once a file has been copied, its entry is removed from the array of file names. In practice it's more efficient to simply flag it as being no longer of interest.

The previous example requires two more elements to make it into a workable procedure. It must deal with disk swaps when the destination disk is full. It must also allow for the possibility of files that are too large to fit on the destination disk even if the disk is completely empty. As things stand now, if such a file were to find its way into the file name array the function would loop forever.

The C language source code for MCOPY is illustrated in 5-2. This is a program I've used for ages, and it has evolved into a fairly streamlined bit of code.

**5-2** The MCOPY.C source code.

```
/*
        MCOPY 2.0 Multiple file copying function
        Copyright (c) 1992 Alchemy Mindworks Inc.
*/

#include "stdio.h"
#include "stdlib.h"
#include "dos.h"
#include "dir.h"
#include "alloc.h"
#include "process.h"
#include "conio.h"
#include "string.h"

#define SCREENBACK      BLUE

#define NORMAL          (YELLOW + (SCREENBACK << 4))
#define BRIGHT          (WHITE + (SCREENBACK << 4))
#define DIM             (LIGHTCYAN + (SCREENBACK << 4))

#define SCREENWIDE      80
#define SCREENDEEP      25

#define STATUSLEFT      6
#define STATUSTOP       10
#define STATUSWIDE      (SCREENWIDE-(STATUSLEFT*2))
#define STATUSDEEP      12

#define COPYFUNCTION    "XCOPY.EXE"
#define BLOCKSIZE        60

struct ffblk *getlist(char *path,unsigned int *count);
unsigned long getfreespace(char *path);
```

```
unsigned long gettotalspace(char *path);
char *screenptr();
unsigned int getcursor();

int attrnormal=NORMAL;
int attrbright=BRIGHT;
int attrdim=DIM;

char copyfunction[128]=COPYFUNCTION;

char *screen;

main(argc,argv)
        int argc;
        char *argv[];
{
        struct ffblk *list;
        char destpath[128],drive[MAXDRIVE],dir[MAXDIR];
        char sourcepath[MAXPATH],file[MAXFILE],ext[MAXEXT];
        char *oldscreen;
        unsigned long freespace,totalspace;
        unsigned long filesizeleft,totalsize=0;
        unsigned int i,count,filesleft,copied,oldcursor;

        setdefaults();

        screen=screenptr();

        i=SCREENWIDE*2*SCREENDEEP;

        if((oldscreen=malloc(i)) != NULL) {
                memcpy(oldscreen,screen,i);
                oldcursor=getcursor();
        }

        if(argc <= 2) {
                puts("MCOPY version 2.0 Copyright (c) 1992 Alchemy Mindworks Inc.\r\n"
                     "____________________________________________________________\r\n");
                puts("Multiple file copying utility "
                     "with optimum density packing\r\n"
                     "              Arguments:              "
                       "   path to source files\r\n"
                     "                                      "
                       "   path to destination\r\n");
                exit(1);
        }

        status(NULL);
        message("Wait...",STATUSLEFT+2,STATUSTOP+4,attrdim);

        strupr(argv[1]);
        strupr(argv[2]);

        if((list=getlist(argv[1],&count)) == NULL) {
                restore(oldscreen,oldcursor);
                puts("File(s) not found or insufficient memory\r\n");
                exit(2);
```

**5-2** Continued.

```
}

    sortlist(list,count);

    for(i=0;i<count;++i) totalsize+=list[i].ff_fsize;

    totalspace=gettotalspace(argv[2]);

    filesleft=count;

    for(i=0;i<count;++i) {
            if(list[i].ff_fsize > totalspace) {
                    status(NULL);
                    fnsplit(argv[2],drive,NULL,NULL,NULL);
                    sprintf(destpath,"%s is too large for drive %s",
                      list[i].ff_name,drive);
                    message(destpath,STATUSLEFT+2,STATUSTOP+4,attrdim);
                    message("Skipping - hit any key or Esc to abort",
                      STATUSLEFT+2,STATUSTOP+5,attrdim);
                    beep();
                    if(getch()==27) {
                            restore(oldscreen,oldcursor);
                            exit(3);
                    }
                    list[i].ff_name[0]=0;
                    –filesleft;
            }
    }

    while(filesleft) {
            filesizeleft=0L;
            for(i=filesleft=0;i<count;++i) {
                    if(list[i].ff_name[0]) {
                            ++filesleft;
                            filesizeleft+=list[i].ff_fsize;
                    }
            }

            freespace=getfreespace(argv[2]);

            for(i=copied=0;i<count;++i) {
                    if(strlen(list[i].ff_name) &&
                        list[i].ff_fsize < freespace) {
                            fnsplit(argv[1],drive,dir,NULL,NULL);
                            fnsplit(list[i].ff_name,NULL,NULL,file,ext);
                            fnmerge(sourcepath,drive,dir,file,ext);
                            fnsplit(argv[2],drive,dir,NULL,NULL);
                            fnmerge(destpath,drive,dir,NULL,NULL);
                            clrscr();
                            status(argv[2],list[i].ff_name,
                                list[i].ff_fsize,freespace,
                              totalspace,filesizeleft,
                              filesleft-1,count);

                            if(copy(destpath,sourcepath)) {
                                    restore(oldscreen,oldcursor);
```

```
                    printf("Error locating %s\r\n",copyfunction);
                    exit(3);
                }

                if(kbhit()) {
                    if(getch()==27) filesleft=0;
                }

                list[i].ff_name[0]=0;
                copied=1;
                break;
            }
        }

        if(!copied && filesleft) {
            fnsplit(argv[2],drive,NULL,NULL,NULL);
            sprintf(destpath,"Please insert another disk in drive %s",
                drive);
            message(destpath,STATUSLEFT+2,
                STATUSTOP+8,attrbright);
            message("(Or hit Esc to abort)",STATUSLEFT+2,STATUSTOP+9,attrbright);

            freespace=getfreespace(argv[2]);

            sprintf(destpath,"%lu bytes free (of %lu bytes total) on %s        ",
                freespace,totalspace,drive);
            message(destpath,STATUSLEFT+2,STATUSTOP+6,attrdim);

            beep();
            if(getch()==27) filesleft=0;
            status(NULL);
        }
    }
    free((char *)list);

    restore(oldscreen,oldcursor);

    exit(0);
}

status(dest,name,size,freespace,totalspace,filesizeleft,filesleft,filestotal)
    char *dest,*name;
    unsigned long size,freespace,totalspace,filesizeleft;
    unsigned int filesleft,filestotal;
{
    char b[81],drive[MAXDRIVE];
    unsigned int i,j,*ip;

    ip=(unsigned int *)screen;

    ip+=SCREENWIDE*STATUSTOP;

    ip[STATUSLEFT]=(attrnormal<<8)+218;
    for(j=0;j<STATUSWIDE-1;++j) ip[STATUSLEFT+1+j]=(attrnormal<<8)+196;
    ip[STATUSLEFT+STATUSWIDE]=(attrnormal<<8)+191;

    for(i=0;i<STATUSDEEP-2;++i) {
        ip+=SCREENWIDE;
```

**5-2** Continued.

```
                ip[STATUSLEFT]=(attrnormal<<8)+179;
                for(j=0;j<STATUSWIDE-1;++j) ip[STATUSLEFT+1+j]=(attrnormal<<8)+32;
                ip[STATUSLEFT+STATUSWIDE]=(attrnormal<<8)+179;
        }

        ip+=SCREENWIDE;

        ip[STATUSLEFT]=(attrnormal<<8)+192;
        for(j=0;j<STATUSWIDE-1;++j) ip[STATUSLEFT+1+j]=(attrnormal<<8)+196;
        ip[STATUSLEFT+STATUSWIDE]=(attrnormal<<8)+217;

        message("MCOPY 2.0 Copyright (c) 1992 Alchemy Mindworks Inc.",
                STATUSLEFT+2,STATUSTOP+2,attrbright);

        if(dest==NULL) return;

        fnsplit(dest,drive,NULL,NULL,NULL);
        sprintf(b,"Copying %s (%lu bytes) to %s",name,size,drive);
        message(b,STATUSLEFT+2,STATUSTOP+4,attrdim);

        sprintf(b,"%u of %u file(s) (%lu bytes) left to copy",
            filesleft,filestotal,filesizeleft);
        message(b,STATUSLEFT+2,STATUSTOP+5,attrdim);

        sprintf(b,"%lu bytes free (of %lu bytes total) on %s",
            freespace,totalspace,drive);
        message(b,STATUSLEFT+2,STATUSTOP+6,attrdim);

        message("Hit Esc to abort after this file",
            STATUSLEFT+2,STATUSTOP+8,attrbright);
}

message(s,x,y,attr)
        char *s;
        int x,y,attr;
{
        unsigned int *ip;

        ip=((unsigned int *)screen)+(SCREENWIDE*y+x);

        while(*s) *ip++=((attr << 8) + (*s++));
}

copy(dest,source)
        char *dest,*source;
{
        return(spawnlp(P_WAIT,copyfunction,copyfunction,source,dest,NULL));
}

unsigned long getfreespace(path)
        char *path;
{
        struct dfree d;
        char drive[MAXDRIVE];

        fnsplit(path,drive,NULL,NULL,NULL);
```

```
        getdfree(drive[0]-'A'+1,&d);

        return((long)d.df_avail*(long)d.df_bsec*(long)d.df_sclus);
}

unsigned long gettotalspace(path)
        char *path;
{
        struct dfree d;
        char drive[MAXDRIVE];

        fnsplit(path,drive,NULL,NULL,NULL);

        getdfree(drive[0]-'A'+1,&d);

        return((long)d.df_total*(long)d.df_bsec*(long)d.df_sclus);
}

struct ffblk *getlist(path,count)
        char *path;
        unsigned int *count;
{
        struct ffblk f;
        char *list;
        unsigned int blocksize;

        *count=0;

        if((list=malloc(BLOCKSIZE*sizeof(struct ffblk))) == NULL)
            return(NULL);

        blocksize=BLOCKSIZE;

        if(!findfirst(path,&f,0)) {
                do {
                        memcpy(list+(*count)*sizeof(struct ffblk),
                            (char *)&f,sizeof(struct ffblk));
                        (*count)++;
                        if(*count >= blocksize) {
                                list=realloc(list,(blocksize+BLOCKSIZE)*
                                    sizeof(struct ffblk));
                                if(list==NULL) return(NULL);
                                blocksize+=BLOCKSIZE;
                        }
                } while(!findnext(&f) &&
                        *count < (unsigned int)(61440L / (long)(sizeof(struct ffblk))));
        }
        else {
                free(list);
                list=NULL;
        }
        return((struct ffblk *)list);
}

sortlist(buffer,count)
        char *buffer;
        int count;
```

**5-2** Continued.

```
{
        int dircheck();

        qsort(buffer,count,sizeof(struct ffblk),dircheck);
}

dircheck(e1,e2)
        char *e1,*e2;
{
        struct ffblk *p1,*p2;

        p1=(struct ffblk *)e1;
        p2=(struct ffblk *)e2;
        if(p1->ff_fsize > p2->ff_fsize) return(-1);
        else return(1);
}

char *screenptr()
{
        union REGS r;

        r.x.ax=0x0f00;
        int86(0x10,&r,&r);

        if(r.h.al==0x07)
           return(MK_FP(0xb000,r.h.bh*0x1000));
        else
           return(MK_FP(0xb800,r.h.bh*0x1000));
}

beep()
{
        sound(660);
        delay(150);
        sound(524);
        delay(75);
        nosound();
}

unsigned int getcursor()
{
        union REGS r;

        r.x.ax=0x0f00;
        int86(0x10,&r,&r);

        r.x.ax=0x0300;
        int86(0x10,&r,&r);

        return(r.x.dx);
}

setcursor(n)
        unsigned long n;
{
        union REGS r;
```

```
          r.x.ax=0x0f00;
          int86(0x10,&r,&r);

          r.x.ax=0x0200;
          r.x.bx=0x0000;
          r.x.dx=n;
          int86(0x10,&r,&r);
}

restore(oldscreen,oldcursor)
          char *oldscreen;
          unsigned int oldcursor;
{
          int i;
          i=SCREENWIDE*2*SCREENDEEP;

          if(oldscreen != NULL) {
                    memcpy(screen,oldscreen,i);
                    setcursor(oldcursor);
          }
          else clrscr();
}

setdefaults()
{
          char *p,s[129];
          unsigned int i;

          if((p=getenv("MCOPY")) == NULL) return;

          i=0;
          while(*p != 0 && *p != ',' && i < 128) s[i++]=*p++;
          s[i]=0;

          if(strlen(s)) strcpy(copyfunction,s);

          while(*p==',') ++p;

          i=0;
          while(*p != 0 && i < 128) s[i++]=*p++;
          s[i]=0;
          if(!strcmpi(s,"MONO")) {
                    attrnormal=0x70;
                    attrdim=0x70;
                    attrbright=0x70;
          }
}
```

The syntax of MCOPY is very much like that of the DOS XCOPY command, for reasons that will become obvious in a moment. To copy all the GIF files from your current directory onto floppy disks in drive A, for example, you'd do this:

```
MCOPY *.GIF A:
```

The MCOPY program implements the optimum copying algorithm discussed earlier in this section. It uses much the same screen handling as was discussed in chapter 1, and by default it spawns the DOS XCOPY command to actually copy files.

It's fairly easy to work through MCOPY. The `main` function begins by getting all the pertinent file names with a call to `getlist`. The `getlist` function is an elementary application of the `findfirst` and `findnext` functions to get file names into an array. The `sortlist` function uses the Turbo C `qsort` library call to sort the file name entries fetched by `getlist`.

The big `while` loop in `main` does all the work. It uses a call to `getfreespace` to work out how much space is left on the target drive. There's a fair bit of juggling with the Turbo C `fnsplit` and `fnmerge` functions to create a complete path for the destination file. The `copy` function does the work of actually copying the file in question.

The `copy` function spawns XCOPY.EXE, which it expects to find somewhere on the current DOS path. You can change this by adding a line to your DOS environment. For example, if you had a hypothetical program to copy files named ZCOPY.EXE, residing in the \STUFF directory on drive C on your hard drive, the following command would set up your DOS environment such that MCOPY would use it, rather than defaulting to XCOPY:

```
SET MCOPY=C:\STUFF\ZCOPY.EXE
```

A great deal of the code in MCOPY.C is tied up with managing the cosmetics of your screen while files are being copied. The `main` function preserves the current state of the screen, draws a status box on it and then restores the original screen when all the files have been copied.

By default, MCOPY displays its text with white characters on a blue background. If you're using a monochrome display card, you might want to modify the previous SET command to be

```
SET MCOPY=C:\STUFF\ZCOPY.EXE,MONO
```

or perhaps just

```
SET MCOPY=,MONO
```

if you want to set the monochrome flag but allow MCOPY to use its default copy function.

As a final note, MCOPY preserves the current screen contents by copying the text mode video buffer to some allocated memory before the program does anything else, and then copies the contents of the memory back to the buffer. It also preserves the current cursor position, which can also be restored. This is something you might want to consider applying to other DOS utilities discussed in this book, as it allows you to use a program and not disturb whatever was on your screen previously. The only catch involved in it is that it will tie up 4 kilobytes of memory for the time your program is running.

## Recurse through a directory tree

As was touched on earlier in this book, recursion is an approach to solving software architecture problems that is elegant in its conception, and almost never actually good for anything. If you have not encountered the expression before, *recursion* is the technique of having a function call itself. For example, this is an application of recursion:

```
DoSomething()
{
  DoSomething();
}
```

This function will print the message "FATAL ERROR: ***Stack Overflow ***".

The usefulness of recursion is not so much in testing the reliability of the stack overflow checking provided by your C compiler so much as it is in handling certain types of data structures. A useful recursive function is one that stops recursing after a number of iterations—preferably before it trashes your stack.

Recursion is usually applied to data structures that vary in more than one dimension. A tree is a good example of this. The mazes generated by the MAZE program in chapter 2 are another. The only practical way to "visit" all the branches of a tree of unknown dimensions is to recurse through them.

Here's how this works in a theoretical sense:

```
VisitBranches()
{
        for(EachBranchFound) VisitBranches()
}
```

Assuming you set this function going at the root of a tree, it would find all the branches in the first level of the tree. Upon finding a branch, it would call itself to find all the branches on that branch, and then return. If any second-level branches existed, the second iteration of the function would call a third iteration, and so on.

A recursive function can't recurse indefinitely, of course, as it will eventually run out of stack space. Each iteration of the function must store its return address, preserved registers, and local variables on the stack. Recursion should be applied to data sets that are of unknown dimensions, but which you can be certain won't become unreasonably deep.

The most common sort of tree-structured data that most PC users encounter is a disk directory tree. A typical hard drive consists of a root directory with a number of subdirectories, each in turn having subdirectories of their own, and so on.

There are numerous applications for functions to "visit" all the subdirectories of a drive tree. You might want to draw a map of your hard drive, as the DOS TREE command does. You might also want to perform a function in each directory, such as killing BAK files. This is the sort of thing that's easy to handle recursively.

A simple example of recursing through a directory tree is shown in 5-3. It will visit every subdirectory on your current drive and keep a running count of the number of files it finds and their aggregate size.

**5-3** The TREESIZE.C source code.

```
/*
        Directory tree recursor
        Copyright (c) 1993 Alchemy Mindworks Inc.
*/

#include "stdio.h"
#include "dos.h"
#include "dir.h"

char *formatlong(long l);

main()
{
        unsigned long size=0L,count=0L;

        _stklen=10000;

        puts("Recursive directory tree size 1.0 "
             "copyright (c) 1993 Alchemy Mindworks Inc.");

        recurse("\\",&size,&count);

        printf("Total file count:\t%s files\n",formatlong(count));
        printf("Total file size:\t%s bytes\n",formatlong(size));
}

recurse(s,size,count)
        char *s;
        unsigned long *size,*count;
{
        struct ffblk f;
        char path[145];
        int i;

        strcpy(path,s);
        strcat(path,"*.*");

        if(!findfirst(path,&f,0x0010)) {
```

```
        do {
                if(f.ff_attrib & 0x0010 && f.ff_name[0] != '.') {
                        strcpy(path,s);
                        strcat(path,f.ff_name);
                        strcat(path,"\\");
                        printf("\rChecking %s",path);
                        recurse(path,size,count);
                        putchar(13);
                        for(i=0;i<79;++i) putchar(32);
                        putchar(13);
                }
                else {
                        (*size)+= f.ff_fsize;
                        ++(*count);
                }
        } while(!findnext(&f));
    }
}

char *formatlong(l)
    long l;
{
    static char b[24];
    char s[16];
    int i,j,n;

    sprintf(s,"%lu",l);
    strrev(s);
    n=strlen(s);

    for(i=j=0;i<n;++i) {
            b[j++]=s[i];
            if(!((i+1) % 3) && i < (n-1)) b[j++]=',';
    }

    b[j]=0;

    strrev(b);
    return(b);
}
```

The Turbo C `findfirst` and `findnext` functions will fetch the first file name to match a file specification and then each subsequent file. They will also fetch the attribute of each file found. If the `ff_attrib` element of the `ffblk` structure filled in by `findfirst` or `findnext` AND 0x0010 is true, the file is actually a subdirectory. Note that the `.` and `..` entries of a subdirectory will appear as valid subdirectory names in this search, but they should be ignored.

The `formatlong` function is a somewhat inelegant but well-used way to format numbers so they're easier to read. It will return a string with the number in the argument passed to it formatted with a comma after every three digits.

## Create a sorted directory command

The DOS DIR command is one of the ugliest things DOS knows how to do. While it serves to tell you what's in a directory—sort of—it's awkward to use. An arcane holdover from the days when everything worth doing could be run from a floppy disk, DIR lives to scroll seemingly endless miles of text past your screen at the speed of sound, should you be foolish enough to use it on a well-filled hard drive directory with no arguments.

Recent improvements to the DIR command make it only slightly less neolithic. You can make it sort and page by adding some cryptic command line switches to it when you summon it forth from its cave, but it's still awkward to use.

Most DOS users have one or more sorted directory programs on hand, little replacement commands for DIR. A sorted directory does almost the same thing that DIR does, but it formats the file names in your directory in a way that makes them easier to scan through.

The drawback to sorted directories is that just about everyone has his or her own idea of how one ought to work. As such, while you'll find a workable sorted directory in this section, plan on customizing it to suit your needs.

The alternative is to create a sorted directory program that configures itself, based on command line switches. This is arguably a bit pointless, as it will quickly turn your sorted directory into something almost as unpleasant to use as the DIR command.

Dedicated Windows users will certainly scoff at the whole notion of having to keep a sorted directory program around. In Windows, one can merely hit Ctrl-Esc, select the Program Manager from the Task Selector dialog, click on the File Manager, click on a drive button, click on a subdirectory, set up the File Manager display options, and quickly see a directory listing. Extraterrestrials who'd never seen a personal computer before could probably look at DOS and Windows and know intuitively they'd come from the same place.

The SDIR program in this section is a C language sorted directory. It accepts the same basic file specification arguments as DIR, or no argument at all to see a listing of the current drive. Suitable arguments could include

- SDIR *.GIF—see all the GIF files.
- SDIR E:*.GIF—see all the GIF files on drive E.
- SDIR \PICTURES*.GIF—see all the GIF files in the directory \PICTURES.

The source code for SDIR is illustrated in 5-4.

There are several considerations in creating a sorted directory program. The first is getting the file names to be sorted and displayed. This can be handled fairly easily through the use of the Turbo C `findfirst` and `findnext` functions. The catch is that ultimately the file names must wind up in a buffer, and it's impossible to know how big to make the buffer when you initially start trolling for names.

**5-4** The SDIR.C source code.

```
/*
        Sorted directory with a side of fries
        Copyright (c) 1993 Alchemy Mindworks Inc.
*/

#include "stdio.h"
#include "dos.h"
#include "dir.h"
#include "alloc.h"
#include "conio.h"
#include "stdlib.h"
#include "time.h"

#define TEXTCOLOUR(foreground,background) (foreground | (background << 4))

#define BACKGROUND      TEXTCOLOUR(WHITE,BLUE)
#define BANNER          TEXTCOLOUR(BLACK,RED)
#define FILENAMETEXT    TEXTCOLOUR(WHITE,BLUE)
#define FILESIZETEXT    TEXTCOLOUR(YELLOW,BLUE)
#define DIRNAMETEXT     TEXTCOLOUR(LIGHTGRAY,BLUE)
#define FILETIMETEXT    TEXTCOLOUR(CYAN,BLUE)

#define HOME            0x4700
#define CURSOR_UP       0x4800
#define END             0x4f00
#define CURSOR_DOWN     0x5000
#define PG_UP           0x4900
#define PG_DOWN         0x5100

#define SCREENWIDE      80
#define SCREENDEEP      25
#define BLOCKSIZE       128
#define ENTRIESPERLINE  2
#define ENTRYSIZE       (SCREENWIDE/ENTRIESPERLINE)
#define PAGESIZE        ((SCREENDEEP*2)/3)

struct ffblk *GetList(char *path,unsigned int *count,unsigned long *size);
char *formatlong(long l);
char *filetime(struct ffblk *fb);
char *screenPtr();
unsigned long getfreespace(char *path);
unsigned long gettotalspace(char *path);

char *screen;

main(argc,argv)
        int argc;
        char *argv[];
{
        struct ffblk *list=NULL;
        unsigned long size,freespace=0L,totalspace;
        unsigned int count=0,line=0;
        char drive[MAXDRIVE],dir[MAXDIR],file[MAXFILE],ext[MAXEXT];
        char b[129];
        int c;
```

**5-4** Continued.

```
clrscr();
screen=screenPtr();

DrawString(0,0,"Wait...",0x07);

if(argc <= 1) {
        strcpy(b,"*.*");
}
else {
        strupr(argv[1]);
        fnsplit(argv[1],drive,dir,file,ext);
        if(file[0]==0) strcpy(file,"*");
        if(ext[0]==0) strcpy(ext,".*");
        fnmerge(b,drive,dir,file,ext);
}

list=GetList(b,&count,&size);
freespace=getfreespace(b);
totalspace=gettotalspace(b);

if(list==NULL) error("File not found");

SortList(list,count);

HideCursor();

ClearScreen(BACKGROUND);
ClearLine(0,BANNER);
DrawString(8,0,"Sorted Directory 1.0 Copyright (c) 1993 Alchemy Mindworks Inc.",BANNER);

ClearLine(SCREENDEEP-1,BANNER);
strcpy(b,formatlong(size));
strcat(b," USED \376 ");
strcat(b,formatlong((long)count));
strcat(b," FILES \376 ");
strcat(b,formatlong(freespace));
strcat(b," FREE \376 ");
strcat(b,formatlong(totalspace));
strcat(b," TOTAL");
DrawString((SCREENWIDE-strlen(b))/2,SCREENDEEP-1,b,BANNER);

do {
        ShowPage(list,line,count);
        switch(c=GetKey()) {
                case HOME:
                        line=0;
                        break;
                case END:
                        line=1+(count/ENTRIESPERLINE)-(SCREENDEEP-1);
                        break;
                case CURSOR_UP:
                        if(line > 0) --line;
                        break;
                case CURSOR_DOWN:
                        if(line < ((count/ENTRIESPERLINE)-SCREENDEEP+2))
```

```
                                    ++line;
                                break;
                        case PG_UP:
                                if(line > PAGESIZE) line-=PAGESIZE;
                                else line=0;
                                break;
                        case PG_DOWN:
                                if((line+PAGESIZE) < ((count/ENTRIESPERLINE)-SCREENDEEP+1))
                                    line+=PAGESIZE;
                                else
                                    line=1+(count/ENTRIESPERLINE)-(SCREENDEEP-1);
                                break;
                }
        } while(c != 27);
        ClearScreen(0x07);
        gotoxy(1,24);
}

ShowPage(list,line,count)
        struct ffblk *list;
        unsigned int line,count;
{
        char *p,b[81];
        int i,j,n;

        list+=(line*ENTRIESPERLINE);
        count-=(line*ENTRIESPERLINE);
        for(i=0;i<SCREENDEEP-2;++i) {
                for(j=0;j<ENTRIESPERLINE;++j) {
                        memset(b,32,ENTRYSIZE);
                        b[ENTRYSIZE]=0;
                        DrawString(j*ENTRYSIZE,i+1,b,FILENAMETEXT);
                        if(count) {
                        if(list->ff_attrib & 0x0010) {
                                sprintf(b,"\\%s",list->ff_name);
                                DrawString(j*ENTRYSIZE+1,i+1,b,DIRNAMETEXT);
                        }
                        else {
                                DrawString(j*ENTRYSIZE,i+1,list->ff_name,FILENAMETEXT);
                                n=strlen(p=formatlong(list->ff_fsize));
                                DrawString(j*ENTRYSIZE+24-n,i+1,p,FILESIZETEXT);
                                DrawString(j*ENTRYSIZE+25,i+1,filetime(list),FILETIMETEXT);
                        }
                        ++list;
                        —count;
                        }
                }
        }
}

struct ffblk *GetList(path,count,size)
        char *path;
        unsigned int *count;
        unsigned long *size;
{
        struct ffblk f;
        char *list,drive[MAXDRIVE],dir[MAXDIR],b[144];
```

**5-4** Continued.

```
        unsigned int blocksize;

        *count=0;
        *size=0L;

        if((list=malloc(BLOCKSIZE*sizeof(struct ffblk))) == NULL)
            return(NULL);

        blocksize=BLOCKSIZE;

        if(!findfirst(path,&f,0x0000)) {
                do {
                        memcpy(list+(*count)*sizeof(struct ffblk),
                            (char *)&f,sizeof(struct ffblk));
                        (*size)+=f.ff_fsize;
                        (*count)++;
                        if(*count >= blocksize) {
                                list=realloc(list,(blocksize+BLOCKSIZE)*
                                   sizeof(struct ffblk));
                                if(list==NULL) return(NULL);
                                blocksize+=BLOCKSIZE;
                        }
                } while(!findnext(&f) &&
                        *count < (unsigned int)(61440L / (long)(sizeof(struct ffblk))));
        }

        fnsplit(path,drive,dir,NULL,NULL);
        fnmerge(b,drive,dir,"*",".*");

        if(!findfirst(b,&f,0x0010)) {
                do {
                        if(f.ff_attrib & 0x0010 && f.ff_name[0] != '.') {
                                memcpy(list+(*count)*sizeof(struct ffblk),
                                    (char *)&f,sizeof(struct ffblk));
                                (*count)++;
                                if(*count >= blocksize) {
                                        list=realloc(list,(blocksize+BLOCKSIZE)*
                                           sizeof(struct ffblk));
                                        if(list==NULL) return(NULL);
                                        blocksize+=BLOCKSIZE;
                                }
                        }
                } while(!findnext(&f) &&
                        *count < (unsigned int)(61440L / (long)(sizeof(struct ffblk))));
        }

        if(*count==0) {
                free(list);
                list=NULL;
        }

        return((struct ffblk *)list);
}

SortList(buffer,count)
```

```
        struct ffblk *buffer;
        int count;
{
        int dircheck();

        qsort(buffer,count,sizeof(struct ffblk),dircheck);
}

dircheck(e1,e2)
        char *e1,*e2;
{
        struct ffblk *p1,*p2;

        p1=(struct ffblk *)e1;
        p2=(struct ffblk *)e2;
        return(strcmp(p1->ff_name,p2->ff_name));
}

DrawString(x,y,text,attr)
        int x,y;
        char *text;
        int attr;
{
        unsigned int a,*ip;

        ip=(unsigned int *)(screen+(y*160+x*2));
        a=attr << 8;

        while(*text) *ip++=*text++ | a;
}

HideCursor()
{
        union REGS r;

        r.x.ax=0x0f00;
        int86(0x10,&r,&r);

        r.x.ax=0x0200;
        r.x.dx=(SCREENDEEP+1)<<8;
        int86(0x10,&r,&r);
}

char *screenPtr()
{
        union REGS r;

        r.x.ax=0x0f00;
        int86(0x10,&r,&r);

        if(r.h.al==0x07) return(MK_FP(0xb000,r.h.bh*0x1000));
        else return(MK_FP(0xb800,r.h.bh*0x1000));
}

ClearScreen(attr)
        int attr;
{
```

**5-4** Continued.

```
        unsigned int i,a,*ip;

        ip=(unsigned int *)screen;
        a=attr << 8;

        for(i=0;i<SCREENWIDE*SCREENDEEP;++i) *ip++=32 | a;
}

error(s)
        char *s;
{
        puts(s);
        exit(1);
}

GetKey()
{
        int c;

        c = getch();
        if(!(c & 0x00ff)) c = getch() << 8;
        return(c);
}

ClearLine(y,attr)
        int y,attr;
{
        unsigned int a,i,*ip;

        ip=(unsigned int *)(screen+(y*160));
        a=(attr << 8) | 32;

        for(i=0;i<SCREENWIDE;++i) *ip++=a;
}

char *formatlong(l)
        long l;
{
        static char b[24];
        char s[16];
        int i,j,n;

        sprintf(s,"%lu",l);
        strrev(s);
        n=strlen(s);

        for(i=j=0;i<n;++i) {
                b[j++]=s[i];
                if(!((i+1) % 3) && i < (n-1)) b[j++]=',';
        }

        b[j]=0;

        strrev(b);
        return(b);
}
```

```
char *filetime(fb)
        struct ffblk *fb;
{
        static char b[24];
        struct date dt;
        struct time tm;

        tm.ti_hund=0;
        tm.ti_sec=(char)((fb->ff_ftime & 0x001f)*2);
        tm.ti_min=(char)((fb->ff_ftime>>5) & 0x003f);
        tm.ti_hour=(char)((fb->ff_ftime>>11) & 0x001f);

        dt.da_day=(char)(fb->ff_fdate & 0x001f);
        dt.da_mon=(char)((fb->ff_fdate >> 5) & 0x000f);
        dt.da_year=(((fb->ff_fdate >> 9) & 0x003f)+80) % 99;

        sprintf(b,"%02d-%02d-%02d %02d:%02d",
            dt.da_mon,dt.da_day,dt.da_year,
            tm.ti_hour,tm.ti_min);

        return(b);
}

unsigned long getfreespace(path)
        char *path;
{
        struct dfree d;
        char drive[MAXDRIVE];

        fnsplit(path,drive,NULL,NULL,NULL);
        getdfree(drive[0]-'A'+1,&d);

        return((long)d.df_avail*(long)d.df_bsec*(long)d.df_sclus);
}

unsigned long gettotalspace(path)
        char *path;
{
        struct dfree d;
        char drive[MAXDRIVE];

        fnsplit(path,drive,NULL,NULL,NULL);
        getdfree(drive[0]-'A'+1,&d);

        return((long)d.df_total*(long)d.df_bsec*(long)d.df_sclus);
}
```

The `GetList` function in SDIR deals with this logistical nasty by allocating a small buffer and adding some names to it. When the buffer is full, it calls `realloc` to make it bigger, and repeats the cycle until all the names have been fetched. In this way, the buffer can expand as more file names are found. It need not be initially allocated so as to be unreasonably large. It also need not arbitrarily refuse to accept more than a fixed number of file names, as some commercial applications do in this situation.

The GetList function will return a pointer to an array of ffblk structures, which are what the DOS directory functions return through findfirst and findnext. An ffblk object includes the name, size, attributes, and creation date of the file it represents. Sorting an array of ffblk objects is handled in SDIR using qsort.

The principal do loop in the main function of SDIR handles displaying the file names in the list array. It calls ShowPage and then updates a pointer into the list array based on the keyboard key it fetches with a call to GetKey. The ShowPage function counts through the list based on the initial line value passed to it and then displays as many subsequent list items as will fit on your screen.

Prior to actually displaying any file names, SDIR prints some disk statistics at the bottom of your screen. Specifically it will tell you the number and aggregate size of the files it has found, the amount of free space on your drive, and the total drive size. You can see how this is handled through the getfreespace and gettotalspace functions.

The ffblk objects stored in the list array contain a wealth of information about the files they represent. You probably won't have much use for all of it, and one of the things that makes a sorted directory program worthwhile is its selection of what is to be displayed. Each listing in the SDIR program displays the file name and file size involved and a somewhat compressed file date and time. Entries that happen to be directory names, as indicated by the ff_attrib of an ffblk object having its fourth bit set, are displayed in a different color.

You'll probably want to customize the information that SDIR displays, and perhaps the way it displays it. You can also fine-tune the colors involved, and so on. You might want to consider using the 50-line display functions from chapter 1 to allow you to get more entries on your screen.

# 6
# Hard copy

*"How can I insert disk number three when only two will fit in the slot?"*

—Graffiti

The last thing a car salesperson wants to see is a customer he or she has just sold a car to. Computer salespeople can have a markedly cheerier outlook, because they know that buying the computer is only the beginning. There's a universe worth of peripherals yet to come, of which printers are by far the most lucrative. Furthermore, people seem to be a lot more prepared to upgrade peripherals than they are to replace a whole computer.

This chapter looks at a few programs for dealing with printers. None of it is particularly difficult in theory, but in theory politicians tell the truth, interchangeable parts interchange, and nobody owns a dog smarter than they are.

The example programs in this chapter have been designed to work with WordStar 3.3 document files. While no longer all that common, they have the advantage of being fairly easy to understand and manipulate. Many word processors and desktop publishing packages can import and export files in this format, even if it might not be their first choice for storing text.

In the event that you thoroughly lack anything that will deal with WordStar 3.3 files, and you'd like to try these programs as they stand before you modify them, you'll find an example document file, MAGCARTA.WS, on the companion disk for this book. It contains the text of the Magna Carta, the great charter of King John. While hardly a model of political correctness or good English by contemporary standards, it has the advantage of being wholly copyright free.

As an aside, history reviles King John for almost everything he did, except for the single noble act of putting his hand to this document. If you read it, rather than merely use it as a test file, you probably won't be surprised to learn that he was largely blackmailed into doing so. It might seem that no medieval king in his right mind would agree to most of it without a gun to his head, or some reasonable facsimile thereof, and so it was.

## Drive a printer port

One of the theories that proves to be even less reliable than the hope of a truthful politician is the one that observes how easy it is to print something from a C program. Should you be unaware of the theory, here's what it looks like. This is how you would print some text to your standard printer device—by default LPT1—using the streamed file functions of C.

```
fprintf(stprn,"This is some %s\n","text to print.");
```

The `fprintf` function prints to a streamed FILE handle, in most cases one that has been returned by `fopen`. However, there are five default file handles created when a C language program starts up, of which `stdprn` is one. It's a handle to your printer port.

The deceptive thing about the previous line of code is that it will probably work. Sending small amounts of simple text to a printer this way is fairly reliable. However, the `stdprn` file handle actually hooks into the DOS printer drivers, which exhibit two distinct problems when they're asked to print large amounts of data. The first is that the DOS printer handlers don't reliably check for the port being ready, and as such may lose some data when the buffer of your printer becomes full. Second, DOS will attempt to convert some control characters, such as carriage returns. This can be nasty if you're actually printing binary data.

Finally, the `stdprn` handle doesn't allow for a convenient mechanism to address ports other than LPT1.

The way to deal with the limitations of the DOS printer drivers is to excise them from your applications entirely. You can perform reliable printing, even of very large amounts of data, if you negotiate directly with the printer BIOS calls. Here's a function to print one character to a printer port through the DOS.

```
p_char(c)
        int c;
{
        union REGS r;

        do {
                r.h.ah = 2;
                r.x.dx = printerport;
                int86(0x17,&r,&r);
        } while(!(r.h.ah & 0x80));
```

```
        r.h.ah = 0;
        r.h.al = c;
        r.x.dx = printerport;
        int86(0x17,&r,&r);
}
```

The value of `printerport` should be the number of the printer port you want to use, where LPT1 is zero, LPT2 is one, and so on.

The `p_char` function will wait until the BIOS says that the printer port in question is free before it sends a character to it. It doesn't attempt to translate anything.

If you write programs to print, this bit of code should be at the heart of them.

## Print to a PostScript printer

Unlike most other types of printers, a PostScript printer does not default to behaving like a dumb teletype. This means that if you send straight ASCII text to one, it won't print anything. If you're lucky, it won't hang.

A PostScript printer is a very elaborate command interpreter. The commands it interprets are in the PostScript language. In effect, PostScript is a programming language that has been fine-tuned to generate text and graphics on a high-resolution imaging device. Unfortunately it has been fine-tuned by martians.

A tutorial on PostScript programming could easily double the size of this book and not begin to get down to all the sorcery and refinements involved. PostScript is easily as rich as the basic function set of C, but it's very much more inscrutable.

One of the things that makes PostScript hard for human beings to read is that it has been designed to be particularly easy for computers to deal with. It's a "postfix" language, which means that whatever is passed to a function appears before the function name.

As a simple example, this is how you might position the screen cursor under C:

```
gotoxy(10,10);
```

This is how you'd perform an analogous function under PostScript:

```
100 100 moveto
```

When PostScript interprets a line of code, what it really does is push everything that isn't a function—or what PostScript calls an "operator"—onto its stack until it runs into something that is an operator, which it calls. The operator is responsible for removing its arguments from the stack. Whoever wrote the PostScript code in the first place is responsible for there being the right number and types of arguments on the stack.

PostScript's error trapping is elegantly simple. If the printer crashes, there must have been an error.

This section discusses a few elemental bits of PostScript to allow you to print with it. If you want to get more deeply into PostScript you'll need the official Adobe PostScript books, known as the red book, the blue book, and the green book, all published by Addison-Wesley. Prepare yourself for a confrontation of epic dimensions.

A PostScript printer supports a selection of fonts, the exact list varying to some extent from printer to printer. It's a safe bet that all the PostScript printers you're likely to run into will have the fonts Times Roman, Helvetica, and Courier. Examples of these fonts are shown in 6-1.

Times Roman
Helvetica
Courier

**6-1** Examples of a PostScript printer's basic text fonts.

Before you can print text on a PostScript printer you must tell the printer to magic you up a font in the size and typeface you require. Here's some PostScript code to do this:

```
/Times-Roman findfont 30 scalefont setfont
```

Note that all PostScript command lines must be followed by a carriage return.

This line tells the printer to fetch the Times Roman font, to scale it to 30 points—or a bit less than a half inch—and then set it as the current font to print text with.

A point is about 1/72 of an inch. This is important to know, as PostScript printers measure things in points.

The next thing you'll have to do to manage basic printing is to position the "cursor" of your printer so your text will appear where you want it to. The coordinate system of a PostScript printer is a bit peculiar. The coordinates (0,0) occur in the lower left corner of the printable page. This will probably sound distantly familiar if you were able to keep awake during high school geometry, but it's not how most coordinate systems work on personal computers, which usually locate (0,0) in the upper left corner of whatever is being printed to.

The dimensions of a PostScript page in points is about 576 by 756 points, allowing that an 8½-by-11-inch page has approximately ¼ inch of margin all around when it runs through a laser printer.

This would position the printing cursor near the top of a page:

```
20 500 moveto
```

Finally, here's how you would print a line of text to a PostScript printer:

```
(Gadzooks! The varlet hath smitten my steed with a polecat!) show
```

You are, of course, free to substitute any text you like between the parentheses.

When you're finished printing you have to tell the printer to eject its current page. The instruction for doing so is:

```
showpage
```

If you imagine the PostScript language to be represented by the time life has existed on Earth, the amount of PostScript that's been discussed in this section would be represented by last week and part of next Friday. Learning PostScript isn't something to be taken on casually after lunch.

## Print a text file to a PostScript printer

Printing a text file to a simple output device, such as a dot matrix printer, involves little more than

```
PRINT TEXTFILE.TXT
```

followed by a trip to the nearest McDonald's for a Coke while your printer sputters and gasps and runs out of ribbon. By comparison, printing a text file to a PostScript printer such that the result looks reasonably attractive is quite an undertaking.

The reason for this is two-fold. As was discussed in the previous section, simply printing text on a PostScript device requires a foray into the somewhat inscrutable operators of PostScript. However, an even more fundamental problem is in the nature of typographic fonts, such as Times Roman. They're proportionally spaced.

The text you're reading at the moment is proportionally spaced. This means that each character on a line of type is allotted only as much space on the line as it requires. The letter *M*, for example, is allowed to occupy a lot more real estate than the letter *i*. By comparison, a conventional typewriter or a dot matrix printer operating in its default text mode will print text with the same amount of space allocated to each character, no matter how wide it actually is. This is called "monospaced" text.

Proportionally spaced text is more attractive, easier to read, and typically allows you to more than double the amount of text you can fit on a page. The only drawback to it is that it's something of a pig to work with.

When you print simple monospaced text it's pretty easy to figure out how many characters will fit on a line—divide the width of a printed line by the width of one character and you're there. In printing proportionally spaced text, the number of characters that will fit on a line depends on the characters involved. A line of *M*s will allow for far fewer characters than a line of *i*s.

To arrive at reasonably well-filled lines, like the ones in this book, the software that drives your printer must split the text to be printed into words. Here's how you'd print lines of text with a proportionally spaced typeface:

```
while(TextIsLeft) {
        FetchWord();
        wordsize=MeasureWord();
        if(linesize+wordsize < PAGEWIDTH)
            PrintWord();
        else {
                NewLine();
                PrintWord();
        }
}
```

Even allowing that this bit of pseudocode ignores things like page ejection, it's remarkably oversimplified. It skips a fairly fundamental issue, that of measuring the size of a word when the characters that make up the word are of varying widths.

Because the characters in a font are of differing and largely unpredictable widths, it's necessary to represent their widths as a table of values, an object usually referred to as a "width table." Width tables are used by any application that must print proportionally spaced text so it can know how wide the text that will appear on paper will actually be.

Width tables are a serious nuisance. Every typeface has a different one. The different effects of a single typeface—bold, italics, and so on—each require a width table of their own. The width table for Times Roman, for example, will be of little use if you want to print with Helvetica.

A still larger nuisance is that there's no readily obtainable source for width table values. While the program to be dealt within a moment includes a width table for the Times Roman font, its derivation was an exercise in digital skulduggery.

There's a final catch to printing simple text files using a proportionally spaced font. You can't do it. At least, you shouldn't. A simple text file has a carriage return at the end of each line. Printed in 12-point Times Roman, a typical word processed text file will print erratically, occupying the left half of the page.

What's really needed is a source file in which carriage returns—or "hard" returns as they're called in typographic circles—only occur at the ends of paragraphs. Most word processing document formats allow for this, as word processors like to reformat text pretty much as a printing program would.

In this section I'll deal with a program to print text from WordStar 3.3 source files. These have the advantage of being exceedingly easy to use, if a bit dated. You might want to see about integrating the WordPerfect document viewer from chapter 1 with the PostScript printing code if you'd like to print from a more contemporary file format.

A WordStar 3.3 file is almost pure ASCII. Some characters, however, have their high-order bits set, which WordStar uses to indicate that some line formatting is to take place. Specifically, the end of each screen line is marked with character 8DH, which is a carriage return with its high-order bit set. The ends of paragraphs are marked with real carriage returns. In addition, if a WordStar file is created with WordStar set up to do right margin justification, character A0H might appear in the line. These are "soft" spaces used to pad out the lines, which can be ignored.

Some text characters might have their high-order bits set. If you AND them with 7FH they'll revert to proper ASCII.

Note that WordStar 3.3 files are read and written by WordStar 4.0. Beginning with WordStar 5.0, the document file format of WordStar mutated somewhat. These later monster WordStars will export the old 3.3 format, but it's not their native document format—their document files can't be used with the program in this chapter.

The source code for PRINT–PS is illustrated in 6-2. This is a simple manuscript printer that accepts a path to a WordStar file as its command line argument and will output the text therein in 12-point Times Roman type, almost filling the pages it generates. It assumes that your PostScript printer is connected to LPT1.

**6-2** The PRINT-PS.C source code.

```
/*
        Simple PostScript text printer
        copyright (c) 1993 Alchemy Mindworks
*/

#include "stdio.h"
#include "dos.h"

#define DEBUG               0
#define DEBUGFILE          "DEBUG.PS"

#define TIMESROMAN          1
#define HELVETICA           0
#define COURIER             0

#define XMPY                12
#define XDIV                720

int TimesRomanWidth[]= {
        250,333,408,500,500,833,778,333,333,333,500,564,250,333,250,278,
        500,500,500,500,500,500,500,500,500,500,278,278,564,564,564,444,
        921,722,667,667,722,611,556,722,722,333,389,722,611,889,722,722,
        556,722,667,556,611,722,722,944,722,722,611,333,278,333,469,500,
        333,444,500,444,500,444,333,500,500,278,278,500,278,778,500,500,
        500,500,333,389,278,500,500,722,500,500,444,480,200,480,541,0,
        };

int HelveticaWidth[]= {
        278,278,355,556,556,889,667,222,333,333,389,584,278,333,278,278,
        556,556,556,556,556,556,556,556,556,556,278,278,584,584,584,556,
        1015,667,667,722,722,667,611,778,722,278,500,667,556,833,722,778,
        667,778,722,667,611,722,667,944,667,667,611,278,278,278,469,556,
```

**6-2** Continued.

```
        222,556,556,500,556,556,278,556,556,222,222,500,222,833,556,556,
        556,556,333,500,278,556,500,722,500,500,500,334,260,334,584,0,
        };

int CourierWidth[]= {
        600,600,600,600,600,600,600,600,600,600,600,600,600,600,600,600,
        600,600,600,600,600,600,600,600,600,600,600,600,600,600,600,600,
        600,600,600,600,600,600,600,600,600,600,600,600,600,600,600,600,
        600,600,600,600,600,600,600,600,600,600,600,600,600,600,600,600,
        600,600,600,600,600,600,600,600,600,600,600,600,600,600,600,600,
        600,600,600,600,600,600,600,600,600,600,600,600,600,600,600,600
        };

#if TIMESROMAN
#define WIDTHTABLE      TimesRomanWidth
#endif

#if HELVETICA
#define WIDTHTABLE      HelveticaWidth
#endif

#if COURIER
#define WIDTHTABLE      CourierWidth
#endif

#define LEFTMARGIN      40
#define RIGHTMARGIN     20
#define TOPMARGIN       20

#define PAGEWIDE        576-(RIGHTMARGIN+LEFTMARGIN)
#define PAGEDEEP        720

#define POINTSIZE       12
#define LEADING         6
#define WORDSIZE        128

#define PRINTERPORT     0

#define TABSIZE         36

double WordSize(char *word);
double CWidth(int c,int tab[],int size);

void writeword(char *word,double *linesize,double *pagedeep);
void newline(double *linesize,double *pagedeep);
void ejectpage(double *linesize,double *pagedeep);

#if     DEBUG
FILE *debug;
#endif

unsigned int pagenumber=0;

main(argc,argv)
        int argc;
        char *argv[];
```

```
{
        FILE *fp;
        char word[WORDSIZE+16];
        double linesize=0,pagedeep=0,spacewidth,tabsize;
        int c,i,n,wordindex=0;
        puts("PRINT-PS version 1.0 Copyright (c) 1993 Alchemy Mindworks Inc.\r\n"
             "______________________________________________________________\r\n");

        #if DEBUG
        if((debug=fopen(DEBUGFILE,"wb"))==NULL) error("Can't create debug file");
        #endif

        if(argc <= 1) error("Argument:          Path to a text file");

        if((fp=fopen(argv[1],"rb"))==NULL) error("Can't open the source file");

        #if TIMESROMAN
        sprintf(word,"/Times-Roman findfont %u scalefont setfont\r\n",POINTSIZE);
        #endif

        #if HELVETICA
        sprintf(word,"/Helvetica findfont %u scalefont setfont\r\n",POINTSIZE);
        #endif

        #if COURIER
        sprintf(word,"/Courier findfont %u scalefont setfont\r\n",POINTSIZE);
        #endif

        p_string(word);

        saypage();

        do {
                if((c=fgetc(fp)) != EOF) {
                        if(c==0x8d) c=0;
                        c &= 0x7f;
                        if(c==32) {
                                do {
                                        if(wordindex < WORDSIZE) word[wordindex++]=c & 0x7f;
                                        c=fgetc(fp);
                                } while((c & 0x7f)==32);
                                word[wordindex]=0;
                                ungetc(c,fp);
                                writeword(word,&linesize,&pagedeep);
                                wordindex=0;
                                word[wordindex]=0;
                        }
                        else if(c==13) {
                                word[wordindex]=0;
                                writeword(word,&linesize,&pagedeep);
                                wordindex=0;
                                word[wordindex]=0;
                                newline(&linesize,&pagedeep);
                        }
                        else if(c==9) {
                                spacewidth=CWidth(32,WIDTHTABLE,POINTSIZE);
                                if(linesize > 0) tabsize=(double)((int)linesize % TABSIZE);
                                else tabsize=TABSIZE;
```

**6-2** Continued.

```
                                n=(int)(tabsize/spacewidth);
                                for(i=0;i<n && wordindex < WORDSIZE;++i)
                                        word[wordindex++]=32;
                        }
                        else if(c=='(') {
                                if((wordindex+4) < WORDSIZE) {
                                        word[wordindex++] = '\134';
                                        word[wordindex++] = '0';
                                        word[wordindex++] = '5';
                                        word[wordindex++] = '0';
                                }
                        }
                        else if(c==')') {
                                if((wordindex+4) < WORDSIZE) {
                                        word[wordindex++] = '\134';
                                        word[wordindex++] = '0';
                                        word[wordindex++] = '5';
                                        word[wordindex++] = '1';
                                }
                        }
                        else if(c > 32 && c < 128) {
                                if(wordindex < WORDSIZE) word[wordindex++]=c;
                        }
                }
        } while(c != EOF);
        writeword(word,&linesize,&pagedeep);
        wordindex=0;
        ejectpage(&linesize,&pagedeep);

        printf("\rAll done...             \r\n");

        fclose(fp);

        #if DEBUG
        fclose(debug);
        #endif
}

void writeword(word,linesize,pagedeep)
        char *word;
        double *linesize,*pagedeep;
{
        double wordsize;
        char b[256];

        if(!word[0]) return;

        wordsize=WordSize(word);
        if((int)((*linesize)+wordsize) >= PAGEWIDE)
            newline(linesize,pagedeep);

        if((*linesize)==0) {
                sprintf(b,"%u %u moveto\r\n (",
                    LEFTMARGIN,TOPMARGIN+PAGEDEEP-(int)(*pagedeep));
                p_string(b);
        }
```

```
        p_string(word);
        (*linesize)+=wordsize;
}
void newline(linesize,pagedeep)
        double *linesize,*pagedeep;
{
        p_string(") show\r\n");

        (*pagedeep)+=(double)(POINTSIZE+LEADING);
        if((int)(*pagedeep) >= PAGEDEEP) ejectpage(linesize,pagedeep);
        (*linesize)=0;
}

void ejectpage(linesize,pagedeep)
        double *linesize,*pagedeep;
{
        (*linesize)=(*pagedeep)=0;
        p_string("showpage\r\n");
        saypage();
}

double WordSize(word)
        char *word;
{
        double wordsize=0;
        int i,n;

        n=strlen(word);
        for(i=0;i<n;++i)
                wordsize+=CWidth((int)word[i],WIDTHTABLE,POINTSIZE);

        return(wordsize);
}

p_string(s)
        char *s;
{
        while(*s) p_char(*s++);
}

p_char(c)
        int c;
{
        #if DEBUG
        fputc(c,debug);
        #else
        union REGS r;

        do {
                r.h.ah = 2;
                r.x.dx = PRINTERPORT;
                int86(0x17,&r,&r);
        } while(!(r.h.ah & 0x80));

        r.h.ah = 0;
        r.h.al = c;
        r.x.dx = PRINTERPORT;
```

6-2 Continued.

```
        int86(0x17,&r,&r);
        #endif
}
error(s)
        char *s;
{
        puts(s);
        exit(1);
}

double CWidth(c,tab,size)
        int c,tab[],size;
{
        return((double)0.06*
               ((double)XMPY/(double)XDIV)*
               (double)size*
               (double)tab[(c & 0x7f)-32]);
}

saypage()
{
        printf("\rPrinting page %u",++pagenumber);
}
```

Prior to getting deeply mired in the workings of PRINT-PS, it's probably worth talking about the Times Roman width table. It appears as the `TimesRomanWidth` array in the PRINT-PS.C listing. As will be obvious, the numbers therein do not have any meaningful relationship to each other. The first entry in the `TimesRomanWidth` table is the width of a space character in the Times Roman font, that is, character 32.

Inasmuch as the design of the Times Roman font, and the characters therein, was fixed around the turn of the century, the width table for Times Roman is a defined entity. Given a particular point size of Times Roman, you could print out each character and measure it to determine how wide they all are. While certainly a workable solution to the problem of generating a width table, this approach is fraught with errors and your eyes would probably leap from your head in rebellion.

A second approach would be to write a PostScript program to measure each character and print the results. This is possible, as PostScript itself certainly knows how big its fonts are. The two drawbacks to this will be fairly obvious. It involves writing a fairly complex program in the PostScript language—something to be avoided—and the result of your labor will be a page full of numbers to be transcribed into a source code file.

The final approach, and the one I used for PRINT-PS, is to observe that other applications that print using the Times Roman font must have width tables. Some of them might even store their width tables in somewhat accessible forms. In the absence of store-bought width tables, you can certainly abstract them from software that's already using them.

One of the best applications to swipe width tables from is Ventura Publisher. You'll need the old GEM version to do this, however, as the current Windows version has largely abandoned the proprietary Ventura width tables in favor of Windows TrueType fonts. It's worth noting that you don't need Ventura to compile and use this program. You might find the following procedure useful if you want to derive width tables for other fonts, however.

Ventura stores its width tables as complex binary files having the extension WID. The 3.0 version of Ventura for GEM included a utility called WIDTOVFM.EXE, which will break these WID files apart into text files with the extension VFM. The VFM files present the width table information as a list of numbers, each number being the character width for characters beginning with ASCII 32.

Under PostScript, character sizes are infinitely adjustable. As a result, these width values don't pertain to a specific point size—they're relative to the size of type you choose to print. Ventura provides a formula for determining the width of a character in points at a specific point size, as follows:

```
0.06 * (XMPY / XDIV) * pointsize * widthvalue
```

The XMPY and XDIV values are provided in the VFM file from which a width table is derived. They're derived like this for the Times Roman font under PostScript:

```
#define XMPY            12
#define XDIV            720
```

The `pointsize` value is the size of the type to be printed in points; that is, in $\frac{1}{72}$ of an inch. The `widthvalue` is the width table entry for the character to be printed.

This might seem like a particularly obtuse way to find width tables—at present, it's one of the few that doesn't require a lot of complex calculations or excessive typing. It's a rich source of them, too, as Ventura's default PostScript WID file includes width tables for dozens of popular fonts.

The PRINT-PS program can be compiled to use one of three fonts: Times Roman, Helvetica, or Courier. Width tables are included for all three. The Courier font is monospaced, and as such its width table entries are all the same. Set one of the TIMESROMAN, HELVETICA, or COURIER defines true to select a font. You might also want to change the POINTSIZE, LEADING, LEFTMARGIN, or RIGHTMARGIN defines to change the appearance of the text PRINT-PS generates. The value of POINTSIZE determines the size of the text in points. The value of LEADING is the number of points of extra space between lines of type. The LEFTMARGIN and RIGHTMARGIN values specify the number of points in from the edge of the page for the area that will enclose the text.

You can see how PRINT-PS works if you look at its `main` function—despite the somewhat exotic calculations involved in working with proportionally spaced type, it's a relatively simple bit of code. It fetches each byte from the source WordStar document file, dealing with the possibility of the high-order bits of some characters being set by AND-ing them with 7FH. It then assembles the bytes into words. A word is considered to be all the characters that aren't spaces or control characters followed by all the characters that are spaces, to a maximum of WORDSIZE bytes.

When a word has been assembled it's passed to `writeword`. The `writeword` function will output the word to your printer and it will measure it, updating the `linesize` and `pagedeep` values accordingly. Specifically, if the length of the word in points plus the current value of `linesize` is greater than the width of the page, `linesize` will be set to zero and the next text to be printed will appear on a new line. Otherwise the length of the word will be added to `linesize`.

The `do` loop in the `main` function of PRINT-PS also handles tab characters, ASCII character 9. In this example it handles them by padding the current word out with spaces until the line length reaches the next tab stop, as defined by TABSIZE. This is unquestionably not the way to handle tabs in a complex typesetting application, as the thickness of a space character is far too coarse to allow for accurate tab alignment. A far better approach would be to readjust the current line position relative to where it was when the tab character was encountered.

Dealing with tabs, on the surface a fairly simple undertaking, is actually quite the seething pit of snakes when you get right down into it. Such snake handling is beyond the scope of this chapter to undertake.

One of the unfortunate aspects of PostScript printers is that if you send them some illegal PostScript code, they usually respond by not printing anything—with no indication as to what has offended them. To this end, the PRINT-PS program can be compiled in debug mode by setting its DEBUG define true. In this mode it will write the PostScript data it generates to a file called DEBUG.PS rather than to the LPT1 printer port. You can look at this file to see what's gone awry.

As a final note, in printing text to a PostScript printer using the `show` operator, it's important to handle any parentheses that occur in your text as a special case. They should be replaced with the octal constants for these characters, `\050` and `\051`, respectively, for opening and closing parentheses. If you fail to do this, the PostScript interpreter in your laser printer might mistake a parenthesis in your text as the one that would appear after all the text has been sent and try to interpret the rest of your line of text as PostScript operators. You can see how this is handled in the `main` function of PRINT-PS.

The PRINT-PS program can form the basis of any application that will work with proportionally spaced type. The only difference between it and a complete desktop publishing package is several million lines of code and a distribution agreement with a large photocopier manufacturer.

## Print text very, very small

The PRINT-PS program in the preceding section had some genuine applications. The SMALL program discussed in this section, while similar in function, defies doing anything useful. It prints text in three columns of very small Courier type. While readable, such text is a bit hard on one's eyes. You could argue that this format is useful for archiving a lot of text in a small space—it would have to be a pretty well thought out argument, however.

As a rough measure of the power of the SMALL to make the fine print of a mortgage look pretty approachable by comparison, it was able to reduce the text for a 150,000-word novel down to 14 pages of laser output.

The SMALL program will drive any PostScript laser printer. It expects to be fed either pure ASCII files or WordStar 3.3 document files. Its source code can be found in 6-3.

**6-3** The SMALL.C source code.

```
/*
        SMALL - diminutive text printing program
        copyright (c) 1993 Alchemy Mindworks
*/

#include "stdio.h"
#include "stdlib.h"
#include "dos.h"
#include "conio.h"

#define columnwide      193     /* width of column */
#define pointsize       4       /* tiny type */
#define titlesize       8       /* page number size */
#define MAX             256     /* useful constant */
#define MAXWIDE         80      /* maximum line width */

FILE *fp;                       /* file pointer */
char footer[MAX+1]="";          /* footer text */
char pathname[MAX+1]="";        /* file to print */

unsigned int line=0;            /* line counter */
unsigned int page=1;            /* page counter */
unsigned int pagetop=770;       /* top of page */
unsigned int pageleft=18;       /* left of page */
unsigned int tabsize=8;         /* width of tabs */
unsigned int pagelines;         /* lines in a page */
unsigned int column;            /* column counter */
unsigned int maxcolumn=3;       /* column limits */
unsigned int printerport=0;     /* the port to print to */

main(argc,argv)
        int argc;
        char *argv[];
{
        char b[MAX+1];
        int c;
```

**6-3** Continued.

```
     puts("SMALL version 2.0 Copyright (c) 1993 Alchemy Mindworks Inc");

     pagelines=(pagetop-30)/pointsize;
     if(argc <= 1) error("Arguments: a path to a text file\n"
                         "Switches    /F<text>    establishes a footer\n"
                         "            /P<number> sets the printer port - LPT1=1, LPT2=2\n"
                         "            /T<number> sets the tab size\n");

        for(c=1;c<argc;++c) {
                if(argv[c][0]=='/') arg(argv[c]);
                else strncpy(pathname,argv[c],MAX);
        }

        if((fp=fopen(pathname,"rb")) == NULL) error("Error opening the source file");

        do {
                startpage();
                printf("Printing page %d.\r\n",page);
                do {
                        line=0;
                        do {
                                c=getst(b,MAX,fp);
                                b[MAXWIDE]=0;
                                writeline(b);
                        } while(c != EOF && line++ < pagelines);
                        ++column;
                } while(c != EOF && column <= maxcolumn);
                endpage();
                ++page;
        } while(c != EOF);
        fclose(fp);
}

arg(s)          /* handle a command line argument */
        char *s;
{
        switch(toupper(s[1])) {
                case 'F':
                        strncpy(footer,s+2,MAX);
                        break;
                case 'P':
                        printerport=atoi(s+2);
                        break;
                case 'T':
                        tabsize=min(atoi(s+2),16);
                        break;
        }
}

writeline(s)        /* write a line of text */
        char *s;
{
        char b[MAX];

        sprintf(b,"%d %d moveto (%s) show \r\n",
```

```
            pageleft+(column*columnwide),
            pagetop-(pointsize*line),s);
        p_string(b);
}
getst(b,l,fp)       /* get a line of text from file fp */
        char *b;
        int l;
        FILE *fp;
{
        int c,r=0;

        --l;
        do {
                c=fgetc(fp);
                switch(c & 0x7f) {
                        case 9: /* tab */
                                do {
                                        *b++=0x20;
                                        ++r;
                                } while(((r+0) % tabsize) != 0 && r < l);
                                break;
                              case 13:  /* cr */
                                c = 0;
                                break;
                        case '\134':
                                *b++ = '\134';
                                *b++ = '1';
                                *b++ = '3';
                                *b++ = '4';
                                r += 4;
                                break;
                        case '<':
                                *b++ = '\134';
                                *b++ = '0';
                                *b++ = '7';
                                *b++ = '4';
                                r += 4;
                                break;
                        case '>':
                                *b++ = '\134';
                                *b++ = '0';
                                *b++ = '7';
                                *b++ = '6';
                                r += 4;
                                break;
                        case '(':
                                *b++ = '\134';
                                *b++ = '0';
                                *b++ = '5';
                                *b++ = '0';
                                r += 4;
                                break;
                        case ')':
                                *b++ = '\134';
                                *b++ = '0';
                                *b++ = '5';
                                *b++ = '1';
```

**6-3** Continued.

```
                                        r += 4;
                                        break;
                                default:
                                        if((c & 0x7f) >= 32) {
                                                *b++=(c & 0x7f);
                                                ++r;
                                        }
                                        break;
                        }
        } while(r < 1 && c != 0 && c != EOF);
        *b=0;
        return(c);
}

startpage()        /* start the page and get the font */
{
        char b[MAX];

        sprintf(b,"/Courier findfont [%d 0 0 %d 0 0] makefont setfont\r\n",
            pointsize,pointsize);
        p_string(b);
        p_string("gsave\r\n");
        line=0;
        column=0;
}

endpage()  /* end the page and eject it */
{
        char b[MAX];

        sprintf(b,"/Courier findfont [%d 0 0 %d 0 0] makefont setfont\r\n",
        titlesize,titlesize);
        p_string(b);

        sprintf(b,"%d 20 moveto (PAGE %d    %s) show\r\n",
            pageleft,page,footer);

        p_string(b);

        p_string("grestore\r\n");
        p_string("showpage\r\n");
}

p_string(s)
        char *s;
{
        while(*s) p_char(*s++);
}

p_char(c)
        int c;
{
        union REGS r;

        do {
                r.h.ah = 2;
```

```
            r.x.dx = printerport;
            int86(0x17,&r,&r);
        } while(!(r.h.ah & 0x80));
        r.h.ah = 0;
        r.h.al = c;
        r.x.dx = printerport;
        int86(0x17,&r,&r);
}

error(s)
        char *s;
{
        puts(s);
        exit(1);
}
```

If you got through the discussion of PRINT-PS in the previous section, you should have little difficulty understanding SMALL. It prints using the Courier font, as this is a monospaced typeface and as such requires no recourse to width tables. If you were to integrate the width table functions from the PRINT-PS program into SMALL you could almost double the amount of text it would print on a page—making the whole works really impenetrable.

Unlike PRINT-PS, the SMALL program allows for a few command line options. Specifically, /F followed by some text will establish a footer. Make sure you surround the complete argument in double quotes if it will contain spaces. The /P argument defines the printer port. Finally, /T allows you to adjust the tab size.

The SMALL program is based on the assumption that its source text files will be formatted to about 64 columns wide. Unlike SMALL-PS, it doesn't do any page formatting of its own.

## Print a text file to a LaserJet printer

If your laser printer doesn't support PostScript it probably speaks in the other common page description language, PCL. This is the native tongue of the Hewlett-Packard LaserJet printers and compatibles thereof. While recent enhancements to the basic implementation of PCL have improved its capabilities considerably, the majority of low-cost laser printers only support the original PCL language.

Compared to PostScript, PCL is a bit brain dead. In its initial incarnation it lacked scalable fonts, much in the way of resident fonts, and most of the graphic facilities that make PostScript such an interesting environment to work in. In addition, rather than being comprised of human-readable operators like PostScript, PCL is handled through singularly cryptic escape sequences.

The advantage of PCL over PostScript is that it requires vastly less printer memory and is much less expensive to implement. PostScript is a copyrighted entity that must be licensed from its creator, Adobe Systems. This license cost adds significantly to the purchase price of a PostScript laser printer. By comparison, the simple nature of PCL has seen many laser printer manufacturers knock it off.

Unlike as with PostScript, a printer that supports PCL will behave like a dumb teletype if it's sent simple text. It will print raw text in 12-point Courier type, and it responds to simple cursor positioning control characters, such as carriage returns and line feeds. The form feed character, ASCII character 12, will cause a LaserJet to eject its page.

The unfortunate aspect of a LaserJet printer is that whereas it can print simple text without involving a lot of sophisticated commands and such, its talents for printing unassisted end about where they begin. Unlike a PostScript printer, a LaserJet cannot generate proportionally spaced fonts for you merely by asking. Its internal 12-point Courier font is the only font it has on hand.

You can print in other fonts on a LaserJet, of course, but you must precede any printing by defining the fonts you want to use. The fonts involved are stored as disk files, called "soft fonts," which include bitmaps for every character in the font in question. Every size and effect of a typeface to be printed requires that you download a soft font for it.

This means that if you want to print in 12- and 14-point Times Roman you have to download two soft fonts. To be able to print in these two sizes in regular medium type, italic type, bold type, and bold italic type you'd have to download a total of eight soft font files. The size of a soft font, and hence the time it takes to download, will increase with the point size of the type it generates. Twelve-point soft font files typically occupy about 30 kilobytes of disk space each.

Once a soft font is downloaded it must be stored in your printer's memory. There is typically a limited amount of memory in a LaserJet to store fonts—one of the attractive things about using the PCL language, at least for a printer manufacturer, is that one can offer a functional laser printer with 1 megabyte of memory rather than the 2 or more megabytes typically required to do anything useful with PostScript. The finite nature of memory on a LaserJet restricts the number of soft fonts that can be stored at one time. This latter issue won't come up in the context of this section—as with PRINT-PS from the previous section, you'll only be dealing with one font here.

There's a subsidiary issue in working with fonts and LaserJets. The typeface names Times Roman and Helvetica are copyrighted entities that are owned by the International Typeface Corporation, a division of Letraset. Adobe Systems, which owns PostScript, licensed these typefaces and their names, and as such it's legal to work with these faces in conjunction with a PostScript output device. By comparison, when Hewlett-Packard created their LaserJet printers they chose to create their own typefaces, and as such they could not use the names Times Roman and Helvetica.

American copyright law states that typefaces themselves cannot be protected as copyrighted entities, although their trade names can. It's legal to create a typeface that looks like Times Roman, for example, as long as you don't call it Times Roman.

The typefaces that look like Times Roman and Helvetica on non-PostScript printers are typically called Dutch and Swiss. The derivations of these names are a bit obscure. Times Roman is a "serif" font—the little picks on the ends of its characters are called serifs. The word serif comes from a Dutch word, *shreef*. The Helvetii were an ancient celtic tribe that lived in what is now Switzerland.

As was touched on earlier in this section, the equivalent to PostScript's operators are escape sequences under PCL. An escape sequence consists of the escape character, ASCII character 27, followed by some additional codes to tell your printer what to do. There are thundering, swollen rivers of escape sequences under PCL, almost all of them irrelevant to the program in this section. Here are a few you'll encounter:

- Esc E—reset the printer.
- Esc * p ### X—set the horizontal cursor position.
- Esc * p ### Y—set the vertical cursor position.

Note that Esc is character 27, the symbol ### is an integer written as an ASCII string, and there are no spaces between the elements of an escape sequence in real life. In the program discussed in this section, the escape character is written as an octal constant; that is, "\033."

You can position the cursor of a LaserJet using a number of coordinate units. In this case I'll be using "decipoints," or units of $\frac{1}{300}$ of an inch.

The source code for PRINT-LJ, the LaserJet equivalent to PRINT-PS, is illustrated in 6-4. The structure of this program will look familiar if you read the previous section of this chapter—it does pretty much the same thing as PRINT-PS did, except that it controls its printer a little differently.

**6-4** The PRINT-LJ.C source code.

```
/*
        Simple LaserJet text printer
        copyright (c) 1993 Alchemy Mindworks
*/

#include "stdio.h"
#include "alloc.h"
#include "dos.h"

#define DEBUG           0
#define DEBUGFILE       "DEBUG.LJ"

#define TIMESROMAN      1
#define HELVETICA       0
#define COURIER         0

#define XMPY            1
#define XDIV            12

int TimesRomanWidth[]= {
```

**6-4** Continued.

```
        48,64,64,152,100,188,164,52,76,76,100,200,48,68,48,56,
        100,100,100,100,100,100,100,100,100,100,56,56,200,200,200,100,
        196,152,136,140,160,140,124,164,164,72,88,148,128,188,152,160,
        120,160,152,108,128,164,152,196,152,152,144,64,100,64,200,100,
        52,96,108,88,108,100,64,96,108,56,52,104,56,164,108,108,
        108,108,76,76,64,108,92,136,88,88,88,100,100,100,200,4,
        };

int HelveticaWidth[]= {
        56,64,64,152,108,168,136,52,68,68,100,200,56,64,56,60,
        108,108,108,108,108,108,108,108,108,108,60,60,200,200,200,104,
        200,128,132,144,140,128,116,148,144,52,100,128,108,168,144,152,
        124,156,132,124,116,144,128,180,124,124,120,72,100,72,200,100,
        52,108,116,104,116,108,52,116,112,40,40,104,40,168,112,116,
        116,116,68,100,56,112,96,144,96,100,96,100,100,100,200,4
        };

int CourierWidth[]= {
        120,120,120,120,120,120,120,120,120,120,120,120,120,120,120,120,
        120,120,120,120,120,120,120,120,120,120,120,120,120,120,120,120,
        120,120,120,120,120,120,120,120,120,120,120,120,120,120,120,120,
        120,120,120,120,120,120,120,120,120,120,120,120,120,120,120,120,
        120,120,120,120,120,120,120,120,120,120,120,120,120,120,120,120,
        120,120,120,120,120,120,120,120,120,120,120,120,120,120,120,120,
        };

#if TIMESROMAN
#define WIDTHTABLE      TimesRomanWidth
#define FONTFILE        "DUTCH12.SFP"
#endif

#if HELVETICA
#define WIDTHTABLE      HelveticaWidth
#define FONTFILE        "SWISS12.SFP"
#endif

#if COURIER
#define WIDTHTABLE      CourierWidth
#define FONTFILE        ""
#endif

#define LEFTMARGIN      100
#define RIGHTMARGIN     100
#define TOPMARGIN       100
#define BOTTOMMARGIN    100

#define PAGEWIDE        2400-(RIGHTMARGIN+LEFTMARGIN)
#define PAGEDEEP        3100-(TOPMARGIN+BOTTOMMARGIN)

#define POINTSIZE       12
#define LEADING         6
#define WORDSIZE        128

#define PRINTERPORT     0
#define TABSIZE         36
```

```
#define points2dots(n)  ((double)n*4.1667)

double WordSize(char *word);
double CWidth(int c,int tab[],int size);

void writeword(char *word,double *linesize,double *pagedeep);
void newline(double *linesize,double *pagedeep);
void ejectpage(double *linesize,double *pagedeep);

#if     DEBUG
FILE *debug;
#endif

unsigned int pagenumber=0;

main(argc,argv)
        int argc;
        char *argv[];
{
        FILE *fp;
        char word[WORDSIZE+16];
        double linesize=0,pagedeep=0,spacewidth,tabsize;
        int c,i,n,wordindex=0;

        puts("PRINT-LJ version 1.0 Copyright (c) 1993 Alchemy Mindworks Inc.\r\n"
             "_______________________________________________________________\r\n");

        #if DEBUG
        if((debug=fopen(DEBUGFILE,"wb"))==NULL) error("Can't create debug file");
        #endif

        if(argc <= 1) error("Argument:          Path to a text file");

        if((fp=fopen(argv[1],"rb"))==NULL) error("Can't open the source file");

        p_string("\033E");

        printf("\rDownloading...");

        if(!DownloadFont(FONTFILE)) error("Can't download the soft font");

        saypage();

        do {
                if((c=fgetc(fp)) != EOF) {
                        if(c==0x8d) c=0;
                        c &= 0x7f;
                        if(c==32) {
                                do {
                                        if(wordindex < WORDSIZE) word[wordindex++]=c & 0x7f;
                                        c=fgetc(fp);
                                } while((c & 0x7f)==32);
                                word[wordindex]=0;
                                ungetc(c,fp);
                                writeword(word,&linesize,&pagedeep);
                                wordindex=0;
                                word[wordindex]=0;
```

**6-4** Continued.

```
                                }
                                else if(c==13) {
                                        word[wordindex]=0;
                                        writeword(word,&linesize,&pagedeep);
                                        wordindex=0;
                                        word[wordindex]=0;
                                        newline(&linesize,&pagedeep);
                                }
                                else if(c==9) {
                                        spacewidth=CWidth(32,WIDTHTABLE,POINTSIZE);
                                        if(linesize > 0) tabsize=(double)((int)linesize %
                                        (int)points2dots(TABSIZE));
                                        else tabsize=points2dots(TABSIZE);

                                        n=(int)(tabsize/spacewidth);
                                        for(i=0;i<n && wordindex < WORDSIZE;++i)
                                                word[wordindex++]=32;
                                }
                                else if(c > 32 && c < 128) {
                                        if(wordindex < WORDSIZE) word[wordindex++]=c;
                                }
                        }
        } while(c != EOF);
        writeword(word,&linesize,&pagedeep);
        wordindex=0;
        ejectpage(&linesize,&pagedeep);

        printf("\rAll done...                \r\n");

        fclose(fp);

        #if DEBUG
        fclose(debug);
        #endif
}

void writeword(word,linesize,pagedeep)
        char *word;
        double *linesize,*pagedeep;
{
        double wordsize;
        char b[256];

        if(!word[0]) return;

        wordsize=WordSize(word);
        if((int)((*linesize)+wordsize) >= PAGEWIDE)
            newline(linesize,pagedeep);

        if((*linesize)==0) {
                sprintf(b,"\033*p%uX\033*p%uY",
                    LEFTMARGIN,TOPMARGIN+(int)(*pagedeep));
                p_string(b);
        }

        p_string(word);
```

```
        (*linesize)+=wordsize;
}

void newline(linesize,pagedeep)
        double *linesize,*pagedeep;
{
        (*pagedeep)+=(double)points2dots((POINTSIZE+LEADING));
        if((int)(*pagedeep) >= PAGEDEEP) ejectpage(linesize,pagedeep);
        (*linesize)=0;
}

void ejectpage(linesize,pagedeep)
        double *linesize,*pagedeep;
{
        (*linesize)=(*pagedeep)=0;
        p_string("\014");
        saypage();
}

double WordSize(word)
        char *word;
{
        double wordsize=0;
        int i,n;

        n=strlen(word);
        for(i=0;i<n;++i)
            wordsize+=CWidth((int)word[i],WIDTHTABLE,POINTSIZE);

        return(wordsize);
}

p_buff(s,n)
        char *s;
        unsigned int n;
{
        while(n–) p_char(*s++);
}

p_string(s)
        char *s;
{
        while(*s) p_char(*s++);
}

p_char(c)
        int c;
{
        #if DEBUG
        fputc(c,debug);
        #else
        union REGS r;

        do {
                r.h.ah = 2;
                r.x.dx = PRINTERPORT;
                int86(0x17,&r,&r);
        } while(!(r.h.ah & 0x80));
```

**6-4** Continued.

```
        r.h.ah = 0;
        r.h.al = c;
        r.x.dx = PRINTERPORT;
        int86(0x17,&r,&r);
        #endif
}

error(s)
        char *s;
{
        puts(s);
        exit(1);
}

double CWidth(c,tab,size)
        int c,tab[],size;
{
        return(points2dots((double)0.06*
               ((double)XMPY/(double)XDIV)*
               (double)size*
               (double)tab[(c & 0x7f)-32]));
}

saypage()
{
        printf("\rPrinting page %u",++pagenumber);
}

DownloadFont(path)
        char *path;
{
        FILE *fp;
        unsigned long size;
        char *p;

        if(!strlen(path)) return(1);

        if((fp=fopen(path,"rb"))==NULL) return(0);

        fseek(fp,0L,SEEK_END);
        size=ftell(fp);
        rewind(fp);

        if(size > 0x0000fff0L) {
                fclose(fp);
                return(0);
        }

        if((p=malloc((unsigned int)size))==NULL) {
                fclose(fp);
                return(0);
        }

        if(fread(p,1,(unsigned int)size,fp) != (unsigned int)size) {
                free(p);
                fclose(fp);
```

```
                return(0);
        }

        p_string("\033*c0F");
        p_string("\033*c8D");
        p_buff(p,(unsigned int)size);
        p_string("\033*c5F");
        p_string("\033&l0O\033(8X");

        free(p);
        fclose(fp);
        return(1);
}
```

The PRINT-LJ program begins by downloading a soft font. There are two of them—DUTCH12.SFP and SWISS12.SFP. You'll find them on the companion disk for this book. The one that gets downloaded is determined by which font you compile PRINT-LJ to use.

The escape sequences in the DownloadFont function will make the font a permanent resident of your printer's memory until your printer is either shut off or reset with the Esc-E sequence. The final sequence after the font has been sent selects this font as the current primary font to print text in.

Note that there is no soft font file to be downloaded if you compile PRINT-LJ with the COURIER define set true. None is needed, as 12-point Courier is the one font a LaserJet knows how to print without being told how to do so. It's worth keeping in mind, however, that it will also use this font if you ask it to print with a different font that it can't find. If your text appears unexpectedly in Courier, something's amiss.

Once PRINT-LJ has downloaded its soft font, its workings are almost identical to those of PRINT-PS. The only catch is that things are measured in points, or $\frac{1}{72}$ of an inch under PostScript, and in decipoints, or $\frac{1}{300}$ of an inch on a LaserJet. As such, in order to port the PostScript text printing program to work with a LaserJet you'll need a function to convert between these two coordinate systems. Actually, a macro will suffice:

```
#define points2dots(n)   ((double)n*4.1667)
```

There's a lot of floating point math used in this program and the preceding one, something that might make some C language programmers a bit suspicious. One of the things that makes C programs unusually efficient in their use of processor resources is the tendency of everything to be done with simple integers. In fact, handling things in floating point doesn't markedly slow the printing speed of PRINT-LJ, because the time it spends waiting for the printer port to be free vastly dwarfs any time it loses in doing floating point math. By comparison, the rounding errors involved in keeping track of line lengths as integers can be quite noticeable. Doing so will convince PRINT-LJ that it has more room on its lines than it actually does, causing the occasional word to spill off the right edge of your page.

Once again, you can modify PRINT-LJ considerably to work with all sorts of other text file types, and to perform much more complex page formatting if you're of a mind to. You'll probably require more soft fonts and width tables to do so, of course, and this is what starts to make word processors and desktop publishing packages that drive LaserJet printers a somewhat daunting prospect. Allow for a reasonable range of typefaces, font sizes, and type effects—with a soft font file for each—and it's not hard to plow 2- or 3-megabytes worth of hard drive space under a crop of LaserJet fonts.

If you can convince all the users of your software to invest in LaserJet 4 printers, which support scalable fonts along the lines of those in PostScript, you can ignore this problem. The rather enormous user base of LaserJet Plus compatible printers already about probably makes this impractical.

# Index

**OBJECTVISION™ PROGRAMMING FOR WINDOWS**—Donald Richard Read

Create your own graphical applications for Windows, or improve old applications in minutes with this easy-to-follow guide—and its 3.5-inch companion disk—to the powerful ObjectVision GUI development package. It will show you how to use ObjectVision's unique "forms" model that makes it easy to adapt dBase, Paradox, and a host of other database programs to the Windows environment. Plus, you'll learn how to design your own Windows databases *visually*, without getting bogged down in complicated source code. 208 pages, 380 illustrations. Book No. 4258, $24.95 paperback, $34.95 hardcover

**NETWORKING WITH LANtastic®**
—Michael S. Montgomery

With this instructive book you'll have an easy-to-read alternative to the program documentation—a comprehensive guide to setting up and running an efficient, high-performance LANtastic network. The author describes proven techniques for sharing files, printing, and using peripherals. Focusing on ways to configure LANtastic to meet specific needs and ensure maximum productivity, he shows you how to plan and design networks, install LANtastic software, use program functions and menus, and more. 632 pages, 199 illustrations. Book No. 4273, $22.95 paperback, $34.95 hardcover

**LAN PERFORMANCE OPTIMIZATION**
—Martin A. W. Nemzow

Resolve your most stubborn network performance problems with this practical resource for LAN managers and consultants. This book/disk package will help you locate and eliminate bottlenecks in local area networks quickly. The diagnostic tools provided are equally effective with Banyan Vines, Novell Netware, UB Access One, Unix, Sun NFS, IBM LAN Server, Microsoft LAN Manager, Ethernet, Token Ring, and FDDI network operating systems. 230 pages, 90 illustrations, 5.25-inch disk. Book No. 4310, $29.95 paperback only

**MICROSOFT ACCESS PROGRAMMING**
—Namir C. Shammas

This hands-on introduction to Microsoft Access database programming is designed for anyone who's familiar with the BASIC language. It's a practical tutorial approach—complete with ready-to-use program code and professional tips, tricks, and warnings. You get up-to-date information on the built-in on-line help that Microsoft Access offers . . . how to craft the visual interface of a form . . . how to fine-tune the control settings to alter their appearance or behavior . . . and much more. 304 pages, 158 illustration, 3.5-inch disk. Book No. 4333, $32.95 paperback

**MD-DOS® BATCH FILE PROGRAMMING—4th Edition**
—Ronny Richardson
Reviewers praised Richardson's previous books:
*"Exhaustive and exhilarating guide. Give this book an A+ for utility."*
***—Computer Book Review***
*"Now, 'The .BAT Book' will set me free!!! . . . I will recommend this one."*
***—Computer Shopper***

Find command-by-command batch file explanation tables, complete DOS command summaries, and a library of practical batch file programs included on disk in this book/disk package. Updated for DOS 6.0, this book has been extensively revised to make it even more helpful to beginning and intermediate-level DOS users. 432 pages, 59 illustrations, 3.5-inch disk. Book No. 4335, $32.95 paperback, $39.95 hardcover

**BOOKKEEPING ON YOUR HOME-BASED PC**—Linda Stern

Written by an award-winning personal finance columnist, this book leads you through the complete process of starting up and running your home-based business—with emphasis on the technology you need to make it work. After an overview of the attractive prospects of the business, the book focuses on how to equip your venture with computer, fax, modem, and telephone systems that fit your specific needs. 256 pages, 50 illustrations. Book No. 4328, $14.95 paperback, $24.95 hardcover

**HEALTH SERVICE BUSINESSES ON YOUR HOME-BASED PC**—Rick Benzel

Find everything you need to know about entering the lucrative health services field in this guide. It focuses on the three most profitable health-related home businesses—billing, claims processing, and records transcription. For each you get a solid plan of action drawn from the real-life experiences of successful entrepreneurs. 208 pages, 50 illustrations. Book No. 4327, $14.95 paperback only

**STACKER®: An Illustrated Tutorial —2nd Edition**—Dan Gookin

Turn your single hard disk into two with this professional guide. Updated through Stacker 3.0, it contains information not found in the manuals. You'll use such features as Express or Custom Setup for Windows and DOS; Windows Stackometer™—a set of real-time gauges showing hard disk capacity, compression ratio, and fragmentation levels. Plus, you'll use Unstack™, a time-saving utility that decompresses files and automatically returns systems to their original state. 208 pages, 50 illustrations. Book No. 4447, $19.95 paperback only

**VISUAL BASIC™ ANIMATION PROGRAMMING**—Lee Adams

Computer animation is more than entertainment. You can use it to give your applications more pizzazz and make them more marketable. This expert guide shows you how to achieve common effects such as run-cycles, background pans, motion blur, and adjustable timers, and how to use different methods to create and store animated images on the Windows platform. Several complete, working programs demonstrate how to tap into Windows's powerful, built-in graphics library, the GDI. 656 pages, 216 illustrations, 5.25-inch disk. Book No. 4224, $39.95 paperback only

# DISK WARRANTY

This software is protected by both United States copyright law and international copyright treaty provision. You must treat this software just like a book, except that you may copy it into a computer in order to be used and you may make archival copies of the software for the sole purpose of backing up our software and protecting your investment from loss.

By saying "just like a book," McGraw-Hill means, for example, that this software may be used by any number of people and may be freely moved from one computer location to another, so long as there is no possibility of its being used at one location or on one computer while it also is being used at another. Just as a book cannot be read by two different people in two different places at the same time, neither can the software be used by two different people in two different places at the same time (unless, of course, McGraw-Hill's copyright is being violated).

## LIMITED WARRANTY

Windcrest/McGraw-Hill takes great care to provide you with top-quality software, thoroughly checked to prevent virus infections. McGraw-Hill warrants the physical diskette(s) contained herein to be free of defects in materials and workmanship for a period of sixty days from the purchase date. If McGraw-Hill receives written notification within the warranty period of defects in materials or workmanship, and such notification is determined by McGraw-Hill to be correct, McGraw-Hill will replace the defective diskette(s). Send requests to:

Customer Service
Windcrest/McGraw-Hill
13311 Monterey Lane
Blue Ridge Summit, PA 17294-0850

The entire and exclusive liability and remedy for breach of this Limited Warranty shall be limited to replacement of defective diskette(s) and shall not include or extend to any claim for or right to cover any other damages, including but not limited to, loss of profit, data, or use of the software, or special, incidental, or consequential damages or other similar claims, even if McGraw-Hill has been specifically advised of the possibility of such damages. In no event will McGraw-Hill's liability for any damages to you or any other person ever exceed the lower of suggested list price or actual price paid for the license to use the software, regardless of any form of the claim.

MCGRAW-HILL, INC. SPECIFICALLY DISCLAIMS ALL OTHER WARRANTIES, EXPRESS OR IMPLIED, INCLUDING, BUT NOT LIMITED TO, ANY IMPLIED WARRANTY OF MERCHANTABILITY OR FITNESS FOR A PARTICULAR PURPOSE.

Specifically, McGraw-Hill makes no representation or warranty that the software is fit for any particular purpose and any implied warranty of merchantability is limited to the sixty-day duration of the Limited Warranty covering the physical diskette(s) only (and not the software) and is otherwise expressly and specifically disclaimed.

This limited warranty gives you specific legal rights; you may have others which may vary from state to state. Some states do not allow the exclusion of incidental or consequential damages, or the limitation on how long an implied warranty lasts, so some of the above may not apply to you.

# Disk Information

The disk included with this book contains four files:

APPS.EXE DPTPE10.EXE
SOURCE.EXE READ.ME

The three executables are self-extracting; in other words, when you type in one of the filenames (without the .EXE extension), that file will unzip itself, unloading its contents into the directory where it presently is.

In light of the fact that these unzipped files will take up more room than the floppy disk can contain, you will want to copy these four files onto your hard drive before unzipping. To create a hard drive subdirectory to store these files in, type

MKDIR directory-name

at your hard drive prompt (most likely C:\), where directory-name is what you want to name the subdirectory.

To copy the files, place your disk in your floppy drive (probably drive B) and type

COPY B:*.* C:\directory-name

The files on the disk will now be copied to your newly created subdirectory.

Run the command

TYPE drive:READ.ME + MORE

for more information from the author about these files, where drive is either B or C (depending on whether or not you've already copies your files onto your hard drive).

## IMPORTANT

Read the Disk Warranty terms on the previous page before opening the disk envelope. Opening the envelope constitutes acceptance of these terms and renders this entire book-disk package non-returnable except for replacement in kind due to material defect.